Understanding Social Movements

Understanding Social Movements

Theories from the Classical Era to the Present

Steven M. Buechler

Paradigm Publishers
Boulder • London

Copyright © 2011 Steven M. Buechler

Published in the United States by Paradigm Publishers, 2845 Wilderness Place, Suite 200, Boulder, CO 80301 USA.

Paradigm Publishers is the trade name of Birkenkamp & Company, LLC, Dean Birkenkamp, President and Publisher.

Library of Congress Cataloging-in-Publication Data
Buechler, Steven M., 1951–
Understanding Social Movements: Theories from the Classical Era to the Present/Steven M. Buechler.
    p. cm.
  Includes bibliographical references and index.
  978-1-59451-915-4 (for the hardcover)
  978-1-59451-916-1 (for the paperback)
1. Social movements—History. 2. Social change. I. Title.
HM711.B84 2011
303.48'401—dc22

2010029208

Printed and bound in the United States of America on acid-free paper that meets the standards of the American National Standard for Permanence of Paper for Printed Library Materials.

Designed and Typeset by Straight Creek Bookmakers.

14 13 12 11 1 2 3 4 5

Contents

Part II: Traditional Theories

Part III: Paradigm Shifts

Foreword

Mayer N. Zald

In the spring of 2007 I was invited to be part of a five person team to give a workshop on social movement theory and research to social science faculty and advanced graduate students from around China. The workshop took place that summer at Renmin University, Beijing. Among other topics, I was asked to lecture on the history of social movement theory and research.

Although I regularly wrote about social movement topics, and had taught courses on it and related topics off and on for more than forty years, I had never actually written about or lectured on the full history of social movement theory. Instead, like many faculty who teach in the general area of collective behavior and social movements, I only discussed enough of the history of the subject to place the current set of interests and topics in context.

I searched for articles and books that bore on the subject, but found only a few. I worked hard on the lecture and presented a talk that not only gave an overview of the history, but also attempted to place that history in a sociological and disciplinary context. I raised the issues of what was going on in the society at the time the scholar was writing and what was shaping the intellectual context in which writings about social movements and collective behavior took place.

As I worked on the lecture I began to think that the topic really deserved a fuller treatment in book form; it seemed obvious to me that it would be really useful to both graduate students and undergraduates. But I knew that I didn't want to write such a book. For one, I already had a pretty full scholarly agenda. I also didn't think I was the best person to write such a book. Although I was competent to give a lecture on the topic, I did not have the depth of background in the history of sociological theory and research to do a really good book.

I began to think about who would be a good candidate to approach about writing such a book, either by themselves or with me. I quickly turned to Steve Buechler. Although I did not know him personally, more than almost anyone else I knew he had shown in his writings a continuing concern about the unfolding history of the field. I offered to give him my lecture notes, and the few articles that I had found discussing one historical development or another.

When we started discussing the project we left it somewhat open-ended as to whether the book would be in some way jointly authored, or solely authored by him. As it has turned out, aside from providing my lecture notes and a few comments on his early drafts of chapters, the book that has resulted has been written solely by him.

My choice of an author has turned out to be felicitous. I think the book is far superior to anything that I could have produced. For one, he has a depth of background in sociological theory that far exceeds my own. For another, he writes just beautifully. The book has a critical edge and a nuanced appreciation of different kinds of work that should be welcomed by its readers.

Introduction

"Steve—This comes out of the blue." This was the first line of an email message I received from Mayer Zald in October 2007. That email began the collaboration Mayer describes in his foreword and led to the book you hold in your hands.

In keeping with Mayer's vision, my goal here is to provide not just a chronological survey but also a sociological history. Such a story must begin with the historicity of the social movement itself. Although there have been many varieties of collective action throughout human history, social movements are distinctly modern.

At the broadest level, social movements subscribe to the basic sociological insight that society is a social construction. For sociology, this construction stands in need of explanation, whereas for social movements, it stands in need of transformation. The premise that society is a human product subject to intervention and transformation is thus the modernist foundation of the social movement (Buechler 2000: 4–11). In slightly different language, "[t]he idea of conscious collective action having the capacity to change society as a whole came only with the era of enlightenment" (Neidhardt and Rucht 1991: 449). As a result, "[s]ocial movements are genuinely modern phenomena. Only in modern society have social movements played a constitutive role in social development" (Eder 1993: 108).

These European scholars echo the earlier insights of an American sociologist who claimed that "the appearance of groups self-consciously oriented to societal change is a peculiar aspect of modern Western social and political life. The idea that change is possible through cooperative activity itself depends on a social and political order that makes such activity possible and probable" (Gusfield 1978: 126).

The origins of the social movement are thus intertwined with the rise of modernity itself. The confluence of capitalism, state building, urbanization, proletarianization, and warfare provided the networks, resources, identities, and grievances for social movements. Great Britain was one such incubator. "Britain's surges of collective activity represented the birth of what we now call the social movement—the sustained, organized challenge to existing authorities in the name of a deprived, excluded or wronged population ... from the 1790s onward we can see a remarkable expansion and regularization of the national social movement not only in Great Britain but elsewhere in the West" (Tilly 1995: 144).

1

The rise of the social movement marked a qualitative shift in collective action as people intervened repeatedly in national affairs to pursue new claims through large-scale coordinated action. This involved a major shift in the prevailing repertoire of contention from actions that were parochial, bifurcated, and particular to campaigns that were cosmopolitan, modular, and autonomous. The social movement was the product of this shift from immediate, localized, and sporadic expressions of revenge or resistance to sustained, cumulative, organized challenges to national centers of decision making (Tarrow 1994; Tilly 1995, 2004).

Social movements thus have a historically specific origin that parallels the origins of sociology itself. Although movements first appeared in the late eighteenth century, sociological discourse caught up with them in 1850 when Lorenz von Stein "introduced the term 'social movement' into scholarly discussions of popular political striving" (Tilly 2004: 5). Given this common heritage, a sociological history of social movement theory seems long overdue.

Just as social movements have been shaped by larger sociohistorical forces, the study of social movements has been influenced by historical, intellectual, and organizational factors. It is not "internal logics but external concerns [that] are vital to understanding the sociological study of social movements" (Gusfield 1978: 122).

Once we recognize that "political and social perspectives and events, external to sociological theory and research, have played a decisive role in the internal logic of this corner of social science," we can also appreciate how "studies of social movements ... are organized as solutions to problematics—to the analysis of problems set by historical events and interests" (Gusfield 1978: 123–124).

In an effort to capture the multiple influences that bear on the study of social movements, the sociological history provided here emphasizes three dimensions.

First, the study of social movements has been shaped by the prevailing matrix of social science disciplines, their intellectual division of labor, and changes in both over time. Thus, some of the earliest work on movements has unusual scope because the lack of rigid disciplinary boundaries allowed scholars to analyze many different aspects of many different kinds of collective action.

As sharper disciplinary boundaries emerged, theoretical conceptions and research agendas changed. With clearer boundaries between history and sociology, the latter developed some new analytical tools for studying movements, but its explanations tended to become ahistorical and overgeneralized. With clearer boundaries between political science and sociology, the former specialized in more formal, organizational, or institutional aspects of movements and politics, whereas sociology gravitated toward less organized, more spontaneous forms of collective behavior (collapsing social movements into this rubric as well).

Changes in the disciplinary matrix of the social sciences and its corresponding division of labor and topics has thus had a profound effect on how social movements have been defined, theorized, and studied in different eras.

Second, the study of social movements has been influenced by shifts in the broader intellectual climate that transcends particular disciplines. Changes in these metatheoretical assumptions and root images have periodically reoriented the study of social movements as well.

Thus, in the late 1950s and early 1960s, an emphasis on game theory and rational actors arose across several social science disciplines. As these ideas filtered into the study of social movements, they reoriented our understanding of movements toward actor-centered approaches emphasizing costs and benefits and pondering dilemmas like the free-rider problem (when actors hope to share in future benefits without paying the current costs of achieving them).

Shortly thereafter, the rise of more critical and radical perspectives in the social sciences dramatically altered understandings of movements by reversing the value biases of earlier approaches. Yesterday's threats to social order became today's victims of oppression, as movements seeking liberation and autonomy were increasingly seen as legitimate and sometimes heroic challenges to repression and social control.

As a final example, the cultural turn in the humanities and social sciences that began in the 1970s substantially redirected the sociological study of social movements by the 1980s. Questions of resources, strategy, interests, and politics were at least partially displaced by issues of symbols, meanings, identity, and culture.

Third, and most obvious, the prevailing movements in a given sociohistorical period have shaped theoretical conceptions of what movements are and questions about how they arise, develop, recruit, mobilize, strategize, and succeed or fail.

Thus, through much of the nineteenth century, movements were often equated—implicitly or explicitly—with revolutionary challenges to the prevailing social order. Whether analysts wrote as sympathetic advocates, neutral onlookers, or conservative reactionaries, movements were often taken to be (or as having the potential to become) foundational challenges to political regimes and social orders.

In the early twentieth century, the confluence of urbanization, industrialization, and immigration created demographic pressures that led to heightened concerns over crowds and crowd behavior. These phenomena were both defined by and feared for their qualities of spontaneity, contagion, irrationality, and extremism, although subsequent sociological work would reveal a more complex reality below this surface appearance.

Moving toward midcentury, global struggles over communism and fascism inevitably shaped how movements were studied. These specters restored a link between politics and social movements. At the same time, this was understood as a politics of extremism and authoritarianism that posed a threat to capitalist democracies. Popular accounts of "true believers" conveyed fears of fanaticism to the broader public.

The protest cycle of the 1960s reoriented conceptions of social movements once again. Sparked by the civil rights movement in the United States and anticolonial struggles abroad, movements came to be seen by many as legitimate and justifiable challenges to political regimes in need of major transformation. For the next thirty years, movements were intensely studied in a climate that was largely receptive to their grievances and goals. This stance has been modified only slightly with more recent reminders that the social movement form can also serve reactionary forces, as evidenced by neo-Nazi, white supremacist, and terrorist cells that have adopted the social movement repertoire.

Although there are subtle and multifaceted ways that prevailing social movements have shaped the agenda for movement theory and research, sometimes the connection is more direct. Many current movement scholars are former movement activists who subsequently acquired academic credentials but still draw upon their activist biography to define the agenda for social movement scholarship. Given the common, social constructionist premise that underlies movement activism and sociological inquiry, such biographies should not be surprising.

This sociological history of social movement theory thus recognizes social movements as a distinctly modernist form and proceeds to trace subsequent theoretical development through a shifting context of disciplinary boundaries, intellectual currents, and movement challenges.

Even with this focus, no single volume can do justice to every permutation in social movement theory over more than a century. Several rather different "sociological histories" could be written, and they would all be unavoidably selective in their content—as is this one.

For instance, this account is more attentive to U.S. contributions, although it begins with and occasionally revisits European work. This bias reflects both the voluminous literature that has been produced on social movements in the United States as well as limitations on my own knowledge and expertise.

This account is also organized around major paradigms and schools of thought because they are convenient organizing principles for the story I seek to tell. Although some attention is paid to internal variations within paradigms and external debates between them, there are more idiosyncratic approaches that fall between the cracks of these major paradigms and are likely to be slighted in this story. Although striving for breadth where possible, it is sometimes sacrificed for a more in-depth analysis of the most prominent approaches to social movements across the decades.

Put succinctly, this is one possible sociological history of social movement theory among others that could be written. If this effort inspires other such histories, then it will have fulfilled one of its purposes.

The book is organized as follows.

Part I begins in the European context that gave birth to the modern social movement and sifts the work of major classical theorists in sociology for insights on social movements and collective action. Karl Marx's theory of revolutionary socialist movements is an obvious point of departure, along with some fateful modifications by the Russian revolutionary Vladimir Lenin. The book then considers the implications of Max Weber's social theory for an understanding of social movements, supplemented by the work of Robert Michels. This section concludes with an appraisal of Émile Durkheim's analysis of social integration and its implications for collective behavior, as complemented by the work of Gustave LeBon.

Part II shifts to the United States and spans four decades from the 1920s into the 1960s. This part of the story begins at the University of Chicago, but distinguishes between two "Chicago Schools" before and after World War II with intriguing differences in their approaches to collective behavior. The story then turns to the rise of political sociology and how this subfield retained a conception of social movements as political actors linked to parties, elections, ideologies, and class cleavages. This part concludes with an overview of several theories that identify social strain or relative deprivation as key mechanisms provoking collective behavior.

Part III traces major paradigm shifts of the 1970s and 1980s in response to new research as well as the 1960s protest cycle. Resource mobilization theory led the challenge to previous approaches and fundamentally reoriented the study of social movements. Soon thereafter, a somewhat parallel approach was recognized as a distinct alternative known as political process theory. Both restored a more political understanding of social movements, but this emphasis was challenged by framing and social constructionist views that reasserted the importance of cultural processes in movement activism. A further challenge to all these U.S. theories came from the European import of new social movement theory, rounding out three decades of active growth in social movement theory and research.

Part IV begins with an overview of this theoretical cross-fertilization, the debates it inspired, and attempts to derive a synthesis out of rival perspectives. At the turn of the century, all these theories (and any possible synthesis) came under a new challenge by an approach emphasizing the dynamics of contention and expanding the field of study far beyond conventional social movements. At the same time, such state-centered theories were challenged by advocates of a more cultural approach to collective action that emphasized the role of emotions in particular. The book concludes by identifying some of the more intriguing or fruitful new directions in social movement theory that promise to reshape the field for years to come.

In closing, I would like to express my appreciation for the wise counsel of Mayer Zald. As noted previously, he supplied the original inspiration for this book. As its chapters took shape, he also offered incisive comments and more references than I felt I could ever track down. He provided a welcome combination of collegial support and intellectual rigor that I'm sure his former students and current colleagues know well. His collaboration has made this a better book than it otherwise would have been.

Part I

Classical Approaches

Chapter One

Marx and Lenin

Karl Marx (1818–1883) is not typically seen as a theorist of social movements. His analysis and critique of capitalism nonetheless led him to develop a robust model of working-class mobilization against capitalists and capitalism. This model remains relevant wherever workers mobilize around their interests, and it also provides a template for analyzing movements launched by other constituencies. As such, Marx provides a logical starting point for our story.

THE CONTEXT

The origin of sociology is conventionally traced to the French social thinker Auguste Comte (1798–1857). As a discipline, however, sociology did not become well-established or clearly recognized in European academic circles until the end of the nineteenth century. Much the same may be said for other disciplines that are now routinely identified as political science, economics, psychology, or anthropology.

As a result, Marx's work was neither framed nor constrained by the now-familiar boundaries between social sciences and their distinctive assumptions, theories, and methods. His training, interests, writings, and life work moved fluidly across the terrain of philosophy, politics, economics, and sociology.

Marx's work also eschewed the social-scientific goal of objectivity or value-neutrality. Throughout his long career, Marx blended scholarly rigor with political advocacy, and fused analysis and critique of the prevailing socioeconomic order. His goal was a type of praxis in which theory and analysis guided political action toward individual emancipation and social transformation. As Marx famously observed, while philosophers have always interpreted the world, the point is to change it.

Marx's work was thus not shaped by a well-defined disciplinary matrix of distinct social sciences. It was profoundly shaped, however, by leading trends and currents in the broader intellectual climate of mid–nineteenth century European

9

society. As a Young Hegelian, Marx seized upon the notion of alienation as a diagnosis of social ills and embraced the Enlightenment themes of progress and perfectibility in fashioning a response to those ills (Coser 1977). Unlike Hegel, however, Marx sought to root his dialectical analysis of the societal totality in the material rather than ideal realm.

These intellectual developments predisposed Marx to a critical analysis of existing society in the name of a preferable and possible future. As that society became more deeply capitalist at its core, Marx joined the chorus responses to the spread and penetration of capitalist social relations into every aspect of life. For many nineteenth century social critics—and most famously for Marx—capitalism brought material progress to a few at the price of alienation and exploitation of the many.

Marx's more specific target was the factory system of industrialized production. With its detailed division of labor, dangerous working conditions, exceedingly long working days, miserably low wages, and abusive child labor, this system offered a wealth of "grievances" that could fuel working-class resistance. Such a system clearly deformed the human spirit, but Marx also documented how countless hours repetitively tending machines literally deformed workers' bodies as well (Marx 1867/1967).

This system provoked numerous ideological challenges, including anarchism, socialism, and communism (often with their own internal divisions and schisms). Marx honed his own ideas in critical dialogue with these ideologies by distinguishing, for example, his version of socialism from those he labeled utopian socialists. At the same time, he was conducting a more academic or "scientific" debate with orthodox political economy and idealist philosophies of the state. Marx used these political and intellectual influences as foils against which to articulate his distinctive vision.

Perhaps the most obvious contextual influence on his work was an array of actually existing social movements, political parties, working-men's associations, and revolutionary brigades that arose throughout much of the nineteenth century. When Marx introduced *The Communist Manifesto* with the words "A spectre is haunting Europe—the spectre of communism," he proceeded to argue that communism was not an abstract, utopian ideal but rather the existing mobilization and movement of workers against capitalism. This movement was already recognized by European elites; indeed, they were already busy repressing it.

Rightly or wrongly, Marx saw himself not prescribing for a future mobilization of working-class resistance but rather describing existing challenges (while also nourishing their potential for revolutionary transformation). His close involvement in the First International was merely one expression of his dual identity as social theorist and political activist. Although the nineteenth century featured a great variety of collective actions and social movements, it was working-class mobilization and its revolutionary potential that was clearly at the center of Marx's work.

Marx is therefore something of an accidental theorist of social movements. He did not identify with a specific discipline such as sociology. He did not operate with a generic concept of social movements that referred to an array of mobilizations by a variety of constituencies. He was instead shaped by a broader intellectual climate that promoted socialist solutions to capitalist problems and advocated working-class mobilization as the key to implementing such solutions. Guided by these lights, Marx nonetheless developed a distinctive approach to the study of social movements.

THE ALIENATION OF LABOR

This approach is a structural theory of social movements because it is the social structure of capitalist society that creates an inevitable conflict of interests between social classes and motivates working-class protest. It is also a relational theory of social movements because an emergent polarization between classes and solidarity within them is vital to the development of such protest.

One way that capitalism harms workers is through the alienation of their labor. This is a grievous violation of humanity itself because Marx viewed labor as central to what it means to be human. Labor is, first and foremost, the activity through which human beings produce their world, reshape their surroundings, and secure their survival. But labor is also the means by which people create and re-create themselves by developing new skills, creatively solving problems, and enhancing their capacities. For Marx, labor is the process that makes us fully human.

Humans also possess a distinctive "species-being" that involves our capacity for self-consciousness and the ability to reflect upon our actions. When this self-consciousness is combined with the ability to labor, humans purposively make and remake their world to their preferences. Labor thereby becomes praxis whereby people plan, act, reflect, react, plan again, modify actions, and so on. As Marx famously noted, these capacities distinguish the worst of architects from the best of bees; the latter may construct elaborate structures, but only on the basis of instinct and only in one way without benefit of self-consciousness and reflexive learning.

Under capitalism, the labor process systematically and insidiously denies these potentials and deforms human beings. The alienation of labor under capitalism takes four interrelated forms.

First, workers become alienated from the product of their labor. All labor involves objectification in which planned activity materializes in some external product. Objectification is not necessarily alienating. It becomes so under capitalism because workers do not own or otherwise control the products of their labor. Moreover, the products they produce bear little or no relation to their own direct needs. Capitalist property relations ensure that ownership of products and decisions about what to produce rest solely in capitalist hands, denying workers the distinctive, positive potential of their capacity for productive labor.

Second, workers become alienated from productive activity itself. The labor process under capitalism denies creative needs and potentials and often reduces work to simplistic, repetitive, deadening activity. Under such a regimen, work becomes something coerced and dominated by external authority rather than flowing freely from the laborer's interests and capacities. The most fundamental expression of this form of alienation is that workers must sell (literally alienate) their labor-power in exchange for a wage if they are to survive. Once sold, they lose effective control over the deployment of that labor. Marx thus likened wage-labor to prostitution in that a vital human capacity is reduced to a commodity serving the instrumental goals of the purchaser and violating the humanity of the seller.

Third, workers become alienated from their species—being under capitalist control of the labor process. Work becomes a mere means of existence rather than an opportunity for self-development. Under these conditions, people are coerced to labor in order to live rather than living in order to labor and develop their capacities for self-reflective activity. Capitalism thereby promotes social dynamics that dehumanize workers and systematically deny their most distinctive attributes.

Finally, all human beings become alienated from all others in such circumstances. The paradigmatic relation is between workers and capitalists, as workers produce the means and transfer the power to dominate themselves and future workers through their productive activity. Workers also become alienated from other workers because all are reduced to cogs in a machine they do not control. Even capitalists experience alienation from their humanity because the rules of the game dictate that they treat others inhumanely if they are to retain their privileges.

There has never been a golden age of unalienated labor, and even Marx conceded that wage-labor was a relative improvement over serfdom and slavery. But alienation is better measured not against the past but rather in terms of the growing gap between the human potential for self-directed labor and the deformations that capitalism imposes on this potential. Seen this way, capitalism is a profoundly alienating form of social organization (Marx 1964). To whatever extent social movements are fueled by substantive grievances, alienation is one way of capturing the grievances experienced by workers in a capitalist society.

THE LABOR THEORY OF VALUE

The centrality of labor remained a central theme as Marx shifted from early philosophical ruminations to later economic analysis. He accordingly appropriated a set of ideas known as the labor theory of value from orthodox political economy. What had been an arid, academic concept in the work of Adam Smith, David Ricardo, and others sparked a blistering critique of exploitation in Marx's hands.

In his efforts to uncover the hidden workings of capitalist economies, Marx probed the origins of profits. The puzzle is how capitalists systematically invest in resources, labor, and technology to create products whose sale results in more money than was there at the beginning. Not every business succeeds, but there is a systematic quality to capital accumulation as a whole that attracts Marx's critical scrutiny.

Any commodity has two types of economic value. It has use-value because it meets some human need. This use-value is realized when someone consumes the commodity. Commodities also have exchange-value. One commodity can be exchanged for another commodity. The exchange-value of a commodity is realized when someone trades it for another. This raises further questions about how the exchange-value of a commodity is determined and why some are more valuable than others.

Mainstream economics points to supply and demand, but this is merely a theory of price fluctuation. Low supply and high demand increase prices, whereas high supply and low demand decrease prices. But what determines the "real" value of a commodity when supply and demand are in balance? The question is difficult because the use-values of commodities are qualitatively different.

The one common feature of all commodities is that they are products of human labor. From this, Marx advocated the labor theory of value: Commodities have economic value because they are the products of human labor. Moreover, the amount of exchange-value that any commodity has is based on the amount of labor that goes into its production. The more labor that goes into the production of a commodity, the greater its exchange-value. Some commodities are more valuable than others because more labor went into their production.

Another defining feature of capitalism is wage-labor. Workers sell labor-power (their ability to work) to capitalists for a wage. In other words, capitalism turns labor-power into a commodity that is bought and sold. Like any commodity, the price of labor fluctuates with changes in supply and demand. But what is the "real" value of labor-power when supply and demand are in balance?

Marx's logic is consistent. If labor-power is a commodity, then its value is determined by the amount of labor that goes into its production. Because labor-power is embodied in a person, the production of labor-power really means the survival of the person. People must consume a variety of commodities to sustain themselves and their ability to labor. So the value of labor-power is equal to the value of all the commodities people need to survive at a culturally acceptable level. If capitalists buy labor-power at its real value, they pay workers wages that allow them to survive and reproduce their labor-power.

The labor theory of value explains the exchange-value of all commodities in terms of the single baseline of human labor. It is the only common element in the production of every commodity, including labor-power itself.

SURPLUS VALUE AND EXPLOITATION

If we assume that commodities exchange at their true values, we still have the question of how profits are possible. Marx argues that labor-power is the only commodity that can create new value greater than its own value. The more productively it is organized, the greater the surplus that will result.

Capitalist production begins with a capitalist who purchases raw materials, means of production, and labor-power. The raw materials and means of production do not create new value when set in motion; their value is simply transferred to the product during the production process. The new value comes from labor and its unique capacity to produce a surplus. The question can now be answered: Profits come from labor.

Starting from a symmetrical situation in which all commodities exchange at their value, we arrive at an asymmetrical outcome. Capitalists create no new value, but receive a systematic profit over their intial investment. This new value is created by workers, but they receive only a portion of it back to reproduce their labor power. The remaining value created by labor goes to capital. When workers create all the new value, and capitalists take a portion of it, that is exploitation. Capitalists exploit workers by taking advantage of labor-power's unique capacity to produce a surplus.

This exploitation is obscured by how workers are paid. Consider economic production on a large scale. Every day some commodities are completely consumed, whereas others are partially consumed. Survival requires that a certain amount of production occur every day simply to replace what is used up. Call this necessary labor. A society could hypothetically do only this much labor and survive. However, there would be no surplus and no growth. In reality, all societies produce some surplus. Put differently, they engage in surplus labor above and beyond the necessary labor needed to ensure survival.

We can thus hypothetically divide a workday into two components. The first is necessary labor required for survival. The second is surplus labor beyond that minimum. The value created during necessary labor comes back to workers as wages. It must, if they are to survive by buying commodities to reproduce their labor-power. The value created during surplus labor goes to the capitalists as surplus value or profits.

It's as if workers work part of the day for themselves and part of the day for capitalists. If the day were really divided this way, logical workers would go home after necessary labor with all their wages and leave capitalists without any income. The wage form prevents this. It takes the money workers need and spreads it out over the entire workday, so they must work a full shift to receive their wages.

Imagine that workers produce eight hours of new value and get four hours back as wages while capitalists take the other four hours as surplus value. This ratio is the rate of surplus value; it expresses what capitalists get relative to workers. It is also the rate of exploitation; it reveals what workers get relative to their contributions. Such exploitation is inherent in capitalism; it makes profits possible.

Capitalism also systematically increases exploitation in two ways. One is by lengthening the working day. If workers can be forced to work twelve hours rather than eight, the rate of surplus value increases dramatically: four hours for workers and eight for capitalists. The other method is to increase the productivity of labor. If workers double their output, necessary labor (and workers' wages) shrinks from four to two hours, and surplus labor (and capitalists' profits) expands from four to six hours. In both cases, workers create all new value, but their share shrinks to an ever-smaller proportion of the total while capitalists' share expands.

Capitalism increases exploitation because capitalists compete among themselves. As powerful as they are, even capitalists are subject to the laws of competition. A primary strategy in the competitive struggle between capitalists is to maximize surplus value by exploiting workers more intensively than rival capitalists. As capitalism becomes more competitive between capitalists, it becomes more exploitative of workers.

Marx recognized the revolutionary power of capitalism to develop the forces of production, but he was highly critical of the price workers paid for such advances. Capitalism inevitably creates increasingly exploitative and antagonistic relations between a wealthy minority and a vast majority. Marx's ultimate target was not capital*ists* but rather capital*ism* because it deforms human relations.

This deformation includes alienating workers from their product, their labor, their potential, and other people. It involves commodity fetishism in which commodities become more important than people. Even though people are required to create them, commodities acquire a life of their own and seem to exist independent of human activity. Marx punctured these illusions by referring to commodities as "dead labor," underscoring that they would not exist without the past efforts of workers. In a similar fashion, the socialist slogan that "property is theft" asserts that what exists now as private property was once the creation of laborers who could not own what they produced. And most generally, Marx insisted that capital is not a thing but a social relationship. It comes into existence through the productive efforts of workers. Its ownership by others should not blind us to how it was created nor to whom was exploited in the process.

To whatever extent workers' movements—and social movements more generally—are motivated by deeply rooted grievances, Marx's analysis of alienation and exploitation provides powerful statements of how such grievances arise. To whatever extent workers' movements—and social movements more generally—arise from structurally rooted conflicts of interest, Marx's dissection of capitalist dynamics provides a logically compelling account of how such conflicting interests generate collective action.

CONTRADICTIONS AND CRISES

Capitalism is a dynamic, unstable system because of capitalist competition and worker resistance. Its instability goes even deeper because capitalism rests on contradictions. Some contradictions develop into major economic crises that threaten capitalism's survival.

One contradiction is between social production and private appropriation. Capitalist production is socially organized; it requires the coordinated activity of many people. Appropriation, however, is private and individual. Resources that are socially produced are privately owned. As a result, capitalism is good at producing private commodities, but bad at producing public goods. The contradiction between social production and private appropriation contributes to capitalist instability.

Another contradiction is between internal organization and market anarchy. Internal organization occurs within the corporation, which becomes a highly rational and bureaucratic firm seeking to control and predict its environment in pursuit of profits. In sharp contrast, there is economic anarchy in the larger society.

There is little economic coordination, no overall plan for utilizing scarce resources wisely, and little regulation of rapid fluctuations in commodity and labor markets. Although the wealthy can survive such instability, it threatens the livelihood of many ordinary citizens.

A third contradiction is the polarization of wealth and poverty. Because capital concentrates in fewer hands, the rich become richer. Even when workers' living standards improve, capitalist standards often improve more rapidly, creating a relative polarization of wealth and poverty. Such extreme inequality creates further instability.

A fourth contradiction is that capitalism produces for profit and not for use. Imagine two circles that partially overlap. One circle represents products that people need. The other represents products that are profitable. Capitalism responds to the second circle. It produces some things that are needed—but it does so because they are profitable, not because they are needed. It also produces some things that are profitable but not really needed. Finally, it does not produce things that are needed but not profitable. Production for profit and not use creates further instability by allowing the extreme affluence of some to coexist with the unmet needs of others.

Each of these contradictions promotes inequality or instability that can spark collective action. Some contradictions, moreover, can become major economic crises. Overproduction or underconsumption is a recurring tendency because capitalism produces more than can be sold at an acceptable profit. Recall that workers produce more value than they receive back as wages, so they don't have the purchasing power to buy all the commodities they produce. Even when capitalist consumption is added to the equation, the tendency toward overproduction or underconsumption persists and periodically becomes an economic crisis. On the production side, profits shrink, investment slows, production declines, inventories accumulate, and productive capacity goes unutilized. Stagnation, recession, or even depression may result. On the consumption side, firms seek new markets, destroy surplus products, rely on government consumption, advertise more heavily, and extend consumer credit so that even people without money can buy.

Another crisis tendency involves a falling rate of profit as capitalists invest in new technology to stay competitive. This means their investment in labor becomes a smaller portion of their total outlay. Because labor is the only source of new value, it becomes increasingly difficult to sustain profits. Again, various strategies come into play. Capitalists may increase exploitation or depress wages to counter a falling rate of profit. In the long term, they must cheapen the cost of new technology to sustain acceptable profits. Unless they can do so fast enough, profits remain low, and the entire economy experiences stagnation.

These contradictions and crisis tendencies cannot be eliminated. What capitalists and their political allies try to do is minimize and redirect their most harmful effects. The value of this crisis theory is that it identifies powerful economic tendencies that trigger social and political instability. Such tendencies can operate both as grievances and as opportunities provoking collective action. Although he never specified a timetable, Marx nevertheless expected that increasing worker poverty, intensifying overproduction crises, and falling profit rates would eventually provoke a working-class revolution.

Marx thereby identifies alienation, exploitation, conflicting interests, structural contradictions, and economic crises as endemic features of capitalist society. Given such a structural backdrop, responses in the form of collective action should come as no surprise. Indeed, it would be more surprising if the social landscape were serene and tranquil under such conditions. Although such collective action could conceivably take many forms, it is obvious for Marx that the most significant social movements will take the form of economically driven class struggle.

CLASS FORMATION

Class for Marx is a dynamic, relational process. Classes emerge and develop over time. Classes bind their members closer together as they distance one class from another. Over time, Marx expected to see increasing solidarity *within* classes alongside increasing polarization *between* classes. Marx called this process class formation or development (Marx and Engels 1848/1964). The logic of class formation is for classes-in-themselves to become classes-for-themselves over time.

As classes-in-themselves, capitalists and workers are necessary if capitalism is to exist at all. Classes-in-themselves are defined by people's relationship to material production. Capitalists own productive property and derive profits and their livelihood from this property. Workers own nothing but labor-power and derive wages and their livelihood from its sale. These differing relations to production distinguish capitalists and workers as classes-in-themselves.

Differing relations to production generate differing relations to consumption. As a general rule, ownership of property yields more income than sale of labor-power; capitalists are wealthier than workers. Hence, distinct lifestyles, consumption patterns, class cultures, and standards of living further distinguish these classes.

Classes-in-themselves also have conflicting interests. What benefits one class typically comes at the expense of the other class. The trade-off between capitalists' profits and workers' wages is the most obvious expression of these conflicting interests because gains for one tend to mean losses for the other. This tension is merely one expression of conflicting interests between capitalism's major social classes.

As classes-in-themselves, capitalists and workers are distinguished by their relationship to production, their relationship to consumption, and their class interests. They are merely categories of people with common characteristics, however. There is no guarantee that these people will recognize their shared characteristics or feel a collective identity with others in the same boat. The latter are outcomes of class formation; with time and nascent conflict, people come to recognize their class position, interests, and allies.

The transformation of a class-in-itself into a class-for-itself happens when people act on their class interests. As capitalists seek the cheapest labor, and workers seek the highest wages, conflicting class interests become evident. Marx placed particular emphasis on the factory system that capitalists created to control workers, manage costs, and enhance profits. Concentrating workers together in the same time and place had the unanticipated consequence of fostering interaction and communication among them. The factory system helped workers see that their fate was closely tied to that of other workers and their class as a whole.

These social dynamics promoted class formation. A *category* of people who shared characteristics became a *group* of people who recognized them as a major determinant of their lives. Feminists speak of "consciousness-raising" to describe women's growing awareness of how gender shapes their lives. Marx had a similar process in mind when he described the emergence of self-conscious classes.

Classes-for-themselves arise when people develop a "we-feeling" or collective identity. This identity emerges as people see the effects of class on their social relationships. Consider how class fosters segregation by sorting people into neighborhoods, communities, schools, and social networks with distinct class privileges and disadvantages. When chronic class segregation combines with acute class conflict, class identity becomes socially meaningful as well as objectively real.

These processes also foster class consciousness, which can be seen as a continuum. At a minimum, class consciousness means recognizing that capitalism is a class-divided society. It means identifying one's class position accurately. It further means recognizing one's class interests. It finally means a willingness to fight on behalf of one's class interests. The ultimate expression of class consciousness is revolution; Marx felt this was most likely when objective economic crises were accompanied by subjective class consciousness.

Class formation culminates with political organization. Collective identity and class consciousness mean little until they fuel a struggle for political power. This requires organization. Whether it takes the form of trade unions, political parties, social movements, or community organizations, classes-for-themselves are most fully developed when they become politically organized (Anderson 1974).

Class formation thus means that both capitalists and workers begin as classes-in-themselves defined by their relation to production, consumption, and class interests. These categories become groups through class conflict that promotes solidarity within classes and polarization between classes. Class formation brings two classes-for-themselves rooted in collective identity, class consciousness, and political organization.

As a factual prediction, this model runs into trouble. History has not followed the script. The model's real value is not as a prediction but rather as an analytical device and a sociological tool.

Consider two cases in which such a device can help frame and explain significant variations across groups or historical periods. First, the model highlights differences in the degree of class formation between highly organized capitalists and less-organized workers. Put differently, Marx was half right; ironically it was the capitalist class that followed his blueprint for class formation much more faithfully than the working class.

This disparity invites sociological explanation. Capitalists are a relatively small and homogeneous group with a tremendous stake in preserving the system that provides their benefits. A high degree of class formation (despite fractional disputes within the class) should come as no surprise in these circumstances. Workers, on the other hand, are a large and heterogeneous group with varying stakes in the system who encounter powerful individualist ideologies that cut against the grain of class solidarity. A lesser and more intermittent level of class formation should also come as no surprise in these very different circumstances.

Second, consider historical variations over time in the degree of working-class formation. In the United States in particular, there have been (relatively brief) periods of high class consciousness, militant activism, and major strike waves interspersed with longer periods of relative quiescence. Marx's model of class formation provides a yardstick for documenting such variations and inviting explanations in terms of shifting opportunities, regional variations, class fractions, industrial sectors, and other processes that may help account for such differential mobilization.

As an analytic device, Marx's model of class formation thus defines critical benchmarks of progress and regress in class formation and development. It will remain useful as long as capitalism generates class conflict.

LENIN'S GHOST

Two decades after Marx's death, Vladimir Lenin was fomenting a revolutionary movement in Czarist Russia that would eventually succeed in overthrowing the old regime and ushering in Lenin's version of the "dictatorship of the proletariat." Lenin was an avid student of Marxist theory as well as a shrewd observer of the political scene. When he concluded that the Marxist script for class formation and proletarian revolution was not unfolding in a natural, organic way, Lenin analyzed the problem and revised the script to speed the pace of social change. In pondering *What Is to Be Done?* (Lenin 1902/1988), he proposed some fateful alterations that go to the heart of many contemporary social movement dilemmas.

Part of Lenin's diagnosis involved the immaturity of the Russian working class. This led him to introduce a distinction between types or levels of working-class consciousness. Workers in Russia—and indeed in many capitalist countries—had little trouble developing what Lenin characterized as trade union consciousness. This led workers to focus on immediate, practical considerations of wages, working conditions, job security, and the like. Although important, this form of class consciousness fell short of the socialist consciousness that was required for a truly revolutionary workers' movement. Without this "higher" level of class consciousness, workers were unlikely to seek broad social transformation (given its attendant risks) and more likely to embrace a reformism that sustained capitalism rather than a revolution that buried it.

The conclusion that the Russian working class was not ready to assume its role as a revolutionary agent of history led to a second fateful revision of the script. Although always vague on precise details, Marx seemed to anticipate a broad, democratic, mass movement of the working class against capitalism. When this failed to materialize in the Russian context, Lenin proposed the substitution thesis. In place of the broad working class (and its limited trade union consciousness), Lenin proposed to substitute a vanguard party of professional revolutionaries (with their expanded socialist consciousness). This small, tightly knit group would do for workers what they were unable to do for themselves: igniting a more basic structural transformation from capitalism to socialism. The substitution thesis thus promoted the vanguard party over the working class as the revolutionary agent of history.

In a third significant contribution, Lenin sketched out a decision-making process for this party known as democratic centralism. According to this doctrine, the vanguard party would initially operate internally in a democratic fashion that invited discussion, debate, and the airing of different points of view. Once a decision was reached by majority vote, however, the party would subsequently operate externally in a centralized fashion that required every member to actively support the majority's decision. In Lenin's view, such an approach maximized input into decision making, but then maximized efficiency in the execution of such decisions.

Even more than Marx, Lenin was an advocate of change, not a dispassionate scholar of social movements. His ideas nonetheless resonate today like seminar topics in social movement analysis. The issue of group consciousness is one example. Debates over "false" versus "true" or rudimentary (trade union) versus advanced (socialist) forms of group consciousness pose complex issues closely related to the equally thorny question of group interests. We have various theories of ideology or hegemony that help explain why people often do not accurately perceive or act on their interests. But who defines those interests if not people themselves? On what basis can the theory or analysis of intellectuals be privileged over the everyday perceptions of ordinary people? Is it possible to identify objective group interests and correct forms of consciousness? Such questions haunt a wide range of social movements down to the present day.

Similar issues arise concerning the substitution thesis. In animal-rights or child-welfare movements, one group acts on behalf of another out of necessity. But what about constituencies that are capable of acting on their own behalf but fail to do so or do so in ways that others deem inappropriate or ineffective? Under what circumstances do some—often elites of some sort—proceed to act on behalf of others? Can such movements ever overcome the gap between leaders and followers or activists and beneficiaries? Once again, these issues are endemic to social movement organizing.

The strategy of democratic centralism also poses crucial questions of movement decision making. It sits somewhere on a continuum between authoritarian, top-down movements that have no room for internal deliberation and participatory, consensus-based movements that sometimes seem to have room for little else. The strategy anticipates yet another familiar set of movement debates over how to balance or maximize commitment and participation on the one hand with effectiveness and coordination on the other.

Lenin's ghost thus provides a bridge between the abstractions of Marx's theory of class formation, more concrete processes of actual mobilization and organizing, and some central debates in the study of social movements today.

Beyond his relevance for understanding the dilemmas of revolutionary action, Lenin's work made another, albeit indirect, contribution to contemporary movement analysis. His study of imperialism as the "highest stage" of capitalism (Lenin 1917/1937) in the early twentieth century inspired the later and enormously influential perspective known as world system theory (Wallerstein 1974, 1980, 1989). This perspective, in turn, has prompted new understandings of global waves of social activism across several centuries (Wallerstein 1990; Martin 2008) that will be examined in the concluding chapter of this volume.

LESSONS FROM MARX

As befits his dual identity, Marx's legacy for the study of social movements is two-fold. His political legacy involves activists who developed social theory as a tool for advancing political struggle and the socialist cause. His intellectual legacy involves scholars who have found rich lessons in Marx's work that also generalize to other constituencies and contexts.

A good example of Marx's political legacy is the work of Antonio Gramsci, an Italian Marxist and founding member of the Italian Communist party in the early twentieth century. Like the German Frankfurt School of the same era, Gramsci (1971) grappled with the question of why a socialist revolution seemed inevitably deferred on the European continent.

His answer pointed not to the material base of economic production but rather to the cultural superstructure of ideas and beliefs. The concept of hegemony referred to the power of ideological beliefs that reflected dominant capitalist interests, but became widely embraced by all social classes. Hegemonic power thus promotes a kind of false consciousness that prevents people from even recognizing—much less acting upon—their class interests.

This concept should resonate with any analyst of social movements who has wondered why potential constituents of a given movement fail to join. Although there can be many obstacles to mobilization, hegemonic control is certainly among them. Overcoming it may require deliberate, counter–hegemonic strategies and ideas. These concepts have obvious relevance to later developments in social movement theory concerning the social construction of grievances and effective forms of diagnostic, prognostic, and motivational framing.

Gramsci also spoke to issues of social movement leadership in his analysis of the role of intellectuals. He initially demystifies this category by observing that all people are intellectuals in terms of their innate capacity to rationally debate and evaluate the validity of ideas, values, and beliefs. Only some people, however, occupy the social role of an intellectual in society, and they subdivide into two categories.

Traditional intellectuals portray themselves as free-floating and detached from social groups, whereas they help construct the hegemonic beliefs that serve dominant powers.

Organic intellectuals, by contrast, emerge "naturally" from specific social classes and become the vehicles through which the interests of such classes are given voice. It is organic intellectuals who are most likely to engage in counter-hegemonic work by puncturing the dominant ideology, revealing its class biases, and articulating the interests of subordinate classes. Once again, Gramsci's analysis of the role of organic intellectuals speaks to the importance of ideology and culture in the identification and articulation of class interests and collective grievances (Gramsci 1971).

A second example of Marx's political legacy is Leon Trotsky (1930/1965). His analysis of the Russian Revolution defined a revolutionary situation as one in which at least two social classes attain simultaneous, significant control over some share of state power. This insight was subsequently reformulated into the notion of multiple sovereignty as the defining characteristic of a revolutionary situation. Such situations, in turn, may or may not produce a revolutionary outcome. These definitions and distinctions have done much to clarify the analysis of revolutions as a specialized case of social movements and collective action (Tilly 1978).

Turning from Marx's political to intellectual legacy, it is worth noting that the power of ideas may sometimes be measured by the volume of criticism they attract. By this standard, Marx's theory of capitalism, class formation, and socialist revolution is powerful indeed. It has been criticized as overly structural, mechanistic, deterministic, reductionistic, and economistic (to name a few criticisms). It privileges one group (workers) and one tactic/strategy/goal (revolution) for resolving grievances. It implies that any other conflict is at best a diversion from the most fundamental divide in a capitalist society. As a theory of social movements, this is clearly too limited, problematic, and even anachronistic. But there is more to be learned here. Rather than engaging in old debates about the relevance of Marxism, it is more productive to identify generalizable lessons contained within this analysis.

Perhaps the most distinctive aspect of Marx's approach is its structural dimension. It offers, in considerable detail and with compelling logic, an analysis of how a certain form of social organization creates deeply rooted conflicting interests between different groups of people. Although Marx may not have identified himself as a sociologist, there is no better example of sociology's power to theorize abstract social structures and trace their impacts on individual human lives (Lemert 2008).

The centrality of conflict in social order and social life is another central theme of this approach. Sociologists have been only intermittently attentive to conflict, and it has sometimes required very circuitous paths tracing the functions of social conflict (Coser 1956) to bring conflict back to center stage in the discipline. For Marx, it was always there and has always been fundamental, as evidenced in the proclamation that "the history of all hitherto existing society is the history of class struggles" (Marx and Engels 1964: 57).

The weight of structure and the centrality of conflict logically lead to a third contribution: a theory of group formation. Marx focused on class, but the model of class formation is eminently generalizable to other groups. It applies to any groups that are initially defined by structurally imposed categories but subsequently undergo a process of group development culminating in collective identity, group consciousness, and political organization. Indeed, the issues of how groups identify their interests; define appropriate forms of collective consciousness; and arrive at effective political strategies, tactics, and organizational forms are familiar to students of many different social movements.

A generic version of Marx's approach is thus applicable to many cases of group conflict, collective action, and social movements. It fits any situation in which categorical identities are hierarchically organized. The identities may involve race, ethnicity, culture, status, gender, nationality, religion, or sexuality. The relation between groups may involve exploitation, oppression, exclusion, colonization, domination, or discrimination. As people identify their interests, act upon them, and engage in overt conflict, we can expect a shift from "groups-in-themselves" based on categories to "groups-for-themselves" based on collective identity, group consciousness, and political organization. The sharper the conflict, the greater the solidarity within groups and polarization between groups.

Two specific examples help illustrate the point. In his critique of the idea that the most isolated individuals are most prone to join social movements, Oberschall (1973) proposes a quasi-Marxist alternative and demonstrates its empirical validity. High degrees of mobilization are much more likely under two conditions. First, the subordinate group has strong preexisting social connections resting upon either communal or associational organization. Second, there is vertical segmentation or distance between dominant and subordinate groups. This more generic model closely parallels Marx's image of class formation (with simultaneous solidarity within classes and polarization between classes) as a precondition for successful collective action.

A second example is Tilly's mobilization model, which he has described as "resolutely pro-Marxian" (Tilly 1978: 48). The model begins with groups' interests and then traces their interactive impacts with organization and mobilization in a broader context of opportunity and power struggles that lead to collective action.

It is at this level of generalization that Marx's insights have stood the test of time and filtered down into contemporary approaches to social movements. The work of Oberschall, Tilly, and others both translates and generalizes Marx's analysis into contemporary language for analyzing social movements. Seen this way, it is evident that Marx's approach is a major contribution to the sociology of group conflict and social movements.

Chapter Two

Weber and Michels

Like Marx, Max Weber (1864–1920) is rarely seen as a theorist of social movements, but his core ideas are rich with implications for the study of collective action. Whereas Marx's ideas congealed into a major paradigm for the study of class conflict, Weber's rich contributions (like his sociology in general) never quite became a unified tapestry. Weber's ideas inform many approaches to social movements while not defining or dominating any particular perspective as a whole.

THE CONTEXT

By the end of the nineteenth century, sociology was becoming an intellectually coherent, academically recognized discipline. Although Weber was initially trained in law, economics, and history, he eventually gravitated toward sociology as his main disciplinary affiliation.

Rather than being shaped by extant sociology, however, Weber helped define what sociology was and would become through a series of foundational proclamations. These statements framed his sociology in general and its implications for social movements in particular.

For example, Weber's famous definition of sociology called for both an interpretive understanding and a causal explanation of social action. From this definition, he derived a typology of social action that in turn led to a typology of authority. Combined with empirical studies of law, religion, capitalism, and bureaucracy, Weber's sociology culminated in a profound ambivalence about Western rationalization and the inescapable iron cage of bureaucracy.

Weber's programmatic statements about sociology included methodological injunctions about the role of *Verstehen,* the function of ideal types, and the nature of causality and probability in sociological explanation. He also grappled with the role of values in social science, rigorously defending a middle ground that recognized the inevitable influence of values on virtually every aspect of intellectual activity while promoting the highest standards of objectivity in the conduct of social science. He thus insisted on distinguishing between the neutrality required in the sphere of science and the commitment—and even passion—necessary in the realm of politics.

Weber's considerable efforts to define the sociological enterprise were inextricably entangled with larger debates that comprised the intellectual climate of his day. One such debate revolved around neo-Kantian idealism, and Weber's engagement with this debate led him to insist that although the natural sciences can only explain events, sociology must also interpret them as culturally meaningful for the social actors who experience them.

Another such debate involved historicism, and Weber's involvement in this dispute led him to another type of middle ground. He rejected the positivist quest for general laws based on the natural sciences. But he also rejected the strict historicist claim that because every society, culture, or historical period was unique, generalization and social science itself were impossible. Weber's compromise endorsed a historical-comparative method that sought patterns in social order while eschewing the search for immutable, general laws of social behavior.

Finally, although Weber underscored the importance of ideas in social action, he was influenced by both Marx and Friedrich Nietzsche, who identified links between ideas and interests. Marx revealed how ideas express and promote class interests, whereas Nietzsche exposed how ideas "became rationalizations utilized in the service of private aspirations for power and mastery" (Coser 1977: 249). For Weber, ideas cannot be reduced to material interests or psychological dispositions, but neither can they be understood apart from them.

Weber's work was thus shaped by the congealing discipline of sociology, by his own efforts to define that field, and by broader debates about the possibility of social science and the role of values and ideas in such an enterprise. His work was also, and even more obviously, influenced by the contours of his own society and its prevailing movements and forms of political conflict.

Weber wrote in the context of a *fin de siècle* German society that had witnessed the consolidation of industrial capitalism, the growth of the administrative state, the extension of voting rights, the institutionalization of party politics, and a rising tide of nationalism and incipient militarism. These social forces inevitably drew his attention and also shaped his sociological ideas.

Whereas Marx channeled optimism about revolutionary transformation in the mid-nineteenth century, Weber articulated classic Germanic pessimism about the rigidity of social order, the futility of revolutionary challenges, and the inevitability of rationalization and bureaucratization. Thus, although Weber acknowledged class inequality and the logic of the socialist challenge to it, he expected (presciently) that socialism would only exacerbate the trend toward bureaucratic domination rather than overturn it.

Weber held strong political views and was actively involved in political debates throughout his long academic career. His views and involvements, however, often

found him between a rock and a hard place. He was frustrated by the traditional-
ism and provincialism of prevailing political parties and ideologies, but even more
distrustful of the rationalization and bureaucratization that seemed poised to replace
it (Coser 1977: 255ff).

Given these influences, it is not surprising that Weber was intrigued by the
possibility of charismatic leaders who might transform ossified social orders. But it is
also not surprising that he was ultimately pessimistic about the probability that any
type of social movement could fundamentally transform society for the better.

THE PROTESTANT ETHIC

Many classic Weberian themes were already evident in his early study of the Protestant Ethic and its relation to capitalism (Weber 1904/1958). In addition to those
discussed previously, three additional key ideas inform this work.

The first is elective affinity. It captures a relationship between social forces that
is not linear and causal but rather recursive and correlational. Thus, the Protestant
Ethic did not cause the spirit of capitalism nor its economic organization, but it resonated with and reinforced both and thereby contributed to their predominance.

The second is the economic relevance of non-economic factors. Turning Marx
on his head, this idea recognizes that economic processes can be profoundly shaped
by beliefs, activities, or forms of organization that are not economically rooted.
Thus, the beliefs that comprised the Protestant Ethic were religious in origin, but
had profound effects on the economic behavior of true believers.

Third, this study illustrates how social action always produces unintended
and unanticipated consequences. The general principle is one of sociology's most
profound insights and applies to innumerable instances of social action. The specific
reference is to how Luther, Calvin, and other religious leaders never intended to
promote the rise of capitalism but nonetheless promulgated values and beliefs that
had precisely that consequence.

The problem Weber addresses in this work is this: Various preconditions of capitalism have been present in many societies and historical periods, but a distinctively
rational-calculative form of capitalism emerged only in the relatively recent history
of European societies. This prompts him to search for the additional factors in this
time and place that, in tandem with the others, produced a unique outcome.

Weber begins with an empirical observation that Protestants—and Calvinists
in particular—are disproportionately found among capitalist entrepreneurs. He
also identifies a distinctive "spirit of capitalism" among this group that underscores
the value of hard work, industriousness, saving, frugality, punctuality, and the like.
Although a secular orientation, this spirit endorses productive work almost as a
religious calling.

There was a strong elective affinity between this secular spirit and Luther's
notion of a religious calling that emphasizes the importance of faithfully fulfilling
duties and meeting obligations as an expression of one's beliefs. Despite their affinity,

there remained a tension between the materialist spirit of capitalism and the religious basis of the Protestant Ethic.

Weber then turns to Calvinism and its core doctrine of predestination. Unlike Catholics who could earn salvation, Calvinists faced the grimmer reality that their fate was utterly beyond their control. It is here that Weber employs his method of *Verstehen* by asking what impact such beliefs might have on true believers. His supposition is that they would produce an intense inner loneliness that would drive people to seek pastoral advice on how to cope with such loneliness.

Weber found that such advice had several themes. First, it was a matter of duty and an expression of faith to consider oneself among the chosen. Even if you couldn't earn your way to heaven, faith required that you act as if you were already on the way. Second, and more practically, believers were encouraged to throw themselves into intense worldly activity and productive labor as a means of reducing anxiety, dispersing doubt, and maintaining faith. Finally, believers were encouraged to renounce earthly sensual pleasures that could undermine faith or promote false hope about one's spiritual destiny.

Although various religious belief systems had either endorsed productive activity or counseled ascetic lifestyles, the Calvinist combination of hard dutiful work while renouncing the pleasures of consumption was unusual. When added to a context that included the spirit of capitalism (and other preconditions), it was unusually powerful at promoting a new form of economic behavior and indeed a new economic system altogether. "When the limitation of consumption is combined with this release of acquisitive activity, the inevitable practical result is obvious: accumulation of capital through the ascetic compulsion to save" (Weber 1958: 172).

Put differently, the Protestant Ethic recast the pursuit of material gain from narrow self-interested acquisitiveness to an expression of, and evidence for, one's religious faith. It equated worth with wealth and cast suspicion on those who were without wealth as also being without worth.

Weber thereby seeks to explain a unique outcome—the rise of rational calculative capitalism in the West—in terms of an unprecedented combination of factors whose elective affinity had the unintended and unanticipated consequence of promoting a new form of economic organization that has now come to dominate the globe.

Although Calvinism doesn't meet most contemporary definitions of a social movement, Weber's analysis is nonetheless rich in implications for how to study such movements. It exemplifies at least part of what has been labeled a Weberian approach to social movements: "a group of people somehow orient themselves to the same belief system and act together to promote change on the basis of the common orientation" (Tilly 1978: 40).

The great irony of Weber's analysis of the Protestant Ethic is that although people were oriented to the same belief system, the macroeconomic change they produced was not a conscious intention but rather an unintended consequence. But the analysis of the belief system itself goes a long way toward addressing the "standard questions" of the Weberian approach: "How do such systems of beliefs arise and acquire followings? How do they constrain their adherents? How do they and the groups which form around them change, routinize, disappear?" (Tilly 1978: 40).

Weber's contribution here is thus to call attention to the role of beliefs, values, and ideas in providing group cohesion and motivating collective action. Such belief-based movements add variety and nuance to standard classifications of movements as either interest-based or identity-oriented. When such beliefs are strongly held, they may even lead groups to support actions against their (material) interests or provide the underlying foundation for some so-called identity movements.

To invoke another Weberian typology, this emphasis on the role of beliefs and values opens the door to analyzing status-based movements alongside class and power-based movements. This has proven to be a viable category for movement analysis all the way from the temperance movement of the late nineteenth century (Gusfield 1963/1986) to many of the movements comprising the "culture wars" of the late twentieth century.

The role of beliefs in constituting collectivities that may subsequently engage in collective action is thus one of Weber's legacies for the study of social movements.

THE SCIENCE OF SOCIOLOGY

As noted earlier, Weber was centrally involved in defining and consolidating the discipline of sociology itself. This project began with his bi-level definition of sociology as a science "concerning itself with the interpretive understanding of social action and thereby with a causal explanation of its course and consequences" (1978: 4). The definition expresses his commitment to sociology as a science, but also as a distinctive type of science that must understand subjective meanings in order to arrive at causal explanations. His analysis of the role of Calvinist beliefs in promoting action that in turn ushered in a capitalist economy is merely one example of this approach in action.

If sociology's subject matter is social action, then the latter requires further specification. Some things people do are mere behaviors, prompted by natural instinct, immediate stimuli, or unthinking habits. They carry no subjective meaning for the actor. Action, by contrast, is behavior to which the actor attaches a subjective meaning of some sort. Action becomes social (and becomes the subject matter of sociology) "insofar as its subjective meaning takes account of the behavior of others and is thereby oriented in its course" (1978: 4). Meanings are thus central to what people actually do as well as to how sociology must explain what they do.

Given its centrality to sociology's goals of interpretation and explanation, Weber proceeded to develop a typology of social action. This is one example of his strategy of developing ideal types for social analysis. Social reality exhibits complex combinations of types and traits, so ideal types are not presented as empirical realities that exist in the world. They are instead meant as conceptual baselines that we can use to examine and clarify the complexity of what does exist in the world.

Weber's first type is purposively rational action. Such action is characterized by efficiency and calculability, both in the selection of ends and particularly in the choice of means to accomplish those ends. Such action is nicely exemplified by capitalist economic activity that is based on rational calculation, cost-benefit analysis, methodical bookkeeping, profit maximization, and the like. The conduct of bureaucracies also exemplifies this ideal type of social action.

The second type is value rational action. This is driven by a conscious belief in, and commitment to, a value for its own sake. This commitment motivates behavior in accordance with this value completely apart from the prospects for successful outcomes. Such action is rational in its overriding orientation to an ultimate value, even if it appears "irrational" by the standards of purposively rational action and its impulse to calculate probabilities of success and alter conduct accordingly. The category of value rational action can thus "make sense" out of deeply committed, highly quixotic, or rigidly fanatical behavior once we understand the underlying value(s) that motivates such behavior.

A third type of social action is affectual action. As the term implies, such action is motivated by feelings, passions, or sentiments. It is not necessarily irrational as much as nonrational, but still subjectively meaningful for the actors involved. Some cases of spontaneous, immediate reactions may not rise to the standard of meaningfully oriented conduct. Action nevertheless qualifies as affectually oriented "if it satisfies a need for revenge, sensual gratification, devotion, contemplative bliss, or for working off emotional tensions (irrespective of the level of sublimation)" (Weber 1978: 25).

The final type of social action is traditional action. This is another type of nonrational action guided by custom or long-standing habits or practices. Weber recognizes that it is also a borderline case because deeply ingrained and habituated conduct may no longer carry any particular meaning for the actor engaged in it. But if the actor could provide an account of the motivation for their behavior, and if that account made reference to social customs or ancestral traditions, those sources could be seen as imparting meaning to the conduct and thereby qualify it as a type of social action.

Recall that these are pure, ideal types. Real action in the world will typically blend two or more of these orientations in complex empirical combinations. But the ideal types are useful concepts for analyzing sociology's core subject matter of social action in whatever setting it occurs. Those settings include situations in which social actors become involved in collective action and social movements.

TYPES OF AUTHORITY

Weber's best-known typology distinguishes three different types of authority. Although this discussion leads us into Weber's political sociology with more direct implications for the study of social movements, this typology is also logically derived from his conception of sociology as a discipline and the types of social action.

Any discussion of authority must first begin with power and domination. Weber's classic definition of power is that it "is the probability that one actor within a social relationship will be in a position to carry out his own will despite resistance, regardless of the basis on which this probability rests" (Weber 1978: 53). The latter phrase implies the breadth and somewhat amorphous character of power; it can arise in a wide variety of circumstances and emerge from a wide range of personal or social characteristics.

For this reason, Weber introduces the more specific concept of domination. This is defined as "the probability that a command with a given specific content will be obeyed by a given group of persons" (Weber 1978: 53). Domination is thus a subtype of the broader category of power, and it is defined in a way that renders it more readily observable.

Weber's concept of power links it to coercion or force. It is evident when one side overcomes the resistance of a rival. Such purely coercive power may be effective in the short run, but is likely to provoke resentment and further resistance in the long run. As a result, raw power is subject to great instability.

The more specific concept of domination may also rest on coercion, but it admits of other possibilities. Thus, people may follow orders that go against their will and do so only under threat of severe sanctions or punishments. On the other hand, people may obey orders out of devotion to a cause or a leader and be in complete agreement with the spirit and goals of the directive they are following. Both are instances of domination, but there is a world of difference between a resistant subordinate and a devout follower.

These variations raise the vital question of whether power or domination is viewed as legitimate by those subject to it. If so, it is likely to be stable and long-lasting; if not, it is likely to be volatile and insecure. Issues of legitimation are thus central to Weber's political sociology.

Reflecting his more general sociology, however, is the ongoing significance of social action, social relationships, and subjective meanings. Legitimation is not a property of superordinates as much as it is an emergent product of the social relationship between superordinates and subordinates. Power or domination becomes legitimate only when subordinates assign to it a subjective meaning that recognizes the right of superordinates to hold and exercise power. In this act of conferring legitimacy upon power or domination, it becomes authority.

If authority means power or domination that has become legitimate, then a logical question concerns how this can happen. Weber's answer is his classic typology of authority that distinguishes between ideal-typical forms of traditional, charismatic, and rational legitimation.

Traditional authority gains legitimation through conformity to age-old rules and long-standing customs that designate leaders who must be obeyed because of their traditional status within the group. This takes the form of personal loyalty to a leader, so that obedience is owed to the person who tradition designates as the leader rather than to some abstract set of rules and procedures (Weber 1978: 226–231).

Rational-legal authority gains legitimation through a belief in the legality of a set of rules and the right of leaders designated by those rules to exercise power and issue commands. In such a system, no one is "above the law." Subordinates owe obedience not to a person but to an office or position, and to the broader set of legal norms and rules that govern the organization as a whole. Despite their authority, superordinates are bound by the same laws, norms, and rules.

Rational-legal authority is the basis for carrying out official business in an ongoing fashion that conforms to established rules. It is organized in a hierarchical fashion that coordinates the activities of various personnel who gain their positions on the basis of specific competencies and carry out their duties according to technical rules and norms. Actions, decisions, and rules are formulated in writing. Members of the staff are separated from ownership of the means of production or administration and are not to use their official positions for private gain or personal ends.

It is no accident that rational-legal authority often goes hand in hand with a bureaucratically organized staff. In such bureaucracies, staff members are organized into a hierarchy of offices based on distinct spheres of competence. Positions are filled through a free contractual relationship and staff remain personally free outside their official obligations. Staff are paid in fixed salaries and are the sole occupants of given offices, and their work history constitutes a career subject to advancement and promotion. These features of bureaucratic organization are thus tailor-made for rational-legal authority, and hence the two are often found in close combination (Weber 1978: 215–223).

Despite their obvious differences, both traditional and rational authority connote a stability, orderliness, and predictability that arises from the "eternal yesterday" and legal codes, respectively. This is only one aspect that sets both sharply apart from Weber's third type of authority.

Charismatic authority is tied to an individual personality who is considered extraordinary and seen as endowed with supernatural, superhuman, or highly exceptional powers and qualities. Whatever these qualities might be, they are not available to the ordinary person; charisma creates a gulf between the charismatic leader and all others. Although all forms of legitimation rest on attributions by followers who accept tradition or obey rules, this is especially true in the case of charismatic authority: "It is recognition on the part of those subject to authority which is decisive for the validity of charisma" (Weber 1978: 242).

The charismatic community is based on emotional communal bonds. The hierarchy, formality, and rules; and positions, salaries, technical qualifications, and spheres of competence that typify legal-rational authority are utterly foreign to this charismatic community. In similar fashion, the customs, precedents, rules, and habits of traditional authority are equally foreign to charismatic authority. This is why Weber noted that at least "in traditionalist periods, charisma is the great revolutionary force" (Weber 1978: 245).

There is a clear and logical path from Weber's conception of sociology as the study of social action through his typology of such action to his discussion of authority as legitimate domination. This is evident in that legitimation depends upon the subjective meanings that people attach to domination, thereby converting it into authority. It is also evident in the relation between these two typologies. Traditional authority is logically derived from traditional action, just as rational authority is derived from purposively rational action. Charismatic authority, in turn, emerges at the intersection of the fundamental commitments of value rational action and the emotional heat of affective action. The combination of these two types of action helps explain the explosively disruptive potential of charismatic authority.

IMPLICATIONS FOR SOCIAL MOVEMENTS

In addition to the role of beliefs discussed earlier, Weber's discussion of authority types suggests additional dimensions of a "Weberian" approach to the study of social movements. We begin with two general observations.

First, Weber's analysis of authority as legitimate power or domination speaks to the venerable question of how we might explain the origin and emergence of social movements. In a social order that enjoys strong legitimacy of any type, there is little "space" for movements to emerge and little basis on which to challenge duly constituted authority. Traditional and charismatic authority—when solidly rooted—seem especially resistant to such challenges. Rational-legal systems of authority make more allowances for political contestation, but if they are conducted according to the rules of the system (through political parties, interest groups, or lobbying organizations), such contests are consistent with that system and lack the transgressive quality usually attributed to social movements.

The implication would be that social movement challenges become more likely as social orders experience legitimation difficulties. Whatever their source, cracks in the façade of authority are crucial to the emergence of social movement challenges. Later theories will characterize such cracks as social strain, structural breakdown, political opportunities, or legitimation crises, but however characterized, their presence is a vital facilitating condition for the emergence of social movements.

Second, movements may be analyzed as a type of social order that requires its own micro-legitimation as a movement by its followers. Weber's general types of authority can thus be translated into a typology of social movements distinguished by how the leadership of the movement derives legitimacy from its members or followers.

A traditionally legitimated social movement may sound like a contradiction in terms. The category applies, however, whenever a social group that is organized around long-standing traditions and customs finds it necessary to engage in contentious politics and organizes its challenge around the traditional authority structure of the group. Movements by indigenous peoples to defend their land or other resources against exploitation by outsiders provide merely one example of this category.

Other movements may present more mixed cases in which traditional legitimation is part of a blend of legitimation strategies in a movement. This is most likely in long-standing movements that have acquired a history and accumulated a culture that survives through cyclical waves of overt activism. Thus, labor movements, women's movements, or civil rights movements have a substantial history that provides traditional legitimation (alongside other types) for particular leaders, issues, campaigns, tactics, or strategies.

Movements legitimated through rational-legal authority are a somewhat more familiar category if only because so many collectivities rest on such legitimation in modern societies. Such movements utilize bureaucratic organization as a means to pursue an agenda of social change. Movements in this category would exhibit a hierarchical, centralized leadership structure; a clear division of labor; specialized competencies in different organizational positions; and clear rules and norms for leadership changes and internal decision making. This organizational form may be becoming increasingly common in what has been called a "movement society" (Tarrow 1994).

Despite this trend, there would seem to be an inherent tension in bureaucratically organized social movements. Put most bluntly, bureaucracies are all about routinization and often lapse into empty ritualism, whereas social movements seek change and transformation. Although it is possible to use bureaucratic organization as an instrumental tool to achieve substantive change, this can happen only if such movements control their inertial bureaucratic tendencies that threaten to derail the battle for social change.

Weber's larger analysis of rationalization in Western societies does not bode well for bureaucratically organized social movements. If the entire society is moving toward an inescapable "iron cage" of bureaucracy, it is highly likely that the same logic will paralyze social movements organized along such lines. The temptations to transform goals, moderate radicalism, maintain the organization at all costs, and ignore rank-and-file members are ubiquitous speed bumps, detours, and barricades on the road to social change. As we will see shortly, such tensions have sparked much fruitful theorizing and research about social movements.

Of the three types, there would seem to be the strongest elective affinity between charismatic authority and social movements. After all, charismatic authority is a revolutionary force that is foreign to all routine, tradition, or instrumental calculation. It appears tailor-made for social movement challenges, and this is why Weber's most obvious contribution to the study of social movements revolves around the role of charismatic leadership.

In a charismatically legitimated social movement, the leader is a powerful, highly revered figure presumed to possess special qualities that separate such individuals from others and uniquely qualify them to lead. Such movements are organized through informal, communal, and emotional bonds rather than the formal, associational ties of bureaucratic authority or the habitual, customary links of traditional authority. The combination of charismatic authority; value rational goals; and emotional, communal membership often produces a depth of commitment to the movement's cause that is rarely found in traditional or bureaucratically organized movements.

Although charismatic leadership and social movements seem made for each other, there is a fatal flaw in this dynamic as well. Because charismatic authority is so closely tied to the personal qualities of the leader, and because even charismatic leaders are mortal, such authority has a limited life span. At the very least, the inevitable death of the charismatic leader poses a major challenge to any organization legitimated along these lines (including social movements). The very nature of charisma, moreover, makes this challenge difficult to meet.

In different ways, both traditional and bureaucratic authority have clear ways of designating a successor when a leader dies or is incapacitated. In movements legitimated in either of these ways, there may be some sort of succession struggle, but there are also traditional customs or formal rules that govern such a struggle and increase the likelihood of a smooth transition of power and movement continuity.

By its very nature, charismatic authority provides no such customs or rules about succession. Movements legitimated by charismatic authority are thus much more likely to experience a major crisis when their leader dies or is incapacitated. Weber's sociology distills several responses that have been made to this challenge, but they all arise from a common "desire to transform charisma and charismatic blessing from a unique, transitory gift of grace of extraordinary times and persons into a permanent possession of everyday life ... Inevitably, however, this changes the nature of the charismatic structure" (Weber 1978: 1121). As powerful as charisma may be, it is thus doomed to be a transitory force.

Members of charismatically organized groups have nonetheless devised a wide variety of responses to the problem of charismatic succession. Sometimes the original charismatic leader will designate a successor. If not, followers may presume that charisma is a hereditary quality to be found in the original leader's offspring. In other cases, followers may look for charismatic qualities in a member of their group, rely upon revelation, seek to transmit charisma through some form of ritual, or designate some administrative staff to select a new leader (Weber 1978: 246–249).

Although one or more of these means may accomplish a relatively smooth transition between leaders, they rarely succeed in transmitting charisma itself. By its very nature, charismatic authority is destined to become routinized. This process affects not just the leader but also the entire organization and the basis of its legitimation. Whether the organization lapses into a more traditional form of organization and legitimation or gravitates toward a more rational-legal mode, charisma is likely to recede in the face of such alternatives. Again, Weber sounds a resigned, pessimistic note about the prospects for social movements; even the most revolutionary force in the world seems destined to burn out in the span of a single leader's lifetime.

MICHELS'S CONTRIBUTIONS

Weber thus recognizes that social movements and charismatic leaders may pose explosive challenges to established order, but he detects an inexorable logic of routinization and bureaucratization that eventually tames them. This logic was explored and elaborated by Robert Michels (1876–1936), a former student of Weber's who made major contributions to the study of elites in politics.

Michels (1915/1958) discovered what he termed an "iron law of oligarchy" in modern organizations. He specifically analyzed this tendency in the operation of political parties in his day, but the logic of his argument is directly relevant to the dynamics of social movements as well.

Michels deployed a methodologically compelling strategy. Some parties and organizations explicitly embrace or implicitly accept hierarchical forms of organization, but their existence doesn't prove there is an "iron law." The strongest argument would emerge from a study of all organizations in a given location and historical period, but this is clearly impractical.

The strategy used by Michels anticipated "critical case" methodology. He deliberately selected an organization—the German Social Democratic Party—that was explicitly committed to democratic, egalitarian principles of organization. If it could be shown that even here, hierarchical, oligarchical tendencies overrode such commitments, then the case for the iron law of oligarchy would be that much more convincing.

Michels began by noting that "democracy is inconceivable without organization" (1958: 25). In social groups of any significant size, direct government and decision making by the masses is a technical impossibility. Leadership—and some gulf between leaders and followers—is an administrative and technical necessity in complex organizations. Although some parties, organizations, and movements may remain committed to democratic principles, the need for organization creates executive authority and a complex division of labor that leads to a "rigorously defined and hierarchical bureaucracy" (1958: 39).

The technical necessity of leadership is reinforced by psychological and intellectual factors. The members of mass organizations feel a deep need for leadership and direction, and leaders who combine professional qualifications and cultural capital fulfill this need. Some of these leaders may be predisposed to autocratic tendencies that heighten the gulf between leaders and followers. Even when such tendencies are lacking, however, Michels argued that the exercise of power will bring about a "psychological metamorphosis" of leaders. "The apathy of the masses and their need for guidance has as its counterpart in the leaders a natural greed for power. . . . What was initiated by the need for organization, administration, and strategy is completed by psychological determinism" (1958: 217).

Although noting such factors, Michels's argument does not rest on psychological reductionism. Organizational dynamics begin the push toward oligarchy, so that the outcome is almost overdetermined. Whatever their psychological predispositions, once leaders are in power they gain access to and control over organizational resources, information networks, and decision-making processes that cannot help but enhance their influence at the expense of rank-and-file members. Psychological factors among both leaders and followers may accelerate the process, but it is deeply rooted in routine organizational functioning.

These general observations are reinforced by a more specific social analysis of leadership in socialist parties. Michels documents the likelihood that "bourgeois elements" and leaders will arise and prevail in such parties. In a revealing footnote, he claims that "the present writer has frequently heard people say: "I have every sympathy with socialism—if only there were not any socialists!" (1958: 269). He thus anticipates later studies of cross-class social movements in which the interests and goals of working-class members are diluted and compromised by the interests and goals of middle- or upper-class leaders (Schwartz 1976). It is no small irony that Michels was offering this analysis at roughly the same time Lenin was advocating that a vanguard party of revolutionary intellectuals act on behalf of a working class trapped in "trade union consciousness."

Michels acknowledges that organizations may attempt to limit oligarchical influences through referenda, recall, or other mechanisms. Such measures, however, will never overcome the fundamentally conservative nature of organizations nor their oligarchical tendencies. If such tendencies emerge even in the German Social Democratic Party with its explicit commitment to democratic principles, then Michels has constructed a powerful argument with rich implications for the fate of not just political parties but also social movements and egalitarian communities of all types.

Michels concludes by noting that the "democratic currents of history resemble successive waves [that are] ever renewed. This enduring spectacle is simultaneously encouraging and depressing" (1958: 425). At best, it seems we can anticipate a circulation of elites as an inevitably oligarchical form of leadership changes hands. Like Weber's iron cage of bureaucracy, Michels concludes that it "is probable that this cruel game will continue without end" (1958: 425).

THE WEBERIAN LEGACY

We can now summarize some of the key insights of Weber's sociology for the study of social movements as well as point to some contemporary examples of work that has continued in, or speaks to, this tradition.

First, Weber's sociology underscores the importance of cultural beliefs and values as underpinnings to all social action, including social movement participation. Just as the Protestant Ethic motivated Calvinist entrepreneurs, other deeply held beliefs and values can create subjective meanings that motivate social activism with rational-legal, value rational, affectual, or traditional orientations.

Second, the concept of authority as legitimate power or domination speaks directly to potential causes of social movements. When societal authority is strong through whatever form of legitimation, movements are unlikely. When authority is weak because its legitimation has been undermined, the social space for social movements increases, and they are more likely to emerge and flourish.

Third, movements constitute social orders that often rest on legitimate domination of followers by leaders. We can thus revisit the types of authority to distinguish among movements that rest upon traditional, charismatic, rational, or some blend of these different types of authority. Moreover, each type of movement legitimation introduces its own tensions with the innovation that movements typically seek,

opening a range of questions about how movements with various forms of legitimation organize, mobilize, strategize, and succeed or fail.

Fourth, Weber's analysis of charismatic authority in social movements suggests
a more specific trajectory for social movements. However disruptive charisma and
the movements it inspires may be, it is inevitably short-lived. Sooner or later, it will
undergo a process of routinization that brings the period of innovation and challenge
to an end and ushers in a more institutionalized and becalmed organization.

Fifth, a "Weber-Michels" model of social movement transformation emerges
by combining Weber's analysis of the routinization of charisma with Michels's case
for the iron law of oligarchy. The combined implication is not just that charisma
and the devotion it inspires are short-lived but also that movement organizations
are inevitably destined to abandon their followers and original goals as oligarchical
leadership emerges.

Moving from Weber and Michels to subsequent work on social movements,
it is evident that their model is the basis for familiar arguments about the trajectory
of social movements. One example involves natural history or life cycle models of
movements that follow a predictable path of growth and challenge followed by dis-
sipation and decline. In a related image, the eventual destiny of movements that do
not immediately fail is not so much success but rather institutionalization whereby
they moderate their challenge in exchange for peaceful coexistence with the status
quo.

One measure of the value of a theory is the empirical research and theoretical specification that it stimulates. By this standard, the Weber-Michels model has
been valuable, indeed.

One of the most well-known challenges to the iron law of oligarchy is a study
of the International Typographical Union (Lipset et al.1956), an organization that
appeared to avoid the trap predicted by the Weber-Michels model. The reasons,
however, may derive from unusual characteristics of this organization rather than
more generalizable elements. A combination of bottom-up origins, local autonomy,
dense interactions, democratic culture, and multiple leadership factions was able
to preserve a meaningful degree of union democracy that resisted trends toward
oligarchy. Although perhaps a unique or at least atypical case, this study challenges
the inevitability of oligarchy in such organizations.

Further refinements to the Weber-Michels model emerged from the work of
Mayer N. Zald and Roberta Ash (1966) on social movement organizations. They
distinguish three types of change implied by the Weber-Michels model: goal transformation, a shift to organizational maintenance, and oligarchization. Although
the model implies that all three inevitably involve greater conservatism, the authors
question this inevitability.

The growth and transformation of social movement organizations are shaped
by the ebb and flow of supporting sentiments, the possibilities of success and failure,
and relations with other organizations. As these factors play out, institutionalization and bureaucratization may be accompanied by greater conservatism, but this
is not a necessary consequence. The authors identify a number of circumstances

in which other outcomes—including radicalization—may also occur. This work further challenges the inevitability of oligarchy while bringing greater specificity to the situations in which it is likely to occur.

Although Zald and Ash add specificity to the oligarchy argument, Pamela S. Tolbert and Shon R. Hiatt (2009) expand it into another arena. Adding to the literature on political organizations and social movements, they bring Michels's logic to the analysis of economic organizations and large corporations in particular. They reinterpret the classic notion of the separation of ownership and control in the modern corporation into an instance of oligarchization whereby managers become an oligarchical elite at odds even with major shareholders. They then link this analysis to recent debates over CEO compensation and policy initiatives that could mitigate the tendency toward oligarchy in such corporations.

Another dimension of the Weber-Michels model looms over Michael Schwartz's (1976) analysis of the Southern Farmers' Alliance. This populist organization emerged toward the end of the nineteenth century and combined both large and small growers into a single organization. Despite progressive origins, its cross-class character proved to be a fatal flaw as large growers came to monopolize control of the organization and its agenda. As they pursued their specific interests as large growers, the organization no longer served and sometimes contradicted the differing interests of the small growers who comprised its mass base.

The Weber-Michels model also serves as a cautionary tale in Frances Piven and Richard Cloward's (1979) work on poor people's movements. For them, effective protest emerges from popular disruption and mass action rather than from organized movements. In a series of case studies, they document a familiar pattern in which disruptive and often effective protest gives rise to movement organizations that in turn create incentives for their leaders to tame protest and seek accommodation with established authorities. In their reading of poor people's movements, once organization appears, effective protest dies.

Counterbalancing this work on the dangers and dysfunctions of bureaucratically organized movements is a historical study that suggests a different conclusion. William Gamson (1990) assembled a sample of fifty-three challenging groups in the United States that appeared between 1800 and 1945. He then analyzed this sample and attempted to distill the characteristics of successful movements. Although various factors interacted in complex ways, bureaucratically organized movements tended to be more successful than their counterparts. The effect was enhanced when bureaucratic organization was combined with centralization of power; such movements were even more likely to be successful than movements lacking those characteristics.

These examples suggest the ongoing robustness of the Weber-Michels model for inspiring new research and theoretical modifications. It has shaped social movement study throughout the twentieth century in the form of natural history, life cycle, and institutionalization approaches to the course of social movements over time. It continues to inspire work on the dynamics of leadership in contemporary movements and the seemingly inevitable tension between bureaucratic and democratic forms of movement organization.

A recent study also suggests the ongoing relevance of Weber's focus on charismatic authority and its relation to movement organization and social institutions.

Joel Andreas (2007) laments the equation of charisma with emotion, irrationality, and social-psychological approaches to social movements, all of which have fallen out of favor in recent decades. In an intriguing analysis of the Chinese Cultural Revolution, he seeks to restore the notion of charisma to its rightful place in analyzing social movements.

Andreas distinguishes between bureaucratic and charismatic forms of mobilization. Although at odds, they often occur together, particularly in radical movements. He suggests that charisma and strategic action are not necessarily incompatible, opening the door to a more nuanced analysis of charisma's role. What emerges is a complex story of the Cultural Revolution in which Mao at the top, and party rebels at the bottom invoked charismatic authority and organization to challenge entrenched party bureaucrats. The result was a redistribution of power away from middle-level bureaucrats back to Mao as well as to mass organizations.

Andreas takes his analysis as confirming Piven and Cloward's suspicions about bureaucratic organization while also suggesting that it remains vulnerable to charismatic upheavals. Indeed, Andreas concludes that Weber's "iron cage" thesis is pessimistic only if "bureaucratic authority is destined to overcome the threat of charismatic challenges once and for all" (Andreas 2007: 455). The Cultural Revolution implies that such challenges always remain possible.

The fact that Weber's most distinctive ideas about social movements remain cogent in social movement theory and research a century after their initial formulation testifies to the value of the Weberian legacy for the study of social movements.

Chapter Three

Durkheim and Le Bon

Alongside Marx and Weber, Émile Durkheim (1858–1917) is yet another classical theorist whose work is rich in implications for studying social movements. Indeed, Durkheim's analysis of social integration spawned an entire category of theories about how movements emerge when such integration breaks down. His analysis of religious ritual also sheds light on solidarity in social groups and anticipates recent work on emotions in collective action. Like Weber, Durkheim's ideas do not constitute a unified theory of social movements, but they are relevant to multiple issues surrounding such movements and have been at the heart of some major debates in the field.

THE CONTEXT

"Emile Durkheim was the first French academic sociologist" (Coser 1977: 143). As such, Durkheim's career was dedicated to promoting sociology as a legitimate science within the French academy. This required defining sociology's distinct niche alongside the other social sciences and philosophy. In doing so, Durkheim became one of sociology's strongest advocates.

Durkheim's case for sociology was situated between at least two poles. In contrast with philosophy and other speculative approaches, he argued for a scientific approach to human behavior rooted in rigorous methods and empirical verification. In *The Rules of the Sociological Method* (1895/1950), he spelled out the basic principles of this newly emerging science of society. In contrast with psychology and other individualistic sciences, he argued for a holistic approach that privileged the social over the individual.

Durkheim conceptualized society as a reality *sui generis*. It is not a collection of individual parts but rather an organic entity that is greater than the sum of its parts. This approach led him to emphasize social facts and the necessity of explaining social facts by other social facts. In Durkheim's sociologistic approach, even seemingly individual acts such as suicide have profoundly sociological causes. For him, even the sacred realm of religion is a projection of the power of society over the individual.

These efforts to define and promote the science of sociology took place in a broader intellectual context as well. Durkheim credited Rousseau's notion of the general will as a testament to the importance of social solidarity, and he also found in Rousseau an early statement of the priority of the social over the individual. Montesquieu, Comte, and St. Simon were other French influences who shaped Durkheim's conception of society as a reality *sui generis* as well as his understanding of sociology as a scientific enterprise (Coser 1977).

Somewhat more surprisingly, the British theorist Herbert Spencer was a major influence on Durkheim's theory of social evolution and the division of labor. Although Durkheim borrowed from Spencer's image of social evolution, he recoiled from the individualistic, egoistic, and contractual premises of Spencer's approach. In Durkheim's model of social evolution, society was a moral order preceding the individual rather than a contractual outcome of individual bargaining and egotistical calculation (Coser 1977).

Like Weber, Durkheim endorsed scientific objectivity in his role as a sociologist while also becoming heavily involved in political disputes as a French citizen. Although his sociological concern with integration has conservative connotations, Durkheim was an avid liberal in the context of the Third Republic and its political disputes. At the same time, he was deeply concerned with the moral foundation of French society, advocating ethical training; civic education; and the role of guilds, associations, and other small groups that would bind individuals within webs of social relationships.

These premises also informed his stance toward socialism as a solution to the ills of industrial capitalism. Here the contrasts among the three classical theorists are clear. Writing in an earlier era, Marx was a strong advocate of socialism. Writing as a contemporary of Durkheim, Weber acknowledged many problems with capitalism, but saw socialism not as a solution but rather as a further step down the problematic road of rationalization and the iron cage of bureaucracy.

Durkheim also recognized problems with capitalism, including the practice of inheritance that sustained an abnormal form of the division of labor that violated meritocratic principles. Despite these problems, he thought socialism was a misguided solution. The most basic problems were not economic but rather moral in nature. For Durkheim, a better solution required reform of industrial society so as to strengthen its social cohesion, meritocratic operation, and moral integrity.

Although Durkheim said little directly about social movements or collective action, his academic sociology, intellectual context, and political orientation fostered a distinctively Durkheimian approach to a number of issues relevant to the causes, consequences, functions, and outcomes of social movements.

THE DIVISION OF LABOR

Durkheim's concern with social integration and solidarity was central in his first treatise on the division of labor in society (1893/1964), which makes three interrelated contributions. First, it provides an evolutionary account of social development from the earliest human societies to the most recent ones. Second, it distinguishes two types of solidarity, uniting societies at the beginning and end of this evolutionary process. Finally, it uses this analysis as a basis for practical recommendations about how to address contemporary social problems.

Durkheim builds upon Spencer's image of social evolution as a transition from incoherent homogeneity to coherent heterogeneity. For Durkheim, traditional societies are distinguished by this homogeneity or lack of differentiation. The people in such societies are overwhelmingly similar to one another in their beliefs as well as their activities and functions.

Such societies survived for long periods of time with these characteristics. Eventually, technological and demographic changes led to more complex forms of communication, transportation, and social organization. These changes, in turn, spurred migration and the concentration of people in villages and towns, and ultimately cities, states, and nations.

These developments were accompanied by population increases as the material base of society was able to support larger numbers of people. Durkheim is at pains, however, to distinguish between population growth and increasing dynamic or moral density. The latter refers to an increase in the rate or frequency of interaction between people rather than a mere increase in their numbers.

The distinction is important in light of Durkheim's injunction about explaining one set of social facts with another. Population growth could be considered a biological rather than a social fact, so it alone is not an adequate explanation of social evolution. Beyond expressing his sociologistic bent, the distinction is important because there could be cases in which increasing population does not necessarily produce increased dynamic density. This could occur if rapid geographical expansion allows increasing numbers to expand over more territory without increasing the frequency of interaction.

Increasing dynamic density is thus the key variable in this evolutionary sequence. When it occurs, it is likely to heighten competition for scarce resources among homogeneous members of society, threatening escalating conflict that could undermine social integration and even social survival. Societies unable to resolve these tensions may indeed have succumbed to disintegrative forces. Others, however, discovered an adaptive mechanism that allowed them to resolve these tensions and continue down an evolutionary path.

That mechanism is the division of labor. By assigning different tasks and resources to different people—by replacing homogeneity with heterogeneity—potential conflicts between all people over all resources are avoided. Moreover, the division of labor creates interdependency among people who are no longer self-sufficient but rather elements in a system where the survival of each is tied to the survival of all. The division of labor is thus the solution to the threat of heightened conflict and the evolutionary turning point into modern society.

The beginning and end points of this process illustrate two dramatically different types of social solidarity. Traditional societies have mechanical solidarity. People and groups are homogeneous; they are linked together as chains of similar elements. Because these elements are relatively self-sufficient, there is little interdependence between them, and this is accompanied by relatively low dynamic density.

Durkheim also notes that such societies have harsh and repressive forms of social control. From this he deduces that deviance of almost any sort is seen as a direct challenge to the core values of the group itself. From this, he further deduces the existence of a powerful *conscience collective* at the heart of such societies. The French term implies both a collective consciousness that privileges the group over the individual and a collective conscience that provides a powerful moral compass and symbolic unity. This *conscience collective* provides people with identity, purpose, and meaning, and it underwrites the integration of the overall society.

At the end of the evolutionary sequence we find modern societies with organic solidarity. Here, social bonds link people and groups that are heterogeneous or very different from each other. They are organically linked into a dense web like the elements of a complex molecule. There is greater interdependence among such organically linked elements, and all this is accompanied by greater dynamic density.

Such societies have less punitive forms of social control. With some exceptions, deviance is more likely to be seen as a technical violation requiring compensation or restitution than a frontal challenge to social order requiring harsh punishment. From this, Durkheim reasons that the collective conscience has lost its central role as guarantor of social integration.

The loss of this source of social integration would seem to pose a major challenge to the survival of modern societies. The decline of the *conscience collective* is compensated for by the rise of the division of labor; it is a functional equivalent in terms of solidarity. Societies that were initially integrated by similarities in what people thought are subsequently integrated by differences in what people do. Put differently, social integration flows from functional differentiation rather than normative consensus.

The collective conscience does not disappear in modern society, but it moves to the margins as its values become as differentiated as the members of the society themselves. As this belief system becomes more secular, it also recognizes the worth and dignity of the individual and the importance of individual rights and opportunities in a society of highly differentiated individuals.

Durkheim even sees the individual as a product of social evolution and differentiation. Traditional societies had "people" but not "individuals" in the modern sense of heterogeneous, differentiated, or even unique members of society. The rise of individuality is a product of the division of labor, and one that is reflected in the more contemporary *conscience collective* and its "cult of the individual."

Despite the logical elegance of his theory, Durkheim recognized that his own society departed from the imagery of a smooth and harmonious organic system. He attributed such problems not to a flaw in his theory but rather to the prevalence of abnormal or anomic forms of the division of labor. Such deviations resulted from rapid change and lack of governmental oversight, and they led to the misallocation of people to roles and functions, unwarranted inequality, and social injustice. With more effective planning, intervention, and regulation, Durkheim anticipated that meritocratic principles and the integrative benefits of organic solidarity would prevail. These concerns about social integration and individualism moved center stage in Durkheim's next study.

THE SOCIOLOGY OF SUICIDE

As a topic of sociological analysis, *Suicide* (Durkheim 1897/1951) was a brilliant choice on several grounds. It was a concrete behavior amenable to empirical study. It made the case for sociology by arguing that even the seemingly personal choice of suicide is best understood as a social fact in need of explanation by other social facts. It illustrated how society was essentially a moral order whose breakdown could create social problems. And finally, it developed a logic that could apply to a wide range of social problems and antisocial behavior while anchoring that logic in the dramatic case of suicidal behavior.

Durkheim conceded that explaining a single suicide involves both social and individual facts. But he redirected attention from individual cases to aggregate rates of suicide and variations across time, space, and social groups. These rates and their variations are social facts requiring explanation by other social facts.

After dispensing with rival theories, Durkheim offers the most concise statement of his argument: Suicide rates vary inversely with the degree of integration in modern societies. This dramatic claim directly links the specific behavior of suicide to broad concerns about integration. The exploration of suicide begins right where the study of the division of labor ended, with concerns about insufficient integration.

Integration problems are expressed in two major ways. Egoism results when the bonds that normally connect people to each other and to social groups are unusually weak or ineffective. The person suffering from egoism (as a social fact, not a psychological condition) is cut free or set adrift from others who might serve as a social anchor in tumultuous times. Egoism is "excessive individuation." With this phrase, Durkheim suggests that it is a pathological exaggeration of an otherwise healthy trend in modern society.

The second sign of malintegration is anomie. It arises when the norms, rules, and guidelines that usually regulate conduct become weak, ineffective, or irrelevant to rapidly changing conditions. When social regulation of individual conduct is absent, people are more prone to act on the basis of underlying passions and ambitions that produce destructive consequences. The two problems are closely related in that social groups or society in general ideally provide both social ties and normative rules.

Durkheim's initial statement can now be expanded to say that societies that are not well integrated will give rise to abnormally high levels of both egoism and anomie that in turn cause higher levels of suicidal behavior. Understood as Weberian ideal types, egoistic suicide is self-destructive behavior resulting from a lack of connections to other people, whereas anomic suicide is self-destructive behavior resulting from a lack of relevant norms for orienting one's conduct.

Durkheim also offered empirical evidence in support of these claims. His case for egoistic suicide rested in part on data revealing higher suicide rates in Protestant regions and countries than in Catholic ones. He reasoned that the highly individualistic nature of Protestant beliefs promoted egoism (and egoistic suicide at the extreme), whereas the more collective nature of Catholicism anchored the believer in the group and provided a buffer against egoism and self-destructive behavior.

The case for anomic suicide was made with comparative data on economic conditions. When such conditions are stable and predictable, familiar norms and rules provide solid guidelines to behavior. When they change rapidly, old guidelines lose their relevance in new situations. Unless new guidelines are found, anomie results, and (in the extreme case) anomic suicide increases. Although suicide in response to financial ruin is not surprising, the argument became more compelling because suicide also increased with rapid improvements in financial condition. The trigger was not material circumstances but rather the presence or absence of normative guidelines for whatever circumstances were at hand.

The crucial subtext of this study of suicide is a distinct image of human nature. Durkheim seems to assume that human beings possess unlimited appetites, insatiable desires, and grandiose ambitions. If these are not sufficiently regulated, people are more likely to take their lives. Much of the power of this study, however, derives from the generalizability of its logic. In principle, anomie and egoism could foster not just higher suicide rates but also higher rates of many forms of self-destructive, antisocial, or otherwise deviant behavior. Durkheim's study of suicide is thus a major treatise on the need for social integration and normative regulation.

This study implies an interesting conception of freedom as well. A libertarian or anarchistic ideal of freedom as involving minimal regulation of individual actions is a Durkheimian nightmare. Real freedom requires a sufficient degree of integration and regulation so that self-destructive tendencies are contained; this allows socially connected, normatively regulated individuals to exercise more limited but more genuine forms of freedom in the conduct of their lives.

The "practical" Durkheim thereby recommended strengthening normative order through civic education and moral training to counter anomic tendencies. He endorsed the role of guilds, associations, and small groups to strengthen social bonds and provide a buffer against egoistic dangers. Throughout this study, then, the dangers of societal breakdown and the need for social integration are ever-present themes.

THE ROLE OF RELIGION

Durkheim's last major work was an analysis of what he called the elementary forms of the religious life (1915/1965). On the surface, it is an anthropological study of totemism among Australian aborigines that might seem of limited interest. It is a methodological claim that leverages this book into a universal statement on the nature of religion. The claim is that all religions share an underlying core that is most evident in the seemingly simpler religions of traditional societies. Totemism is thus a methodologically convenient window into broader truths about religion in general, just as suicide is a specific indicator of broader fissures in social integration.

Durkheim proposes that what is common to all religions is a distinction between the sacred and the profane. The profane refers to practical, mundane, everyday aspects of life with little overarching significance. The sacred refers to transcendent, holy, or suprahuman aspects of life that are the focus of religious belief and ritual. The sacred is often surrounded by prescriptions and prohibitions spelling out how true believers are to relate to this realm. The diversity of religions persists in the variety of objects that are placed in one or the other category. The universality of religion resides in the drawing of this distinction in the first place.

Upon this foundation, many religions add more complex beliefs about the specific objects in such categories. They also develop rituals through which people can participate in religious practices, express their beliefs, and create solidarity with other believers. Finally, many religions also develop elaborate institutional structures defining authority figures and power relations between religious leaders and followers. Although acknowledging these embellishments, the core of every religion remains the dichotomy between the sacred and the profane.

Durkheim's study builds upon this definition to advance three major hypotheses. They are illustrated in detail with reference to totemism, but they are intended as much broader statements about the role of religion in social life in all times and places.

The most straightforward hypothesis concerns the positive functions of religion in providing the social integration required by all healthy societies. Religion was central to the collective conscience of traditional societies and thereby directly related to their integration. More specifically, religion appears tailor-made as a solution to, or buffer against, the problems of anomie and egoism.

Thus, religion is often a source, if not the major source, of the norms, rules, and laws that govern organized social life. Although external social controls may always be necessary, the internalization of religious norms and beliefs goes a long way toward instilling the conformity and guidance needed to avoid anomie and promote integration. Many (if not necessarily all) religions also pull people into some kind of community of worshippers, creating and strengthening social bonds and anchoring the individual in the group. As such, religion also makes a significant contribution to avoiding or resolving the dangers of egoism.

Although religion may have lost some of its previous centrality in more modern and secular societies, Durkheim clearly regarded it as crucial to social integration for most of human history. He moreover used it as a template for discovering functional equivalents that could operate alongside religion in modern societies to provide the necessary degree of social integration in these more complex social systems.

A second and somewhat more speculative hypothesis concerns the origins of religion in society. This illustrates another classic Durkheimian theme of the priority of the social over the individual. In this case, the social is represented by a force that Durkheim refers to as "collective effervescence." It arises when large numbers of people are present together with a common focus of attention and a mutual awareness of each other's presence.

Such conditions are a powerful social force that can create strong group identity. Moods, beliefs, sentiments, and even visions can pass throughout such groupings in a contagious fashion. Under such conditions, emotional energy and commitment are high, and a kind of social electricity reinforces group solidarity.

If we acknowledge the power of such moments, it is not too far-fetched to suggest that religion may have originated out of situations of collective effervescence when people are highly energized by the co-presence of others and their absorption into a larger collectivity. Such an argument seems even more plausible at those moments when communities confronted natural disasters or cosmic events that begged for some explanation. In such circumstances, the "invention" of religion seems like a plausible response.

The power of the collective is also seen in the plethora of rituals that accompany many religions. As periodic, communal gatherings, rituals re-create the collective effervescence and social community that may have given rise to religion in the first place. Given Durkheim's functional hypotheses about religion, the repetition of these rituals and their periodic revival of collective effervescence may be central to sustaining social integration.

Durkheim's causal hypothesis about the origins of religion shades over into his third and most distinctive interpretive hypothesis of religion. Articulating a logic at the heart of the sociology of religion, he took a middle ground on the issue of validity. On the one hand, the near universality of religion in human society suggests that it cannot be dismissed as purely illusory. It refers to and is about something that sociologists need to take seriously. On the other hand, the near universality of religion does not prove its validity. Indeed, beliefs in different societies often contradict one another while also reflecting the spatio-temporal contours of the society that gave rise to them.

Pursuing this logic, Durkheim argues that the supernatural, sacred, or transcendent object of religious belief is not a deity but rather society itself. Religion is both a conscious acknowledgment of a higher power and an unconscious recognition that that higher power is the collectivity of people comprising society.

This initially bizarre claim gains some credence if one considers the qualities often attributed to gods and the sacred. This realm often has the attributes of exteriority, constraint, obligation, and eternality in relation to the individual. Stripped of their religious overtones, however, they are precisely the qualities that society possesses in relation to the individual. It is society, not god, that comprises a larger totality, exists outside ourselves, constrains our actions, obligates its members, and transcends the lifespan of any particular individual. For Durkheim, religion is thus people's recognition of the higher power and greater force we call society.

IMPLICATIONS FOR MOVEMENTS

Marx and Weber devoted a considerable portion of their sociological work to conflict, stratification, politics, and the like. Although they may not have used the term "social movement" in its contemporary sense, it is relatively easy to derive lessons about such movements from their work.

Durkheim, by contrast, said relatively little about such topics, and it is not as obvious how his work might inform the study of social movements. It would be a mistake to dismiss it on this basis, however. There are several provocative links between Durkheim's work and the study of collective action, and it is appropriate to speak (as we will soon) of a Durkheimian legacy in this field.

It is a distinctive legacy as well. Whereas Marx retained optimism about the prospects for change through collective action, and Weber expressed resignation over inevitable cycles of change and ossification, Durkheim saw collective behavior as yet another symptom of underlying tensions and problems of social integration.

One lesson for studying movements concerns the types of social integration Durkheim distinguished. It is not just entire societies but social groups of all types that depend upon certain mechanisms to ensure group integration. Because social movements are groups, it follows that they can be integrated in one of two ways.

Movements integrated through mechanical solidarity derive their unity from the homogeneity of their members and the similarity of their beliefs. It is these beliefs that are central as a movement *conscience collective* that is embraced by all members. Building further on this type of solidarity, we would expect such movements to be highly intolerant of internal dissent and disagreement (mirroring the stance of traditional societies toward all forms of deviance).

Speculating further, we might predict that when such disagreement does occur, it is likely to create fissures and schisms, whereby dissenting groups spin off to form new groups that will be equally intolerant of internal dissent. We are likely to find all these processes in play wherever the ideological purity of beliefs is central to the movement. The dynamics of many cults and some religious sects and political parties provide some obvious examples.

Movements that are integrated through organic solidarity derive their unity from the heterogeneity of their members and the interdependence of their activities. These groups will have a more complex organizational structure with a division of labor that assigns different movement tasks to different individuals and subgroups. Such movements will be less threatened by diversity of opinion in their ranks because their solidarity derives more from their interdependence than their belief system.

Such movements may be more stable and more able to incorporate large numbers of members. At the same time, they will be unlikely to inspire the passion or even fanaticism that drives movements based on ideological purity. Speculating further on this type of solidarity, their tolerance of diverse views may backfire by fostering a degree of individuality that undermines movement solidarity and collective identity, and promotes microforms of egoism and anomie at the expense of effective movement functioning. When recast at the level of social movement groups, Durkheim's types of solidarity are rich in hypotheses that foreshadow more recent work on social movements.

Durkheim's work also provides a broadly conceived mechanism that causes collective action. For Marx, this mechanism was the structural conflict of interests between social classes. For Weber, it was the erosion of the legitimate authority of a given regime. For Durkheim, it is chronic strain or acute breakdown in social integration. If these three were to debate how and why social movements emerge, the discussion would surely revolve around these different mechanisms.

Such a debate would reveal the distance between at least two of these approaches. For Marx, conflicting class interests are so fundamental to capitalist society that working-class mobilization and class conflict are all but inevitable. It is the lack of conflict that would require a special explanation in terms of false consciousness, overwhelming repression, or an utter lack of working-class capacity.

For Durkheim, socially integrative forces are so fundamental to both traditional and modern society that social stability, consensus, and interdependency are the normal if not inevitable conditions of social life. For him, it is conflict that would require a special explanation as a condition that deviates from this normal state of society. That explanation, in turn, would point to the breakdown of social integration that normally precludes such conflict.

This lack or breakdown of social integration may take several specific forms. It might involve a forced division of labor and a misallocation of people into roles and functions for which they are not suited. It might involve an anomic division of labor in which clear rules and guidelines for such allocation are lacking. It might involve a broader social condition of anomie in which rapid change renders all familiar guidelines for everyday conduct irrelevant, and people are cut adrift from the social gyroscopes that normally orient them. It might be exacerbated by a lack of moral, ethical, or civic forms of education to shore up social integration in times of stress.

Alongside the anomic path to the breakdown of social integration is the egoistic one. When the individuation that is a normal and even desirable feature of modern society goes too far and becomes "excessive individuation," the social bonds that link people together and inhibit dangerous or destructive behavior become frayed, and people are cut adrift. The erosion of small groups and intermediate levels of social association may increase the likelihood of this particular form of breakdown.

Durkheim's image of human nature imparts ominous overtones to this outcome. As noted earlier, without the beneficial influence of social integration and normative regulation, people may become slaves to passions, drives, desires, and ambitions that can be highly destructive to selves and others. The extreme case is suicide, but the same logic could also make people more susceptible to mass forms of collective behavior that further threaten social integration.

Although these implications can be extracted from Durkheim's work on types of solidarity and forms of suicide, his work on religion has additional implications for social movements. The role of ritual is one example. An astute student of Durkheim interprets his argument to be that ritual precedes and gives rise to collective representations and beliefs, and that although ritual generates belief, symbols, and language, the ritual itself retains primacy as a moral force that provides social cohesion (Bellah 2005).

Rituals are thus vital social processes that create symbolic meanings through redundancy. Although they are a pathway to the sacred in their religious form, their more mundane function is to establish the routines, social conventions, and moral order that make for social integration. Without ritual, there could be no society: "if rational action were all there is, there would be no solidarity, no morality, no society, no humanity ... Only ritual pulls us out of our egoistic pursuit of our own interests and creates the possibility of a social world" (Bellah 2005: 194).

Conceived in this way, it would seem that ritual would be a force for social conservation. However, "Durkheim believed that through experiences of collective effervescence, not only was society reaffirmed, but new, sometimes radically new, social innovations were made possible" (Bellah 2005: 190–191). Thus, even with its routine and redundancy, the social energy generated by ritual can help people envision alternative worlds and generate the beliefs that support those visions. Rituals can thus be cauldrons in which people not only reaffirm established beliefs in the sacred but also nurture beliefs about newer, better, and even utopian alternatives to the status quo.

Although the circumstances under which ritual nurtures alternatives rather than affirming the status quo remain murky, there is a clear role for ritual in the maintenance of social movements. Successful movements require strong collective identity to sustain commitment and motivation, and they derive less from the rational calculation of self-interest than from the solidarity bonds that ritual can create and sustain.

The value of ritual in sustaining solidarity is often overlooked when frustrated activists lament that their movement has become "only" or "merely" ritualistic; the implication is that nothing important is going on. A more Durkheimian view would underscore the latent function of seemingly empty rituals in sustaining collective identity, core beliefs, and commitment levels that might otherwise wither away. When movements have momentum, such processes happen almost automatically; when they lose momentum, ritual can become vital to survival. Ironically enough, ritual may perform its most vital function of movement maintenance precisely when movements have been reduced to what some interpret as "empty" ritualism.

Closely related to the role of ritual in sustaining social movements is the emotional energy created by situations of collective effervescence. Movements are by definition social, and their action is collective, so these qualities are central to understanding them. Like religion, many movements may originate in situations of collective effervescence and rely on re-creating such conditions to sustain their efforts. Emotional energy rather than rational cognition is the fuel for this process.

Social assembly and collective effervescence "can, at their height, generate 'a sort of electricity' which launches people to an 'extraordinary' state of 'exaltation' ... collective effervescence induces changes in individuals' internal bodily states which have the *potential to substitute the world immediately available to our perceptions for another, moral world in which people can interact on the basis of shared understandings*" (Schilling 2005: 215; italics in original).

The emotional energy generated by collective effervescence is relevant to collective action of at least two types. For broader social movement campaigns and organizations, tactics often include periodic protests, marches, demonstrations, and rallies. Although deliberately orchestrated, such events are still capable of generating powerful and often unpredictable emotional responses for all the reasons Durkheim has explored.

Collective behavior also encompasses less structured, more spontaneous, short-lived, mass gatherings in which collective effervescence and the emotional energy it generates are even more obvious. Under this heading, later sociologists would analyze panics, crazes, and riots as instances when the co-presence of large numbers generates considerable emotional heat and symbolic energy. Outside the context of religious ritual (or even social movement campaigns), such energy may lack a clear focus, and its impact and consequences become more difficult to predict.

LE BON'S CROWD

Recall Durkheim's image of human nature implicit in his study of suicide. Without adequate social controls, our underlying impulses can readily lead to destructive behavior. This is why religious ritual and the emotional energy created by collective effervescence are crucial: They provide the cohesion that reins in dangerous impulses and subordinates them to the moral force of the collective.

When ritual, collective effervescence and emotional energy unfold outside the sacred canopy of religious belief, however, the picture changes. Rather than bringing people back into the social fold, these forces could help unravel it by unleashing destructive impulses. Although Durkheim did not explore this possibility in any systematic way, some of his contemporaries went down this path. One might say that Durkheim opened the door to irrationality and Gustave Le Bon (1896/1960) and other European crowd theorists walked through it to examine the psychology of the crowd.

In this perspective, whatever rationality people may possess as individuals is seriously compromised when they become members of any sort of crowd. Often under the sway of a powerful leader, people in crowds become highly credulous and suggestible. The energy generated by the co-presence of others erodes individual judgment and rational thinking, so that people support ideas and actions that they would never embrace as rational individuals. This outcome is not an aggregation of individual changes as much as it is the product of contagion as irrational views spread like a virus through the collective body of the crowd.

It is not that crowds are completely incapable of reasoning, but rather that their reasoning is markedly inferior. Crowds embrace extreme simplifications that deny any ambiguity or shades of gray. In higher-order thinking, ideas are linked through logic and reason; in crowds "there are only apparent bonds of analogy and succession ... Whatever strikes the imagination of crowds presents itself under the shape of a startling and very clear image, freed from all accessory explanation ... " (Le Bon, cited in Smelser 1962: 80).

As a product of his times, Le Bon was drawn to newly emerging theories of the unconscious. He asserted that the energy created by proximity to others in a crowd overwhelms the conscious personality, which gives way to an unconscious personality that is even more susceptible to contagion. For some crowd theorists (echoing a very Durkheimian theme), this produces "a release of repressed impulses which is made possible because certain controlling ideas have ceased to function in the immediate social environment" (Martin, cited in Gurr 1970; 287).

For Le Bon, these dynamics mirror the psychoanalytic process of regression. Crowds reduce otherwise mature adults to the "impulsiveness, irritability, incapacity to reason, the absence of judgment and the critical spirit, the exaggeration of the sentiments" (cited in Rule 1988: 94) one typically finds in neurotics and children. To become part of a crowd is paradoxically a highly social and yet desocializing experience as crowds erode adult moral judgment and rational functioning, only to replace it with unconscious and even infantile impulses.

It would be a mistake to attribute Le Bon's logic to Durkheim himself. Durkheim did not draw such a sharp dichotomy between reason and emotion, and he did not necessarily equate emotion with irrationality. Moreover, as James Rule (1988: 92) notes, the irrationalists such as Le Bon saw the problem as arising from too much social influence in the form of crowd psychology; Durkheim saw it as deriving from too little social influence in the form of anomie and egoism.

Having said that, it remains true that Durkheim's logic opened the door to theorizing that too readily saw collective action as irrational, apolitical, deviant, extremist, and dangerous. As we will see shortly, many of these themes migrated from the late nineteenth century European continent to the early twentieth century United States.

DURKHEIM'S LEGACY

Although he never developed a systematic analysis of social movements, Durkheim's work speaks indirectly to several issues shaping movements and directly to some processes involved in collective behavior. We conclude with just a few examples of this legacy.

It was suggested earlier that Durkheim's two types of social integration could be used to characterize different ways of integrating social groups including social movements. Anthony Oberschall's (1973) more recent distinction between communal and associational organization is one example.

Communally organized groups are based on long-standing traditional ties with strong symbolic and moral overtones; such mechanical solidarity provides one basis for movement integration. Associationally organized groups are based on contractual ties deriving from the self-interest of differentiated groups; it mimics organic solidarity as another basis of movement integration. Interestingly enough, if a group is not integrated in either of these ways (perhaps suggesting high degrees of anomie or egoism), Oberschall predicts that it will be unlikely to generate a social movement at all.

Perhaps Durkheim's biggest contribution to the study of social movements is the implication that the breakdown of social integration can be a major factor in the emergence of collective action. One descendant of this logic is Neil Smelser's (1962) elaborate stage model of how collective behavior emerges. Strains, tensions, and ambiguities in social order facilitate its initial emergence, whereas the breakdown of social control (in tandem with other factors) all but assures its ultimate eruption.

Smelser's theory is broadly gauged to address not just social movements but other forms of collective behavior as well. It typifies a generic logic that attributes social order to social control and challenges to order to breakdowns in control. This logic has been used to explain everything from ephemeral crowd behavior, to prolonged riots and rebellions, to large-scale revolutions. Despite this diversity, the underlying logic of how the breakdown of social order facilitates collective action owes a heavy debt to Durkheim's analysis of social integration.

A complementary logic may be found in mass society theory, which also has a Durkheimian point of departure. Mass society consists of large institutions and isolated individuals with few small-scale, intermediate social groups that could provide membership, connections, or guidance. Because such intermediate groups are scarce, mass society is prone to high levels of anomie and egoism. This, in turn, makes individuals more available for participation in collective behavior. Although this prediction has found little empirical support, its logic is quintessentially Durkheimian.

The diversity of social integration (and its breakdown) allows for many variations on breakdown theories of collective behavior. David A. Snow et al. (1998) bring a phenomenological twist by underscoring the quotidian nature of much social life and the natural attitude that supports it. When events undermine this taken-for-granted reality, this disruption or breakdown can facilitate participation in collective behavior. It is especially likely to do so when people retain strong ties to others within social groups. This more nuanced version of the theory thus recognizes a combination of anomie (disruption of the quotidian) without egoism (group bonds remain strong) as most likely to generate collective behavior.

A final twist on this theme may be found in the work of Piven and Cloward, who are especially interested in the circumstances that give rise to non-normative forms of mass defiance and popular protest. In a study of poor people's movements (1979), they argue that such periods are rare precisely because social structure and the rhythms and routines of daily life within those structures normally preclude such activities. It is only in atypical periods of disruption and instability that social controls are weakened, and people become available to participate in social protest. Under the right circumstances, such protest can be dramatically successful. It is also likely to be short-lived because social control and routine rhythms reassert themselves and often reverse the gains derived from the short-lived period of mass protest.

Although one part of Durkheim's work speaks to the origins of collective behavior, another speaks to the processes that constitute such behavior. Although formulated in the context of his study of religion, the study of collective effervescence and ritual enactments finds a natural application to what Herbert Blumer (1951) would subsequently call the elementary forms of collective behavior. The stimulation and contagion deriving from the co-presence of many people in one time and place that Durkheim found in totemism and Le Bon found in crowds became a centerpiece of the collective behavior theory that prevailed in much of twentieth century American sociology. This tradition will receive closer scrutiny in the next chapter.

Alongside the origins and processes of collective behavior, Durkheim shed light on the "fuel" of such activity by analyzing the emotions deriving from ritual and collective effervescence. Once again, what he found in a religious setting may also be found in secular forms of collective behavior. Such a translation is provided by Randall Collins's (2001) examination of how collective rituals amplify and transform intense emotional states in the specific case of social movements. This is merely one indication that after a long hiatus, the study of emotions that was always part of the Durkheimian canon is finally returning to our understanding of social movements.

Marx, Weber, and Durkheim predated the subdivision of sociology into specialties such as collective behavior and social movements. They did not use the generic category of social movements as a basis for systematic theorizing about the causes, processes, and consequences of collective action. Nevertheless, even this perfunctory treatment of these theorists demonstrates how their work is rich in implications for the study of social movements. They represent three largely distinct paradigms for understanding collective action. As a result, their work has informed many subsequent schools of thought and lines of research in the field of social movements.

Part II
Traditional Theories

Chapter Four

The Two Chicago Schools

This chapter moves us from pre-1920 Europe to post-1920 Chicago. Despite shifting geography and chronology, there are threads of continuity. Like Weber and Durkheim, the Chicago School practiced sociology in a distinctive way. Its analysis of collective behavior has obvious debts to Durkheim's ideas about social disorganization, ritual, and emotion; clear links to Weber's emphases on symbolic meanings and cultural beliefs; and vague echoes of Marx's interest in social change and reform. Building on these and other sources, the Chicago School forged a vision of collective behavior that dominated sociology for several decades in the mid-twentieth century.

THE CONTEXT

The ambitions of the Chicago School to define the field of sociology are evident in an early publication by Robert Park and Ernest Burgess. Their *Introduction to the Science of Sociology* (1921) runs more than 1,000 pages, and addresses science, human nature, the self, personality, and the group, as well as social interaction, social forces, competition, conflict, accommodation, social control, collective behavior, and progress.

In this and other statements, Chicago School sociology analyzes society as a fluid interactive process rather than a static institutional system. This processual approach examines "organization and disorganization, conflict and accommodation, social movements and cultural change. It imagines society in terms of groups and interaction rather than in terms of independent individuals with varying characteristics. Methodologically, it is quite diverse, but it always has a certain empirical, even observational flavor" (Abbott 1999: 6).

Chicago sociology "was a change from the concern with abstractly formulated laws, from cut-and dried-pronouncements about statistical regularities; it was an introduction of vividness and immediacy. It linked sociology with journalism and literature. It opened it to a wider audience. It gave it a new strength" (Shils 1980: 185). The Chicago School had three broad foci: social psychology, social organization, and social ecology (Abbott 1999: 6). The former analyzed individuals in a social context, while studies of organization and ecology helped interpret that context.

Chicago sociology and its approach to collective behavior were forged in a distinctive intellectual climate. In some respects, Chicago sociology was an emergent product of behaviorism and pragmatism. When the behaviorist emphasis on close scientific observation of human behavior was tempered with a pragmatist appreciation of interactively negotiated meanings and symbols, a distinctive sociology was created. The pragmatist premises of social philosophers John Dewey and George Herbert Mead thus helped see "human behavior as problem-solving and emergent rather than controlled and shaped by external 'forces'" (Gusfield 1978: 129).

Pragmatism thereby reinforced the processual approach of the Chicago School. It helped its practitioners see social reality not as static or fixed, but rather as an interactive outcome of people's actions in the world. Pragmatism also helped avoid the trap of reification by emphasizing how concepts were simply convenient labels for dynamic, ongoing social processes that must remain the focus of study.

Alongside intellectual influences, Chicago's social and political climate shaped the sociology that emerged there. Although change was widespread, "few cities anywhere in the Western world changed more rapidly in such a short time than did Chicago in the decades at the end of the nineteenth and beginning of the twentieth centuries" (Lemert 2008: 62). This rapidly growing metropolis was a naturally occurring sociological laboratory, and multiple "experiments" were underway involving industrialization, urbanization, immigration, Americanization, social disorganization, crime, and delinquency. The city and its urbanizing processes were the setting and the topic of much Chicago School sociology.

Indeed, there was "a 'demand' for sociology in the city of Chicago. Movements to improve the condition of the poor and to improve the quality of public institutions were also very active and from the first they drew to themselves the professors of the new university ... It was perhaps the first time that academic sociologists as a class were welcomed by reformers with much practical experience" (Shils 1980: 183).

The Progressive Era embraced the pragmatist belief that science and knowledge were instrumental in the analysis and resolution of social problems. Successful reform, however, required accurate description and analysis, and sociology provided the tools to accomplish these goals.

A process-oriented sociology was thus reinforced by a pragmatist philosophy and a political reformism that encouraged active engagement with the social world. All these forces shaped an understanding of collective behavior as both outcome and cause of social change.

PARK AND BURGESS

Robert Park (1864–1944) was a leading figure in the Chicago School. In the 1880s, he studied literature, history, and philosophy with John Dewey at Michigan. In the

1890s, he worked as a newspaper editor and reporter and studied philosophy with William James at Harvard. In 1899, he went to Germany, studied with Georg Simmel, and wrote a dissertation on *The Crowd and the Public* in 1904.

This text provided a bridge between late nineteenth century European crowd theory and early twentieth century U.S. collective behavior theory. Gustave Le Bon's treatment of the crowd is a major pillar of that bridge. The first of Park's three chapters is an extensive and largely positive discussion of Le Bon's work on crowds.

Thus, Park notes that for Le Bon, the crowd is less a matter of spatial concentration than a psychological condition in which individual self-consciousness disappears as feelings and thoughts move in a similar direction. The process sounds like evolution in reverse: "a heterogeneous mass under previous conditions is transformed into a homogeneous entity" (Park 1972: 13). With this blending, people in crowds lose the capacity for intelligent action as the crowd reduces their capacities to the lowest common denominator.

Crowds thereby exhibit some standard characteristics: heightened emotional sensitivity and capriciousness, increased suggestibility and credulity, exaggerated and one-sided opinions, intolerance and despotism, and personal disinterestedness and unselfishness (Park 1972: 15–16). Park argues that all these traits are different manifestations of the same underlying condition of suggestibility that is a defining feature of the crowd. This suggestibility "is generated by the reciprocal influence of individual emotions and ... affects all members of the crowd in the same way" (Park 1972: 16).

Park's discussion of the public is more scattered and less complete, but it is evident that publics are a fundamentally different form of collective behavior. Although instincts dominate in the crowd, reason prevails in publics. Indeed, critical attitudes, diverse opinions, prudent judgments, and rational reflection are defining elements of publics that set them apart from crowds.

Whereas crowds erase individual differences and reduce their members to a lowest common denominator, publics recognize such differences as the basis for reasoned discussion and debate. Publics can thus arrive at a consensus through discussion without necessarily imposing a unanimous stance on their members (Park 1972: xiv). This discursive capacity of the public sets it apart from the crowd; however "[w]hen the public ceases to be critical, it dissolves or is transformed into a crowd" (Park 1972: 80).

Although much of Park's dissertation underscores the differences between the crowd and the public, a second theme concerns their similarities compared with routine institutionalized behavior. Thus, both crowds and publics are temporary, spontaneous, and fleeting forms of association. Unlike institutional behavior, crowds and publics have no traditions and they do not flow predictably from past to present and future.

Despite their ephemeral nature, the crowd and the public are two fundamental mechanisms for producing social change because they exist outside the normative guidelines and institutional patterns of everyday society. In highlighting these two forms, Park transplanted European assumptions about crowd behavior while juxtaposing publics as a more rational and deliberative type of collective behavior.

One of the earliest codifications of the Chicago approach to collective behavior is in *An Introduction to the Science of Sociology* (Park and Burgess 1921). The book contains an eighty-five-page chapter on collective behavior, situated between equally long chapters on "social control" and "progress." The chapter is an amalgamation of original text, lengthy excerpts from Le Bon's work and Park's dissertation, and adaptations from other writers describing examples of collective behavior. Because it sets the stage for decades of work on collective behavior, it merits a closer look.

The chapter begins by noting that when people gather together, their behavior is social to the extent that each individual is influenced by the action of other individuals. It becomes collective when each acts under the influence of a shared mood or state of mind. "Collective behavior, then, is the behavior of individuals under the influence of an impulse that is common and collective, an impulse, in other words, that is the result of social interaction" (Park and Burgess 1921: 865).

The most elementary form of collective behavior is social unrest. It involves milling that stimulates circular reaction as people react to each other's initial actions and subsequent responses in an escalating fashion. The stage of social unrest is significant because it represents "a breaking up of the established routine and a preparation for new collective action" (Park and Burgess 1921: 866).

Turning to the topic of crowds, the authors follow Le Bon's analysis of how milling in crowds creates social contagion and a collective impulse to act, concluding that "[w]hen the crowd acts it becomes a mob" (Park and Burgess 1921: 869). This is in sharp contrast with publics, with their capacity for critical discussion, diverse opinions, and rational reflection.

Although acknowledging the public, it is the crowd that frames the subsequent discussion of collective behavior. To clarify the nature of crowds, the text reproduces descriptions of "animal crowds," including sheep flocks, cattle herds, and wolf packs. Although acknowledging that human crowds can mimic animal crowds when they dissolve into a panic or stampede, they also distinguish human crowds on the basis of common purposes and collective representations that are absent in animal crowds.

The text then reprints several pages from Le Bon (1896/1960) on the "psychological crowd" that reiterate some of his more dubious and stereotypical characterizations of crowds as involving irrational impulses, unconscious personalities, mass contagion, diminished intelligence, criminal tendencies, and the like.

This is followed by a briefer passage from Park's dissertation that underscores the role of rapport (involving "contagious excitement and heightened suggestibility") in crowd behavior. Such rapport, along with a common focus of attention and collective representations, seem to be the defining elements of the crowd for Park and Burgess. The authors say little more about these components, leaving the impression that their analysis of the crowd remains heavily indebted to Le Bon's work.

When the chapter finally moves from crowds to mass movements, it consists entirely of excerpts from other writers on various movements. The chapter concludes with brief comments that dispense with mass movements in fewer than two pages and bundle together "fashion, reform and revolution" in an equally brief treatment.

Although collective behavior may not be reducible to crowds for the early Chicago School, it is evident that the crowd provides a fundamental template for analyzing collective behavior and that Le Bon's work is central to this template. As the authors conclude, "[a]ll great mass movements tend to display, to a greater or less extent, the characteristics that Le Bon attributes to crowds" (Park and Burgess 1921: 871).

BLUMER'S COLLECTIVE BEHAVIOR

Eighteen years after the Park and Burgess text appeared, Herbert Blumer published his overview of collective behavior theory (the 1939 original was prominently reprinted in 1951). It is often taken as the definitive statement of the early Chicago School on this topic. As such, it is striking how closely it follows earlier treatments of the crowd while expanding the analysis of social movements.

Blumer notes that virtually all of sociology's subject matter could be considered collective behavior, but then distinguishes behavior that is routinely governed by norms and traditions from more elementary, spontaneous, unregulated forms. As a subfield within the discipline, collective behavior studies the latter and the manner in which it may develop into more organized social behavior.

"Circular reaction is the natural mechanism of elementary collective behavior" (Blumer 1951: 171). Through interstimulation, people's behavior reproduces and amplifies some initial stimulation. Given Blumer's subsequent establishment of the symbolic interactionist tradition, it is striking that he distinguishes circular reaction from interpretative interaction. The interpretation that intercedes between stimulus and response in most human interaction is absent in circular reaction.

Elementary collective behavior is likely to arise "under conditions of unrest or disturbance in the usual forms of living or routines of life" (Blumer 1951: 171). When "restlessness" is part of circular reaction, it becomes contagious and leads to social unrest. In this state, people are highly sensitized to each other's presence, and rapport develops.

Once social unrest occurs, people's behavior becomes random, erratic, aimless, excited, apprehensive, irritable, and suggestible. "In a state of social unrest, people are psychologically unstable, suffering from disturbed impulses and feelings" (Blumer 1951: 173). Despite—or perhaps because of—this disorientation, "social unrest may be regarded as the crucible out of which emerge new forms of organized activity—such as social movements, reforms, revolutions, religious cults, spiritual awakenings, and new moral orders" (Blumer 1951: 173).

Several mechanisms spark elementary collective behavior. Through milling, individuals become highly sensitized to each other's presence. Like Park and Burgess before him, Blumer cites animal herds (and hypnotic subjects) to describe how this heightened rapport leads people to respond to one another "quickly, directly, unwittingly" (Blumer 1951: 174). Milling and rapport can lead to collective excitement that heightens emotional arousal and makes people more unstable and irresponsible. These mechanisms may then culminate in social contagion, as the "relatively rapid, unwitting, and nonrational dissemination of a mood, impulse, or form of conduct; it is well exemplified by the spread of crazes, manias, and fads" (Blumer 1951: 176).

Blumer then provides a taxonomy of collective behavior. Predictably enough, crowds are the first type to be discussed. Crowds emerge when some exciting event sparks milling, leading to a common object of attention and impulses leading to action. Casual crowds (watching a street performer) and conventionalized crowds (attending a baseball game) are two rudimentary types.

The acting, aggressive crowd is one in which individual self-concern and critical judgment are overwhelmed by the suggestibility, rapport, and common focus of attention of the group. Blumer thus notes, as Park and Burgess did before him, that a common strategy of crowd control is to redirect attention from its original focus.

The expressive or dancing crowd is a more introverted group that has no external goal or plan of action. Its behavior often involves rhythmic expression and catharsis. Following Durkheim, expressive crowds can create collective ecstasy that may be projected onto objects or symbols that become sacred to the crowd.

Both types of crowds have the potential to break up old forms of social organization and promote new ones. Acting crowds seek this externally through purposive social change and a new political order. Expressive crowds seek this internally through collective rituals and a new religious order.

The mass is another type of collective behavior. Its members are heterogeneous and anonymous. They have little interaction with each other, so the mass is more loosely organized than the crowd. Masses consist of alienated individuals who have become detached from localized cultures and groups. This recalls Durkheim's analysis of anomie and egoism while also anticipating mass society theory.

The public is the final type of elementary collective grouping. Echoing Park, publics are defined by issues that generate divided opinions and ongoing discussion. Unlike later approaches to public opinion that would merely aggregate individual attitudes, Blumer's concept retained an emphasis on how interaction within the public collectively shaped their views. At the same time, publics are fleeting and spontaneous groups with no tradition, we-feeling, or conscious identity.

The crowd, mass, and public are thus the major elementary collective groups; they signal social change. "They have the dual character of implying the disintegration of the old and the appearance of the new" (Blumer 1951: 196). In virtually every respect, Blumer's analysis to this point is a faithful if slightly updated rendition of the Park and Burgess approach.

Where Blumer departs from this approach is in the more detailed and analytical treatment of social movements. Movements are conceptualized as "collective enterprises to establish a new order of life" (Blumer 1951: 199). They begin, however, on the "primitive level" of the collective behavior already discussed; they are initially "amorphous, poorly organized, and without form" (Blumer 1951: 199). Only in the later stages of a movement career does it acquire traditions, customs, and leadership that allow a more stable form of social organization.

"Cultural drifts" are gradual but pervasive changes in people's values and self-conceptions that may trigger general social movements as vague, indefinite responses. Given their inchoate nature, general social movements resemble the mass and emerge when people are detached from localized social moorings. Both masses and general social movements remain "formless in organization and inarticulate in expression" (Blumer 1951: 201).

Just as cultural drifts are the crucible for general social movements, the latter are "the setting out of which develop specific social movements" (Blumer 1951: 202). These crystallize previously vague and amorphous sentiments and orient them to a particular objective. Such movements become minisocieties, with organization, structure, leadership, culture, a division of labor, and we-feeling.

The emergent quality of this process is captured in a stage theory of social movements that foreshadows other approaches that describe movement stages, life histories, or careers that culminate in either movement decline or institutionalization.

Blumer's first stage is the social unrest already discussed as the starting mechanism of elementary collective behavior. Recall that "[i]n a state of social unrest, people are psychologically unstable, suffering from disturbed impulses and feelings" (Blumer 1951: 173). Blumer sees the role of the agitator as central to creating and spreading social unrest.

The second stage is popular excitement, which relies on milling while developing more focused objectives. Here, leaders are more likely to be prophets or reformers. The third stage is formalization, when "the movement becomes more clearly organized with rules, policies, tactics, and discipline" (Blumer 1951: 203), and its leader more closely resembles a statesman.

The final stage is institutionalization, in which "the movement has crystallized into a fixed organization with a definite personnel and structure to carry into execution the purposes of the movement" (Blumer 1951: 203). In this final stage, leadership has evolved from agitator, prophet, and statesman to administrator.

Distinct mechanisms propel movements through these stages. Agitation arouses people and makes them available for the movement. Successful agitation must gain attention, excite people, arouse feelings, and provide direction. When it works, it changes people's self-conception.

The development of *esprit de corps* is a second mechanism; it foreshadows more recent work on collective identity. *Esprit de corps* develops by underscoring the relation between the in-group and out-group(s), by fostering informal fellowship, and by engaging in ceremonial behavior that reinforces social bonds.

A third mechanism is morale; it creates a stronger group will and commitment to a collective purpose. Morale reinforces "a conviction of the rectitude of the purpose of the movement" (Blumer 1951: 208), and it may invoke sacred symbols; patron saints; and various creeds, myths, and literatures that elucidate its *raison d'être*.

A fourth mechanism is group ideology. It often serves multiple purposes as a statement of objectives, a condemnation of the status quo, a justification of the movement, and a repository of movement myths. Effective ideologies often blend both a scholarly and a popular dimension to achieve these multiple objectives.

The final mechanism involves tactics. These must address three basic tasks of "gaining adherents, holding adherents, and reaching objectives" (Blumer 1951: 211). Successful movements rely upon all five of these mechanisms to move from initial social unrest through popular excitement and formalization to institutionalization.

Blumer's treatment of social movements concludes with a loose typology. Perhaps the most significant aspect of his discussion of reform and revolutionary movements is an unwillingness to see even these forms of collective behavior as political phenomena. Thus, the "primary function of the reform movement is probably not so much the bringing about of social change, as it is to reaffirm the ideal values of a given society" (Blumer 1951: 213). Revolutionary movements, on the other hand, seek to create an "uncompromising group" out of "have-nots", which "makes its function that of introducing a new set of essentially religious values" (Blumer 1951: 214).

Blumer's work has been summarized in such detail because it is arguably the most-often cited example of the early Chicago School's view of collective behavior. As such, three conclusions are worth noting. First, Blumer's treatment of collective behavior is heavily indebted to Park and Burgess, who in turn relied heavily on Le Bon's analysis of the crowd. Second, Blumer departs most significantly from them in his more extensive treatment of social movements. Third, however, even this more extensive treatment of movements sees them as originating in more elementary processes of collective behavior. For Blumer, movements remain derivative of elementary collective behavior in general and the crowd in particular. That idea would subsequently attract much criticism from proponents of a more political view of social movements.

THE CONTEXT REVISITED

This early and foundational work on collective behavior appeared at the height of the Chicago School's prominence. "From about the outbreak of the First World War to the end of the Second, the Department of Sociology of the University of Chicago was the center *par excellence* of sociological studies in the United States and in the world, although in the last decade of its dominance it was living from the momentum of the preceding two decades" (Shils 1980: 215).

The relative decline of the Chicago School after World War II involved internal and external factors. Internally, some of the major figures of the school either departed or retreated from the forefront of sociological work. There were sharp disputes among remaining members about the direction of the department, prompting additional departures (Abbott 1999, Ch. 2). As a result, "the fundamental ideas of Chicago sociology were coming to a standstill and were not being extended or deepened" (Shils 1980: 217).

Externally, other universities were challenging Chicago's predominance and advocating different approaches. From its unrivalled preeminence between the wars, Chicago lost ground to Harvard and Columbia after World War II. Although its approach to doing sociology remained distinctive, it was now one among several competing approaches rather than the *sine qua non* of sociological scholarship.

Like most "rise and fall" narratives, this is a bit simplistic. Closer inspection reveals a "second" Chicago School that consolidated in the post-war period (Fine 1995). The members of this second school both continued and modified the approach of the first, and this is nowhere more evident than in the study of collective behavior.

The continuities are evident in an ongoing emphasis on emergent interactive processes. The distinctiveness of this approach actually became more evident as rivals appeared. Although the Chicago School emphasized process, the Harvard approach postulated strains as the root of collective behavior. Somewhat later, a more politically oriented Michigan approach would emphasize resources as crucial (Snow and Davis 1995).

Perhaps equally significant, the second Chicago School departed from its predecessors on several key issues. "They tended to demystify the concept of impulse, reject the mechanical nature of circular reaction, and abandon the pathological connotations of contagion. They emphasized the continuity of collective and institutional action, rejecting or qualifying the classical assertion of Le Bon ... that crowds are characterized by spontaneity, suggestibility and mental unity" (Snow and Davis 1995: 193). The second Chicago School thereby avoided some of the pitfalls of its predecessor.

TURNER AND KILLIAN

The first edition of Ralph Turner and Lewis Killian's seminal text on collective behavior appeared in 1957, and substantially revised versions followed in 1972 and 1987. Each mirrored the Park and Burgess (1921) volume by interspersing original text with supporting case material from others. This book is a core statement of the second Chicago School that illustrates both continuity and transformation in this approach.

The authors define collective behavior as "forms of social behavior in which usual conventions cease to guide social action and people collectively transcend, bypass, or subvert established institutional patterns and structures" (Turner and Killian 1987: 3). Their focus is thus group behavior that lacks conventional organization or departs from established institutional patterns.

Turner and Killian distance themselves from a "pathological view" of crowd behavior exemplified by Everett Martin's early characterization of the crowd as "people going crazy together" (cited in Turner and Killian 1987: 5). Although they acknowledge that Park and Blumer may have relied too heavily on Le Bon's view of the crowd, they assert that a "conscientious reading" of the Chicago School tradition would show that its major writers "all have rejected the assumption that collective behavior is necessarily less rational than institutional behavior" (Turner and Killian 1987: 5)

The authors proceed to argue that the terms "irrational" or "emotional" refer to individuals rather than groups. To characterize groups in either of these ways is untenable. The imputation of individual characteristics to collective entities is logically fallacious, and the assumption that members of collectivities are homogeneous in cognitive and affectual states is empirically dubious. They further challenge the duality of rationality and emotion, concluding that both are always elements of human behavior whose meanings are socially constructed in specific cultural contexts.

Any plausible theory of collective behavior must answer three questions for Turner and Killian. The first concerns extra-institutionalism: Why do people act outside of normal, routine, established channels? The second concerns action: Under what circumstances do values, attitudes, or beliefs get translated into action? The third is about collectivities: When do people decide to act collectively rather than individually?

Their answer to the first question involves emergent norms, which they contrast with two other views. Collective behavior is sometimes explained as a deviant, irrational, or anomic rejection of social norms. It is alternatively explained as a manifestation of rational interests overriding normative conformity. Their approach preserves the role of norms in guiding behavior while underscoring circumstances when new norms emerge and redefine right and wrong in ways that require extra-institutional behavior.

Their answer to the second question about action involves feasibility and timeliness, which they again distinguish from other views. The tipping point from feeling to action is often understood mechanistically: Some initial state is simply intensified to a threshold that sparks action. Although intensification may play a role, these are also matters of interpretation and social definition. When people not only have strong feelings but also believe that new circumstances favor acting, they are more likely to do so. A sense of feasibility and timeliness is thus crucial to translating feelings into action. The latter becomes especially likely when accompanied by emergent norms justifying action.

Their answer to the third question of *collective* action involves a combination of extraordinary events and preexisting social groups. The event provides a common focus of attention that requires interpretation. The preexisting ties among people facilitate the flow of information. These interacting factors lead to a collectivity rather than isolated individuals. Although described schematically through these concepts, the actual emergence of collective behavior is a complex interactive process.

Rival approaches include convergence and contagion theory; both attempt to explain the unanimity or homogeneity of crowds. The authors' point of departure, however, is the empirical reality that "the crowd is characterized not by unanimity but by differential expression ... [t]he illusion of unanimity arises because the behavior of part of the crowd is perceived both by observers and by crowd members as being the sentiment of the whole crowd" (Turner and Killian 1987: 26).

It is this seeming unanimity that emergent norm theory is meant to explain. Emergent norms are collective redefinitions of a situation that create an illusion of unanimity through differential expression; they simultaneously obscure persisting variations in the motives and types of people who comprise crowds.

Addressing the emergence of collective behavior, the authors define social order as consisting of three elements: a normative order, a social structure, and a communication system. This order is reinforced by the taken-for-granted basis of everyday life, which may lead people to assume that their social world is more solid and orderly than it actually is.

This definition of social order suggests what conditions are conducive to the emergence of collective behavior. The first is challenges to the normative order. Whenever there is a "real or perceived conflict, ambiguity, or change in the normative order" (Turner and Killian 1987: 40), collective behavior becomes more likely. Parallel changes, weaknesses, or inconsistencies in the social structure or the flow of information also increase the likelihood of collective behavior. The greatest likelihood is when there is a dynamic combination of broad social instability alongside the specific mechanisms that produce extra-institutional, collective action.

The text also discusses rumor as the mechanism of communication in collective behavior. They use this term to underscore "the tentative, shifting, questioning nature of the communication which goes on until a definition is collectively constructed" (Turner and Killian 1987: 75). These insights on process, emergence, and communication comprise a general theory of collective behavior that is subsequently used to analyze crowds, publics, and movements. Although Park and Burgess had little to say about movements, and Blumer began to expand that discussion, Turner and Killian (1987) devote more pages to social movements than to crowds and publics combined.

The authors walk a delicate line on how and why social movements should be analyzed as a type of collective behavior. They define a social movement as "a collectivity acting with some continuity to promote or resist a change in the society or group of which it is a part" (Turner and Killian 1987:223). Social movements are part of collective behavior because the latter studies "phenomena that fall between group and organizational behavior organized on the basis of rules and tradition or intimate personal relations, on the one hand, and disparate individual behavior on the other" (Turner and Killian 1987: 230).

They acknowledge, however, that "social movements fall near the boundary that separates collective behavior from strictly organized and institutionalized behavior. Movements that persist over time increasingly lose the distinctive features of collective behavior" (Turner and Killian 1987: 230). They conclude that to understand "true social movements, principles from collective behavior and organizational behavior must be conjoined to provide adequate understanding" (Turner and Killian 1987: 230).

Having acknowledged that movements cannot be understood solely with collective behavior theory, and that movements routinely become something other than collective behavior, the authors nonetheless extend their underlying model of collective behavior to the analysis of social movements. This yields more specific answers to the original questions of why people act in extra-institutional ways, how feelings are translated into action, and why action is collective rather than individual.

Emergent norms remain central to explaining the extra-institutional dimension of social movements. In contrast to more transitory forms of collective behavior, however, social movements frequently build upon an emergent norm of injustice to offer more elaborate ideologies and goal hierarchies that "emphasize the obligatory nature of the movement's mission" (Turner and Killian 1987: 241).

Feasibility and timeliness likewise remain central to the translation of feelings into action. In the case of social movements, feasibility means "a sense that it is possible to correct the unjust situation" (Turner and Killian 1987: 241), whereas timeliness involves a sense of urgency that change is more possible now than before. Feasibility and timeliness are vitally affected by the material resources available to a movement and by the degree of hope among members.

Finally, recall that action becomes collective through two interacting factors. The first is some extraordinary event that orients people to others for an interpretation and response. In the case of social movements, this is more likely to be an enduring social condition rather than a passing occurrence. The second factor is preexisting group organization that allows the free flow of information through the group. In the case of movements, this often requires formal leadership, stable constituencies, and dense networks to sustain the movement over time.

Having adapted their general model of collective behavior to social movements, the authors analyze goals, grievances, and ideologies; strategies and tactics; conflict and violence; recruitment and commitment; and forms of movement organization. As such, this text is the most systematic effort to extend the tradition started by Park and Burgess and sustained by Blumer into the closing decades of the twentieth century.

Although direct acknowledgements are understated, this final edition of *Collective Behavior* (Turner and Killian 1987) clearly reflects the influence of rival paradigms. The recognition that movements have sustained, organizational aspects and that preexisting social networks are often crucial to movement emergence and maintenance surely reflects the impact of resource mobilization approaches that appeared a decade before this edition was published.

Subsequent scholarship has sought to redefine the central contributions of Turner himself. Although emergent norm theory has historically been seen as the most distinctive aspect of Turner's work, his more lasting contribution may be in identifying the interrelated themes of normative coordination, emergent phenomena, symbolization processes, and interactive determination in crowds and movements (Snow and Davis 1994). These themes serve as potent reminders of the close links between the study of collective behavior, the orientation of the Chicago School, and its roots in the perspective of symbolic interaction.

OTHER EXEMPLARS

As central as Turner and Killian's work has been, the second Chicago School included many scholars who developed additional permutations on these ideas. One authoritative source identifies the group as consisting of "Joseph Gusfield, Morris Janowitz, Lewis Killian, Orrin Klapp, William Kornhauser, Gladys and Kurt Lang,

E. L. Quarantelli, Tamotsu Shibutani, and Ralph Turner" (Snow and Davis 1995: 188). The topics of their work ranged from collective dynamics to rumors, disasters, mass media, mass society, riots, violence, and more. Here we will briefly consider two works to illustrate the second Chicago School's approach to social movements in particular.

Given the Chicago School's aversion to seeing collective behavior as a political phenomenon, William Kornhauser's (1959/2008) analysis of the politics of mass society is an intriguing exception (Buechler, forthcoming). Written in the 1950s in the shadows of fascism and communism, mass society theory sought to explain the rise of extremism abroad and the dangers to democracy at home. Recalling Durkheim's analysis of egoism and anomie, mass society emerges when small local groups and networks decline, leaving powerful elites and massive bureaucracies on one side and isolated individuals on the other.

"Mass society is objectively the *atomized* society, and subjectively the *alienated* population. Therefore, mass society is a system in which there is *high availability of a population for mobilization by elites … [p]eople who are atomized readily become mobilized*" (Kornhauser 2008: 33; italics in original). Put slightly differently, mass society is one in which "*both elites and non-elites lack social insulation; that is, when elites are accessible to direct intervention by non-elites, and when non-elites are available for direct mobilization by elites*" (Kornhauser 2008: 43; italics in original).

In a healthy pluralist democracy, both groups are partially insulated, intermediate groups are strong, and normal channels of influence are robust. In mass society, both groups lose this insulation, intermediate social buffers erode, normal channels are ineffective or bypassed, and extremism becomes more likely.

Mass movements pursue remote, extreme objectives and mobilize uprooted, atomized people (Kornhauser 2008: 47). Thus, "[m]ass movements mobilize people who are alienated from the going system, who do not believe in the legitimacy of the established order, and who therefore are ready to engage in efforts to destroy it. The greatest number of people available to mass movements will be found in those sections of society that have the fewest ties to the social order" (Kornhauser 2008: 212).

Mass movements are not the only type of movement, but in some respects they are closest to the collective behavior tradition because they arise out of mass behavior with a remote focus of attention; a declining sense of reality and responsibility; and a highly unstable, shifting focus of attention and intensity of response (Kornhauser 2008: 43–46). Thus, in this relatively rare statement about the politics of collective behavior, they are depicted as an unreasoning and extremist threat to social order.

Subsequent analysis and research have led many to conclude that the idea that the most socially isolated are most likely to engage in mass politics "is almost certainly false" (Rule 1988: 109). Those who are socially isolated are actually less likely to join, whereas those who are embedded in preexisting social ties are disproportionately likely to join (Oberschall 1973: Ch. 4). Turner and Killian (1987: 390) note that "[s]ubsequent study of totalitarian movements has raised serious questions about the applicability of Kornhauser's concept of mass movement."

In a different vein, Blumer once claimed that the main function of a reform movement is to reaffirm societal values. This might be seen as the point of departure for Joseph Gusfield's (1963/1986) study of the American temperance movement, which provides a second example of the Chicago approach to social movements. Gusfield calls this movement a "symbolic crusade," a label that could apply to many moral reform movements.

Whereas class movements and politics are about the distribution of material resources, status movements and politics are about the prestige of groups making claims. The conflict is over values and styles of life, and the status group that prevails in such a conflict sees its values become dominant and perhaps codified into law.

Through much of the nineteenth century, the temperance movement had a dual focus as a type of status politics. On one hand, it was a form of social control whereby white, native-born Protestants sought to reshape the behavior and values of immigrant groups whose culture differed from the mainstream. On the other hand, practicing temperance was also thought to be crucial to the success and social mobility of the dominant group. Temperance was thus a way of sanctioning those who were different and reinforcing the values and standing of one's own group.

Over time, the temperance movement shifted from assimilative reform (saving the drinker) to coercive reform (punishing the deviant). The campaign culminated in the passage of Prohibition in 1920, which was a potent symbol of native-born, Protestant, middle-class domination. By the same token, its repeal only thirteen years later symbolized the decline of this status group, its values, and its lifestyle.

Gusfield interprets temperance as a form of status politics that is more prevalent among middle classes, in which material comfort often combines with status anxiety. Status politics often appeal to a fundamentalist strain in society and express unease with change, modernity, and diversity. The value of this approach to understanding the "culture wars" and their associated movements of recent decades is readily apparent.

Much the same may be said for Gusfield's summary of his work as a "dramatistic theory of status politics." This is "because, like drama, it represents an action which is make-believe but which moves its audience" (Gusfield 1986: 166). It is also a way of studying symbolic action in which "the object referred to has a range of meaning beyond itself" (Gusfield 1986: 167). Gusfield thereby deploys Chicago sociology and symbolic interactionism to provide an incisive analysis of an important type of social movement and its associated politics.

CONCLUSION

The Chicago School(s) arose in a specific sociohistorical setting and developed an equally distinctive approach to the study of collective behavior. It dominated U.S. sociology from the 1920s into the 1950s, and it survives today in several guises, including framing and social constructionist approaches to social movements.

Partly because of its prior dominance, the Chicago School came in for more than its share of criticism as rival approaches sought to create space for their alternatives in the 1960s and 1970s. Critics argued that the Chicago approach was too individualistic or psychological, that it ignored the political dimension of collective action, that it failed to recognize persisting organizational features of collective action, and that it ignored "solidarity" as a better predictor of collective action than "breakdown." Finally, critics claimed that despite protestations to the contrary, this approach still viewed collective behavior in a negative light and as an expression of underlying irrationality (Currie and Skolnick 1970; Tilly, Tilly, and Tilly 1975; McAdam 1982).

As often happens when new paradigms challenge old ones, the critics sometimes overstated their case and glossed over variations and distinctions among their targets. This provoked selective defenses of the collective behavior tradition (G. Marx 1972; Aguirre and Quarantelli 1983; Turner and Killian 1987; Snow and Davis 1994). This is not the place to reiterate the debate, but rather to offer some brief conclusions based on a close reading of the Chicago School texts summarized in this chapter.

Concerning the "first" Chicago School, it seems undeniable that the writings of Park, Burgess, and Blumer rely heavily on Le Bon's analysis of the irrational crowd as a template for collective behavior. In part, this reflects the sociohistorical climate of the time and the fears provoked by fascist and communist movements that were explicitly referenced in Blumer's (1951: 209) discussion of social movements.

At the same time, Park in particular recognized the positive, creative potential of collective behavior and refused to reduce it to a purely destructive, negative force (Rule 1988: 97ff; Oberschall 1973: 14ff). Perhaps it is fairest to say that the early Chicago School displayed a profound tension between the irrationalist tradition it inherited from European crowd theorists and its own efforts to move toward a more well-rounded approach to collective behavior.

Concerning the "second" Chicago School, Turner and Killian (1987: 13–15) explicitly repudiated the presumption of irrationality that haunted earlier work. This repudiation was not always recognized by critics who tended to collapse both schools together, although it was acknowledged by more sympathetic interpreters (Snow and Davis 1995).

There remained a different kind of tension, however. Having set aside the irrationality issue, it became clearer that the inclusion of social movements with more elementary forms of collective behavior (out of which they supposedly originate) was becoming increasingly strained. In introducing a discussion of emergent norms, Turner and Killian say that "[t]he crowd, the most easily observed type of collectivity, will be used as the model" (1987: 75). In fact, the crowd seems to be the template not just for emergent norms but also for their overall theory even as they seek to extend it to other types of collective behavior.

As a result, their later treatment of social movements incorporates much work from other traditions that feels tacked on rather than logically derived from their underlying premises. Perhaps recognizing this, the authors eventually note that "social movements fall near the boundary that separates collective behavior from strictly organized and institutionalized behavior" (Turner and Killian 1987: 230).

Proponents of the collective behavior tradition have sought to maintain the linkage between elementary collective behavior and social movements. Others have noted that "[s]urely there is something ironic about this concern with saving the *concept* of collective behavior. The term was originally put forward to designate a category of phenomena whose conceptual unity was considered apparent. Now that unity appears more obscure, and analysts resort to increasingly tortuous rules to propound a conceptual rule that will include the changeful processes of original interest" (Rule 1988: 115; italics in original). In the end, the Chicago approach may have lost its dominance not so much over the issue of irrationality as over the implausibility of analyzing social movements through the lens of collective behavior.

Chapter Five

Political Sociology and Political Movements

This chapter moves from Chicago to New York. The relative decline of Chicago sociology was accompanied, and partially caused, by the rise of rival approaches at other institutions, including Columbia University. The approaches discussed here contrast sharply with the Chicago School because they view social movements as a form of political contention. At the same time, one aspect of this political approach examined psychological dynamics that predisposed some people to join extremist movements. The premise of irrationality that had haunted the Chicago School thus found a new niche in studies of extremist politics.

THE CONTEXT

From a contemporary perspective, the disconnect between collective behavior and political conflict in Chicago School sociology is one of its most puzzling features. From a historical perspective attuned to sociological patterns of disciplinary and intellectual development, it becomes more understandable.

In the late nineteenth century, the boundaries between political science and sociology began to sharpen. This brought benefits to both disciplines by allowing them to ask more focused questions and develop more sophisticated methods and analytical techniques to pursue their respective questions.

This process also had drawbacks. The sharpened boundaries around these disciplines left some issues on the margins of both. Although some topics were readily adopted by one discipline or another, others were "ontological orphans." They existed in the real world, but they were not adopted by either of the more sharply differentiated disciplines.

Such was the fate of social movements. Sociology largely ceded questions of politics to its sister discipline of political science. The latter, in turn, defined its subject matter as the organized and institutional dimensions of states, governments, elections, and parties. Because social movements involve extra-institutional elements, they were off the radar screens of political scientists.

Thus, sociology analyzed collective behavior as an apolitical phenomenon, and political science studied politics as an institutional system; neither was conceptually predisposed to examine the politics of social movements. Movements were too political for sociology and too unorthodox for political science. As a result, important questions about movements and the political system were not addressed.

This situation was partially redressed with the rise of political sociology as a subfield within sociology. While examining some of the same topics as political science, political sociology placed the institutional political system within a broader context that included economic, social, cultural, and extra-institutional political dynamics. In some respects, it was a return to questions (if not necessarily answers) posed by Marx and Weber. This contextualization opened the door to studying social movements.

One important incubator of political sociology was Columbia University, which "by the early 1950s markedly surpassed Chicago as a center" (Shils 1980: 219). Columbia's impact on sociology as a whole is often attributed to "two major intellectual personalities, Robert Merton and Paul Lazarsfeld, who combined what was most 'needed' in sociology: ingeniously contrived techniques of survey research with interesting, quite specific substantive hypotheses" (Shils 1980: 219). This new style of sociology was institutionalized in the Bureau of Applied Social Research at Columbia.

Sociology at Columbia also reflected broader trends in the social sciences and intellectual climate. Across many disciplines, there was a renewed emphasis on forging genuinely scientific approaches on a par with the natural sciences. This required solid empirical data that, in turn, prompted the development of new statistical tools, sampling techniques, and research methodologies to deliver the data and redeem the promise of a scientific approach.

At Columbia, these broader intellectual ambitions were married to specifically sociological concerns. Lazarsfeld not only advocated survey methods and quantitative analysis of topics like political attitudes; he also linked individual attitudes to group memberships and social influences through cluster sampling. Although these approaches informed research on many issues, it was Seymour Martin Lipset (trained at Columbia) who did more than anyone to deploy them in the study of political sociology in general and political movements in particular.

Another example of new rigor in analytical methods was the revival of comparative-historical methods in the social sciences generally and in sociology specifically. Lipset, along with Stein Rokkan (1967), was a part of this development through work comparing political party systems and voting patterns across industrial democracies. This revival was also evident in the ambitious comparative and historical approach of Barrington Moore Jr. to reveal differing paths to modernity.

The renewed interest in political movements was also sparked by movements and challenges on the domestic and global scene. The Great Depression sparked both revolutionary and reactionary movements in the United States while fascism abroad helped trigger World War II. Social movement scholars therefore returned to "big questions" about broad movement ideologies, social class bases, and shifting political alliances that sustained movements across the political spectrum.

One subset of these questions examined the appeal of Nazism, fascism, and other right-wing political movements. Such questions were raised by Hitler's rise to power and transplanted to the United States by émigré German intellectuals. There was a domestic version of these questions as well, as McCarthyism prompted both popular and scholarly studies of extremist movements.

Under all these influences, the study of social movements underwent some major transitions in a relatively brief time. This chapter documents some of these transitions.

A EUROPEAN IMPORT

Before turning to Columbia and Lipset's impact, we begin with a significant text by Rudolf Heberle (1951). Its very title illustrates the theme of this chapter: *Social Movements: An Introduction to Political Sociology.* Heberle wrote a dissertation on the Swedish labor movement while in Germany, studied in the United States, returned to Germany, and then fled back to the United States when Hitler's rise to power interfered with the publication of several studies he had conducted on political movements. When his text appeared in 1951, he was a sociology professor at Louisiana State University.

The status of Heberle's text is suggested by an unlikely source. In the first edition of Turner and Killian's book on collective behavior, they list Heberle's book at the top of a list of recommended readings on social movements. They include the annotation that "[a]lthough slanted toward political organization rather than collective behavior, this book is the most adequate sociological treatment of social movements available" (1957: 535). The understated compliment illustrates the tension between these approaches while according a prominent status to the German émigré scholar.

Heberle conceptualizes a social movement as a social collective whose intention is to change the patterns of human relations and social institutions that characterize a society. Group identity and solidarity are essential elements, as social movements are akin to Marx's notion of a fully developed social class. Movements must therefore be treated as groups, and they must furthermore be distinguished from trends, tendencies, pressure groups, or political parties. Movements also involve ideologies or constitutive ideas that provide integration and inspire followers. Summarizing a sociological approach to the field, Heberle counsels students of social movements to dissect their ideologies, social psychology, social foundations, structure, strategy, tactics, and functions.

Movement ideologies are broadly conceptualized to include ideas, theories, doctrines, values, and strategic and tactical principles. The constitutive ideas of movement ideologies typically specify the movement's goals, identify means for attaining those goals, and provide a rationale for the movement's endeavors. Analysis of movement ideologies should include their stated goals, historical origins, assumptions about people and society, and the reasons for their appeal to followers.

At the same time, Heberle cautions that proclaimed goals are not always the real goals, so that the sociological analysis of ideology may involve an "unmasking" function exemplified by Mannheim's (1936/1952) study of ideology and utopia. Heberle utilizes this framework to provide detailed analyses of the historical roles of liberalism, conservatism, and socialism as the ideological foundations for a broad range of political movements.

Turning to the social psychology of movements, Heberle cites Weber's ideal types of social action as a means of understanding people's motivations to join social movements. Although acknowledging a limited role for "abnormal psychology" in the analysis of movements, Heberle cautions against explanations that invoke personality, psychopathology, or psychoanalysis. A more sociological approach would reframe the issue to ask what social conditions allow psychopathic leaders such as Hitler to rise to power. In the end, good sociology must distinguish between the enthusiast who is creatively inspired by the movement and the fanatic seeking action for its own sake.

Weber's work also illuminates the social-psychological "texture" of a particular movement. His ideal types help distinguish between 1) the spiritual community or fellowship of a value-oriented movement, 2) the following oriented around a charismatic leader, and 3) the association arising out of the rational-utilitarian calculations of its members. Heberle's text is just one example of how a political approach to social movements almost inevitably leads back to Marxist and Weberian concepts.

Concerning the social foundations of movements, the typical carriers of movements have been religious groups, status groups, ethnic groups, and social classes (or portions of them). Many movements blend together more than one social base. In the modern era, Heberle contends that most movements revolve around social classes. Class position, however, does not guarantee class consciousness or political organization, and there are many reasons why the correlations between class, consciousness, parties, and movements are imperfect.

The class base of movements and parties, moreover, is often concealed by the need to garner support from multiple classes and groups if a movement or party is to succeed. In the end, however, class antagonisms shape political parties and struggles more than any other cleavage, and all social and political movements aim at some type of redistribution of power between classes. Writing at the midpoint of the twentieth century, Heberle thus summarizes the "old" social movement theory that subsequently became the target of late twentieth century, "new" social movement theory.

Heberle then tailors his analysis to the U.S. context, identifying its historically major conflicts as involving not only capital versus labor but also commercial or industrial capitalists against farmers. He reviews the distinctly American impediments to class consciousness (despite some violent class struggles) and the relatively non-class character of U.S. political parties when compared with their European counterparts. As a result, the two-party system in the United States rests more on tradition than class antagonism, and the latter tends to be conducted directly rather than politically mediated.

Even so, studies of political ecology, polls, and elections reveal that the two major parties are widely perceived to represent "workers" and "business," even in regions with little overt class conflict and low levels of class consciousness. Rather than a complete exception to the European norm, class, politics, and movements are simply woven together in a different way in the United States.

Analysis of the structure and organization of social movements and political parties reveals many similarities. Once again, Weber proves a reliable guide for distinguishing between charismatically and bureaucratically organized parties and movements, and Michels's analysis of oligarchical tendencies is favorably cited. Heberle then anticipates more recent comparative work by applying these principles to the development of political parties in Britain, Germany, France, and the United States.

Totalitarian movements receive special attention in Heberle's discussion; their defining feature is the denial of legitimacy to any opposing group. Marxist movements are not necessarily totalitarian, although Lenin's strategy in the Russian situation moved this way, as have subsequent Leninist movements and parties.

Both fascist and communist movements and parties often resemble religion in their "all-embracingness," reliance on revealed authority, techniques of sanctioning, and definitions of heresy. Although recruitment, indoctrination, and discipline may be similar, there are also differences. Fascist movements are not class movements as much as movements of *déclassé* and socially insecure elements. Fascist movements often embrace charismatic models of leadership, whereas communist movements (at least officially) repudiate them. Heberle thus offers a nuanced analysis of what were widely perceived to be the most significant movements of the day.

An analysis of strategy and tactics reveals that tactical controversies are endemic in social movements. One common controversy involves political action (oriented to the political system) compared with direct action in the form of boycotts, sabotage, strikes, and the like. With a concluding section on the functions of movements and parties (forming consensus, shaping public opinion, selecting elites), Heberle thus provides an exhaustive survey of the field of social movements at mid-twentieth century.

Although some aspects of Heberle's work are obviously dated, it is striking how many ideas were ahead of their time. These include the emphasis on the politics of movements, their relation to political parties, their organizational forms, and cross-national comparisons. The book concludes with a discussion of differing opportunities for social movements in open versus more closed political systems that foreshadows the much more recent "dynamics of contention" approach to social movements. Heberle thereby earned a prominent place in the history of social movement analysis.

LIPSET'S POLITICAL SOCIOLOGY

Although Heberle's text provided an overview of movement topics, the "Columbia School" steered the field in a more empirical direction. It encouraged research using new data collection techniques, cross-comparative methods, and middle-range theory.

Seymour Martin Lipset quickly became the model for this style of research. He received his degree from Columbia in 1949 and published major works in political sociology and political movements for the next five decades. In his early career, he was a democratic socialist; he subsequently identified more as a political centrist. He studied unions, movements, politics, and inequality. He also used a comparative perspective to explore the preconditions and correlates of democratic governments in industrial societies.

"No phenomenon is more urgently in need of study today than the conditions under which new social movements may emerge in our society." These words open Robert Lynd's foreword to Lipset's (1950: vii) revised dissertation and first major book on agrarian socialism in Saskatchewan. Lipset's own preface acknowledges theoretical debts to Marx, Weber, and Durkheim as well as Robert Lynd and Robert Merton. He also acknowledges his support for democratic socialist movements while noting the discrepancy between the ideology and behavior of democratic socialist governments.

Lipset observes that although many of the world's governments are moving in a collectivist, socialist, or totalitarian communist direction, the United States and Canada "are the foremost exceptions to the growing collectivist trend" (Lipset 1950: 1). There is an important exception to this exceptionalism, however.

In 1944, "the first electorally successful North American socialist movement, the Cooperative Commonwealth Federation (CCF), came to power in the almost completely rural province of Saskatchewan" (Lipset 1950: 3). This can only be understood, Lipset proposes, by examining how the social and economic position of farmers in the United States and Canada sparked a radical response to their situation. This, in turn, may require a modification of the "exceptionalist thesis" that recognizes this homegrown radicalism.

In sketching the history of this movement, Lipset cites Weber's work on how organized group action can convert a mass of individuals into a self-conscious class, or what Marx would call a class-for-itself. This happened in the Saskatchewan agrarian movement in the early twentieth century as wheat farmers gradually became convinced that they were the victims of a highly monopolistic system of distribution that benefited "vested interests" at their expense (Lipset 1950: 71ff). This became the soil out of which a more explicitly socialist challenge would grow.

There were inevitable divisions within this movement between more conservative reformers and class-conscious radicals. The radical voice became more prominent as a result of a conference held in Calgary in 1932 that is credited with bringing together "Marxian socialists from British Columbia, men raised in the tradition of the British labor movement, and the agrarian radicals" (Lipset 1950: 87). It was this conference that founded the CCF, linking agrarian radicals and urban labor groups in a common fight against the domination of capitalist markets and interests.

The Great Depression increased support for this radical agrarian movement. As the CCF began to seriously contest for power within Saskatchewan, it encountered predictable schisms, rivalries, and divisions. Although many farmers sought radical economic change, the socialist label was problematic for some and a target for critics. The CCF thereby moderated some of its policies and forged practical alliances in order to win political power. These strategic moves paid off in 1944 when "[a]fter thirteen years of organization, the Saskatchewan CCF took over as the first 'socialist' government in the United States or Canada" (Lipset 1950: 121).

A closer examination clarifies what "socialist" meant in this context. The most successful socialist or protosocialist parties in the United States and Canada did not follow the Marxist script of class struggle by a permanently exploited proletariat. They rather framed their politics as a traditional struggle of common people against powerful vested interests and a defense of people's opportunities for good jobs, family farms, and small businesses (Lipset 1950: 154ff). The CCF illustrates how broad ideologies must acquire some cultural resonance to be effective.

Lipset offers three broad conclusions. First, Saskatchewan politics reveal that mass passivity and political apathy are not inevitable in modern society. Second, even successful movements that attain formal political power confront ongoing tensions between the need for change and the requisites of holding power. Finally, the bureaucratic nature of modern government continues to undermine the prospects for genuine democracy.

Lipset's study of agrarian radicalism thereby combines classical sociological theory and innovative methodological techniques to analyze the fate of a socialist movement that attained formal political power and became an intriguing exception to the "exceptionalism" of North America.

This penchant for studying exceptions to familiar patterns was also evident in Lipset's next major work, a collaborative study of union democracy (Lipset, Trow, and Coleman 1956). Although the original research is confined to a single union known as the International Typographers Union (ITU), a "larger objective of this book ... is to illuminate the processes that help maintain democracy in the great society by studying the processes of democracy in the small society of the ITU" (Lipset, Trow, and Coleman 1956: ix).

The study reconsiders Michels's iron law of oligarchy that predicts an inevitable evolution from formal organization to oligarchical domination of the many by the few. Many factors produce and reinforce this tendency; the authors highlight three to couch their study.

First, the large size of most unions leads to a bureaucratic hierarchy in which union officials enjoy a near-monopoly of power. Second, leaders once in office typically seek to stay in office. Third, members typically do not participate in union politics. The net effect is a strong tendency toward oligarchy even in unions and other voluntary organizations that formally proclaim a commitment to democratic principles of operation.

Countervailing approaches ask what factors might promote democracy rather than oligarchy. For Aristotle, democracy requires a middle-class society; for others, it can only thrive on a small scale. For Lipset, a third factor is more important, and it is suggested by two seemingly opposed theories of political pluralism and mass society.

Whereas mass society theory reaches the "pessimistic" conclusion that without intermediate groups, the masses are atomized and easily dominated, political pluralism reaches the "optimistic" conclusion that when such groups are present and vibrant, meaningful democratic input to the larger polity becomes possible through these intermediate groups. In other words, "democracy is strengthened when members are not only related to the larger organization but are also affiliated with or loyal to subgroups within the organization" (Lipset, Trow, and Coleman 1956: 15). Indeed, it is the multiplicity of groups seeking particular goals while maintaining a larger loyalty to the overall polity that fosters the tolerance that is one hallmark of democratic governance.

The history of printers' unions reveals a fundamental cleavage that goes back at least to the late nineteenth century. In the early twentieth century in the ITU, this took the form of an Administration Party (in power at the time) and an Anti-Administration Party. The former group advocated moderate or conservative tactics, whereas the latter favored militant trade union tactics.

After a period of internal schisms and shifting alliances among multiple groups, this two-party system was reconstituted in 1932 as a competition between Progressives and Independents. The authors underscore that "these are real rather than formal alternatives ... [because] ... most shifts in ITU administration have meant sharp reversals in collective bargaining tactics pursued by the international union" (Lipset, Trow, and Coleman 1956: 53).

Other unions have similar histories of internal conflict and division. The important question revolves less around the early history of the ITU and more around how it sustained its internal democracy when so many other unions succumbed to oligarchy.

Broader political theory once again illuminates specific ITU characteristics. Although a lack of secondary groups often leads to mass society and oligarchical domination, secondary groups that are present but controlled by the government often lead to revolutionary totalitarianism. Democracy thus requires relatively *independent* secondary groups that can be a genuine basis of opposition to dominant power. Such was the case in the ITU, and that reality distinguished it from many other unions.

There were also aspects of the occupational community that fostered internal democracy. In addition to the two-party system, there was an extensive network of social clubs that promoted participation and crosscut political cleavages, thereby encouraging involvement while also moderating internal conflict. The printers interviewed by Lipset and others also saw their work as a high-status craft that gave them pride and motives to associate with other printers. These factors, along with the prevalence of night shift work, all strengthened the social integration of printers and reinforced their endorsement of, and participation in, union democracy.

Turning to union politics in operation, this craft identification, relative material security, and security of status created a significant pool of union members available for political involvement and leadership. The latter factor—security of status—means a belief that "active opposition to the incumbent administration will not be penalized by a marked loss of prestige and standing in the union" (Lipset, Trow, and Coleman 1956: 211). This is one reflection of the larger normative climate of ITU politics that recognized the legitimacy of opposition within the union while also placing union above party. The balance is crucial; the "party system in the ITU could hardly exist if it were not for the variety of mechanisms that have developed to permit freedom of opposition without allowing such opposition to destroy the cohesion and effectiveness of the organization" (Lipset, Trow, and Coleman 1956: 252).

In the end, the authors do not see their analysis as refuting Michels's theory but rather as identifying some of the relatively rare circumstances under which oligarchy may not be inevitable. Some of them are specific to the printing industry, but the broader principle is that internal democracy is possible only when an "incumbent administration does not hold a monopoly over the resources of politics" (Lipset, Trow, and Coleman 1956: 413). Although unions are not identical to social movements, the challenge of maintaining democracy in both is similar enough to make this work on union democracy of great relevance to students of social movements.

A final dimension of Lipset's political sociology deserving recognition is his work on cross-national comparisons of party systems and voter alignments (Lipset and Rokkan 1967). The basic question concerned how various cleavage structures that divide or polarize a population translate into different political party systems, party affiliation, and voter alignments.

Such work was relevant to later social movement analysis in at least two ways. First, parallel questions were asked about recruitment patterns into social movements. Second, multiple political systems were compared to reveal the differential opportunities they provided for social movements to arise alongside political parties as expressions of underlying cleavage structures. In both his studies of specific movements and his broader political sociology, Lipset thus made a substantial contribution to the study of political movements in the 1950s and beyond.

CONFRONTING TOTALITARIANISM

While Heberle, Lipset, and others were developing a political sociology of social movements oriented to "big" questions of macrostructures, political systems, and social change, others were working on more specific questions about totalitarian movements. Such concerns were obviously inspired by the rise of fascism abroad, but there was also an American version of these questions centered on radical right movements at home.

Columbia University played an important role here as well. The Frankfurt School had been established in Germany in 1923; its members developed an incisive brand of critical theory that fused Marxist sociology and Freudian psychology. Within a decade, Hitler's ascension created an increasingly hostile climate for leftist Jewish intellectuals, and the Institute for Social Research essentially disbanded.

Max Horkheimer, a leading member of the group, managed to reassemble the institute in the United States in the late 1930s through an affiliation with Columbia University. With this institutional base, the group continued publication of its influential journal. Right after the war, "Horkheimer became research director of the American Jewish Committee which granted him a sum of money ... to conduct a widely ranging study of anti-Semitism" (Shils 1980: 191). The study appeared shortly thereafter under the title *The Authoritarian Personality* (Adorno et al. 1950/1982); it was arguably the most significant statement of this genre.

Other scholars had already tilled the soil in which this massive work would take root. Erich Fromm had explored totalitarianism as an escape from freedom (1941). For Fromm, the rise of individualism in the modern age brought freedom from traditional bonds while also creating existential anxiety that could drive people "into new submission and into a compulsive and irrational activity" (Fromm 1941: 103).

Several mechanisms of escape are available for such troubled individuals. Authoritarianism involves a fusion of self with someone or something outside the self to compensate for what is felt lacking. It can involve a striving for submission and domination and be accompanied by masochistic feelings of inferiority, powerlessness, and individual insignificance. Destructiveness is a more extreme response that aims not at symbiosis with an object but rather its elimination. The response that Fromm finds of the greatest social significance, however, is that of automaton conformity in which "the individual ceases to be himself; he adopts entirely the kind of personality offered to him by cultural patterns" (Fromm 1941: 185–186).

This is the foundation for Fromm's analysis of the psychology of Nazism. He distinguishes between the working class who grudgingly submitted to the Nazi regime and the lower middle class who actively supported it. He then traces the resonance between the status anxiety of the lower middle class and Hitler's authoritarian personality. Although Nazism cannot be reduced to psychological processes, Fromm traces how the Nazis perfected a variety of techniques to transform psychological anxieties into mass support for the movement and subsequently the regime.

At the height of World War II, Sigmund Neumann's (1942) study of dictatorship complemented Fromm's psychoanalytic approach with a more macro-level political analysis. He detects a latent threat of fascism in all industrial societies, but sees Germany as the most fully developed fascist dictatorship. Like Fromm, Neumann locates the social base of fascism in the "new middle classes" as a group "between big capital and labor that was always in danger of being crushed by these two impersonal forces" (Neumann 1942: 107).

The actual nature of their support, however, is best understood in terms of Le Bon's crowd psychology. In a chapter ominously titled "The Amorphous Masses Emerge," Neumann traces how mob psychology undermines individuality, rationality, and complex social groups as all are melted into "one gray mass." The "modern dictatorship in its sociological meaning is nothing but the substitution of crowds for society.... The transformation of the spontaneous social groups of a pluralistic society into the totalitarian mass state is the real background of Fascism" (Neumann 1942: 115).

With massification, many social controls become even more effective. A one-party state is able to emerge that can mobilize state bureaucracies, armed forces, churches, schools, and even families as props for dictatorship. With propaganda techniques shaping public opinion, the totalitarian control of society through dictatorship at home and permanent war abroad became complete.

These works set the stage for the ambitious study of the authoritarian personality funded by the American Jewish Committee, brokered by Horkheimer, and ultimately published by Adorno and others in 1950. The study focused on the "potentially fascistic individual" and confirmed that "individuals who show extreme susceptibility to fascist propaganda have a great deal in common" and "exhibit numerous characteristics that go together to form a 'syndrome'" (Adorno 1982: 1).

Given the Frankfurt School's critique of empiricism in social science, this study was remarkable for its elaborate methodology and empirical grounding. Carefully designed questionnaires were initially distributed to large numbers of subjects who responded to factual questions, opinion-attitude scales, and projective questions.

A subset of respondents who expressed antidemocratic tendencies were then recruited for interviews designed to probe more deeply into the subject's personality through such projective techniques as the Thematic Apperception Test. College students were used initially; with increased funding, the broader population was studied.

This research is perhaps best known for developing distinct scales to measure different dimensions of the totalitarian mindset. The anti-Semitism scale included subscales measuring the degree to which respondents found Jews to be "offensive," "threatening," or "seclusive or intrusive." The authors concluded that although people have different "triggers" for prejudicial beliefs, anti-Semitism is a broad, coherent ideology heavily reliant on stereotypes.

The ethnocentrism scale included subscales tapping attitudes toward Negroes, minorities, and Jews, as well as a "patriotism" subscale. Once again, ethnocentrism appears to be a consistent ideology rooted in a basic distinction between in-groups and out-groups, and "the *generality* of out-group rejection. It is as if the ethnocentric individual feels threatened by most of the groups to which he does not have a sense of belonging" (Adorno 1982: 147; italics in original). Ethnocentrics endorsed stereotyped negative imagery toward out-groups, stereotyped positive imagery toward in-groups, "*and a hierarchical, authoritarian view of group interaction in which ingroups are rightly dominant, outgroups subordinate*" (Adorno 1982: 150; italics in original).

The authors then devised the fascism-, or F-scale, to measure "the potentially antidemocratic personality" (Adorno 1982: 157). The scale combined some fascinating themes: rigid conventionalism about middle-class values combined with authoritarian submission within the group and authoritarian aggression toward out-groups; opposition to the subjective or tender-minded combined with superstition and stereotypy; a preoccupation with power, toughness, destructiveness, and cynicism; projectivity about wild and dangerous things going on in the world alongside an exaggerated concern with sexual "goings-on" (Adorno 1982: 157–170).

Interviews provided a richer picture of the authoritarian personality revealing repression, conventionalism, and rigidity as major components. The symmetry of attitudes about many issues in this personality syndrome was intergenerationally transmitted: "a basically hierarchical, authoritarian, exploitive parent-child relationship is apt to carry over into a power-oriented, exploitively dependent attitude" (Adorno 1982: 475) toward sexuality, religion, politics, and social life. Although the authors are careful not to reduce fascism or totalitarianism to psychological attitudes, they provide provocative arguments about the elective affinities between the psychological, political, cultural, and social dimensions of authoritarian movements and regimes.

While German scholars investigated the roots of Nazism, American writers were addressing some parallel issues, albeit sometimes with a very different tone. Whereas the Adorno volume was rigorous, scholarly, and even pedantic, a freelance writer and longshoreman named Eric Hoffer (1951) published a study of the true believer that was anecdotal, reductionistic, and sensationalistic. For Hoffer, fanatics joined extreme movements to give meaning to their guilt-ridden existence (as the cover blurb proclaimed). Hoffer thus posited the "interchangeability of mass movements" because people did not join for coherent ideological reasons or enlightened self-interest but rather as an expression of deep-rooted psychological pathologies.

While Hoffer's book became a best seller, political sociologists began a more nuanced investigation into extremist movements. For example, Kornhauser's (1959/2008) analysis of mass society (discussed in the previous chapter) attributed extremism less to a social class or psychological disorder than to the lack of intermediate social groups that might constrain predispositions to join extremist movements.

In the mid-1950s, other sociologists examined right-wing radicalism in the United States. Once again, the sociohistorical context shaped the concerns of these scholars. "The effect of McCarthyism on the intellectual life of the United States during the early 1950s is difficult to overestimate. Coming after the experience of Nazism in Europe, it was responsible for an anxious foreboding among many American academics about the future of liberal political institutions in the United States" (Gusfield 1978: 143).

One of the earliest expressions of this concern was Daniel Bell's edited book on the new American right (1955). Richard Hofstadter's contribution calls this movement a pseudoconservative revolt. He acknowledges borrowing this term from Adorno et al.'s study of the authoritarian personality and uses it to describe those who display "conventionality and authoritarian submissiveness" along with impulsive, anarchic, and occasionally violent tendencies. Hofstadter contrasts this with "the temperate and compromising spirit of true conservatism" (Bell 1955: 35). He subsequently analyzes this movement as an instance of status politics and projective rationalizations rather than interest politics driven by material grievances.

Talcott Parsons's essay addresses McCarthyism specifically, but analyzes it as a symptom of much broader strains resulting from fundamental changes in American society. He hesitates to call it a movement because of its overwhelmingly negative content and utter lack of a solution or program for change. The negativity, in turn, is seen as an expression of fear, anger, and frustration with the loss of American self-confidence (Bell 1955: 138–139ff).

Lipset's entry returns to the distinction between class and status politics, using the latter to characterize the radical right's appeal to status anxieties. Although government can address economic grievances, there is no comparable "fix" it can provide for status concerns. "It is not surprising, therefore, that the political movements which have successfully appealed to status resentments have been irrational in character, and have sought scapegoats which conveniently serve to symbolize the status threat" (Bell 1955:168). He traces the long and varied history of right-wing politics in the United States, culminating in McCarthyism as the unifying ideology of the right in the 1950s.

This academic line of inquiry persisted into the 1970s and beyond. Bell's reader was reissued in 1964 with updated essays and new attention to the John Birch Society. Lipset and Raab published two editions of *The Politics of Unreason* (1970, 1977) surveying the entire history of right-wing extremism in America, including George Wallace's electoral campaign. This work demonstrates that right-wing political movements have a long history, and sociologists have fashioned useful tools for understanding them.

ON DICTATORSHIP AND DEMOCRACY

The political sociology developed by Heberle, Lipset, and others identified the social class base of movements as an important factor. Scholars of totalitarian movements also described certain class (and status) dynamics that fed them. An even broader question asks what class dynamics produce totalitarian outcomes in some settings and democratic results in others.

It was this question that led Barrington Moore Jr., a Yale-trained political sociologist teaching at Harvard in the 1960s, to explore the social origins of dictatorship and democracy (1966). Tackling this question required a broad historical canvass and a historical-comparative method. Moore's work is one of the most ambitious examples of the political sociology approach to social movements and revolution.

In recent centuries, much of the world underwent a transition from agrarian to industrial societies. There have been several paths through this transition, however. Capitalist democracies, exemplified by England, France, and the United States, resulted from successful bourgeois revolutions. Fascist regimes, exemplified by Japan and Germany, resulted from aborted bourgeois revolutions that did not fully break from the past. Communist regimes, exemplified by China and Russia, were the outcomes of peasant revolutions. Although this summarizes historical outcomes, the power of Moore's work is in understanding the processes behind these outcomes.

Social class plays a crucial role in Moore's story, but not as a static or isolated factor. It is rather the dynamics between classes—their development, struggles, alliances, and balances of power—that are crucial in explaining the differential outcomes of dictatorship and democracy.

Moore sees the development of democracy as requiring "three closely related things: 1) to check arbitrary rulers, 2) to replace arbitrary rules with just and rational ones, and 3) to obtain a share for the underlying population in the making of rules" (Moore 1966: 414). In contrast with many other societies, Western feudalism contained some of the seeds of this democratic outcome in the partial immunity of certain groups from the power of the ruler, in rights of resistance to unjust authority, and in the notion of contracts as freely undertaken mutual engagements (Moore 1966: 415).

"This complex arose only in Western Europe. Only there did that delicate balance occur between too much and too little royal power which gave an important impetus to parliamentary democracy" (Moore 1966: 415–416). This balance put checks on both the monarchy and the nobility, which in turn allowed a healthy bourgeois class to emerge as an incubator of democratic ideas and institutions.

The commercialization of agriculture also played a crucial role in fostering democracy, especially when it strengthened the urban bourgeoisie and weakened the landed aristocracy. Crosscutting class cleavages were also favorable to a democratic outcome by preventing a strong coalition between the aristocracy and the bourgeoisie against the peasants and workers, which might steer development down the fascist path. "Where lines of social, economic, religious and political cleavage do not coincide too closely, conflicts are less likely to be passionate and bitter to the point of excluding democratic reconciliation" (Moore 1966: 425–426).

While recognizing national variations, Moore asserts that these factors were crucial in the emergence of capitalist democracy in England, France, and the United States. He also examines India as an intriguing non-European nation on the path to democracy, but notes that without a revolutionary break with the past, it will be difficult for India to complete a transition to capitalist democracy.

The second path to modernity involves revolution from above that culminates in fascism. In this case, capitalism also takes hold in both agriculture and industry, but in the absence of any popular revolutionary upheaval, it veers off in a fascist rather than a democratic direction. The development of a profitable but labor-repressive agricultural system is a telling indicator. Such systems require strong political controls that often strengthen the monarchy and support a military ethic among the nobility.

Such labor-repressive economies eventually encounter strong competition from more efficient systems. This often strengthens authoritarian and reactionary tendencies among the landed upper class. When such groups are unable or unwilling to change their social structures to foster modernization, it is likely to intensify militarism and push the society farther down the fascist path.

Fascism requires a veneer of democracy because it attempts to make reactionary conservatism popular by appealing to the masses. It thereby taps into the insecurities of the lower middle classes in the cities as well as the peasants in the countryside.

Thus, "the glorification of the peasantry appears as a reactionary symptom" in fascist regimes in both Asia and Europe. This constellation of class forces and an inability to break with the past routes capitalist modernization down the path of fascism rather than democracy.

The third path to modernity involves peasant revolutions leading to communist regimes. Moore argues that compared with feudalism's diffuse and decentralized powers, centralized agrarian bureaucracies are especially vulnerable to peasant challenges. This becomes even more likely if the landed aristocracy does not develop commercial agriculture but rather seeks to enhance its lifestyle by extracting more surplus from the peasantry.

When the landed upper classes "did not make a successful transition to commerce and industry and did not destroy the prevailing social organization among the peasants" (Moore 1966: 467), the ingredients for a peasant revolution and communist outcome fell into place. The major remaining question was whether the peasantry could attract leaders from, and establish alliances with, other classes in order to realize their revolutionary potential.

Moore's analysis is complex and multifaceted, but can also be simplistically summarized as "no bourgeois, no democracy" (Moore 1966: 418). In tracing interactive class conflicts over centuries across six national cases, Moore offers a magisterial survey of how different combinations of these factors set modernizing societies on a path to democracy, fascism, or communism.

CONCLUSION

The "Columbia School" of the 1950s never matched the unrivalled dominance or unitary identity of the Chicago School in the 1920s and 1930s. It nevertheless inspired a new approach to the study of social movements that analyzed them through the lens of political sociology; focused on macro-level processes of social change; explored the links between movements, classes, ideologies, and parties; and employed new empirical techniques to answer all these questions.

Although the answers may have been more precise because of these techniques, many of the questions harkened back to Marx and Weber. They also saw movements as largely political in nature, as reflecting underlying group interests and ideologies, as gaining solidarity through conflict with out-groups, as pursuing goals that reflected class interests and status politics, and as part of much larger processes of social change as they interacted with each other and the larger political system.

Although the political approach resonates with Marx and Weber, it shares relatively little with the Chicago School. The former's macro-orientation to long-term, political struggles expressing group interests and broad ideologies contrasts sharply with the latter's micro-orientation to fleeting, social-psychological gatherings reflecting group dynamics and interpersonal interstimulation.

Perhaps the closest point of contact between the two came when the political approach analyzed totalitarian movements. For example, Neumann's description of the mass, crowd, public opinion, and propaganda could well have been written by an early Chicago sociologist. The difference is that he offers it as a historically specific analysis of the appeal of Nazism rather than a broad generalization about collective behavior. Perhaps that is why the imputation of irrationality that seems dubious as a generic feature of collective behavior sounds at least somewhat more plausible in this case.

Although the strengths of the political approach derive from its macro-orientation, its weaknesses flow from its relative inattention to micro-level processes. This approach has little to say about motivation, recruitment, conversion, or interpersonal dynamics within movements. Although identifying the broad social base of a movement is helpful, the tougher question is differential recruitment: Why do some members of a given class or status group join while others do not? This approach is largely silent on such questions. This is less a criticism than a reminder that all perspectives are necessarily partial; they inevitably illuminate some questions while leaving others in the shadows.

There is a more basic issue with the political sociology approach to social movements. This chapter opened by identifying movements as ontological orphans not fully claimed by a sociology studying collective behavior and a political science addressing institutional politics. Political sociology began to bridge this gap, but even here social movements typically remain tangential to the main story. Put differently, social movements become of interest to this approach when they interact with other parts of the polity rather than having enough intrinsic interest to place them center stage. Thus, Lipset's study of agrarian socialism is really about how a movement became a party, whereas his work on the printers' union is a study of organizational behavior rather than a social movement per se.

The nebulous status of social movements was also reinforced by the social climate of the late 1950s. Proclamations about the affluent society and the end of ideology reinforced a sense that major social conflicts and struggles over material redistribution were rapidly becoming a thing of the past. A focus on the affluent problems of angst, anxiety, alienation, and the "lonely crowd" was displacing older materialist concerns with conflict, coercion, control, and class struggle.

Characterizing the marginality of movements up to the early 1960s, one authority noted that "[a]s a field, social movements remain diffuse and fluid; fitting in different ways into the corpus of contemporary sociology. One leg stands in the field of collective behavior and the other, in political sociology. One arm is extended toward the study of social change and the other waves at the field of social control" (Gusfield 1978: 135).

At the risk of a tortured metaphor, perhaps it could be said that with the development of political sociology in the 1950s, social movements went from ontological orphans to foster children of the discipline. It would take another decade of social change and two decades of theoretical development before they became full-fledged members of the family.

Chapter Six

Strain and Deprivation Models

The collective behavior approach and some versions of the political sociology perspective traced movements back to strains or deprivations in social order. By the 1960s, this logic appeared in several guises linked to distinct theoretical paradigms and contexts. Their convergence around the notion of social strain or deprivation as the cause of social movements is sufficient, however, to treat them together in this chapter.

THE CONTEXT

Strain and deprivation models relegate Marx and Weber to supporting roles while bringing Durkheim back for an encore. As sociology's preeminent classical theorist of social integration, his work provides clues for detecting the strains, disintegration, and breakdown that can precipitate collective action.

By the 1950s, however, sociology also had a new theory of social order in the guise of structural-functionalism. Like Durkheim's theory, it focused on the forces that provide social integration. It also recognized, however, that the complexity of modern social structures all but guaranteed episodes of strain, ambiguity, deprivation, or breakdown. One manifestation of these pressures was collective action.

Although there was no single institutional center for strain theories of social movements, Harvard University was the closest candidate for the role. The sociology department at Harvard was established later than at Chicago or Columbia, and it "lacked the high degree of consensus among its central personalities which was possessed to such a degree at Columbia" (Shils 1980: 224). Nonetheless, by the late 1940s under the leadership of Talcott Parsons, "a deliberate attempt was made to integrate the theories of social structure, culture, and personality" (Shils 1980: 224).

The most obvious result of this attempt was *The Social System* (Parsons 1951). The concepts of structure and function had a long history in social thought (Turner and Turner 1990: 120 ff), but Parsons restored them to prominence. In his view, social order involved the interlinking of cultural, social, and personality systems whereby culture provided values and beliefs; socialization implanted them into people (personality systems); and properly socialized individuals enacted status-roles in the social system.

Systems survive, moreover, by meeting functional requisites of adaptation, goal attainment, integration, and latency. In complex systems, distinct subsystems and structures evolve to meet these requisites. When they work, social order is maintained. When they falter, strain, disequilibrium, and disintegration can occur and set other dysfunctional processes in motion alongside efforts to restore social equilibrium.

On the relatively rare occasions when Parsons addressed conflict and change, strain was a crucial explanation. As we saw in the previous chapter, he cited strains that triggered anxiety, aggression, and wishful thinking to explain the appeal of McCarthyism. Daniel Bell (1955) similarly referenced strain as an explanation for the appeal of right-wing movements. More globally, Chalmers Johnson used the notion of a system out of equilibrium to explain revolutionary situations and movements worldwide (Snow and Davis 1995:190).

As structural-functionalism addressed macro-level strains, social psychology analyzed micro-level deprivation manifested in individuals. Robert Merton's work on reference groups (1957) demonstrated how individuals interpret their experience by reference to existing or desired group memberships. Such groups provide a basis of comparison for one's own position or a legitimation of beliefs or actions accepted by such groups.

Relative deprivation may be one result of such comparisons. When people judge themselves to be deprived relative to a plausible reference group, that grievance may provoke them into collective action. Other strands of social psychology were also relevant. Solomon Asch (1952) had documented the influence of the group on individual judgments, whereas Leon Festinger (1957) had explored the motivation provided by cognitive dissonance and the lengths to which people would go to resolve it.

These disciplinary ideas were accompanied by broader intellectual currents that continued to push sociology (and other disciplines) in a scientistic direction. This spirit was evident in Samuel Stouffer's logical positivist declaration of faith "that there can be developed in the social sciences a body of theory, operationally formulated and empirically tested, from which predictions can be made about what will happen in practical situations" (cited in Turner and Turner 1990: 112). This scientism filtered into sociology in the emphasis on middle range theory, in methodological specifications of independent and dependent variables, in hypothesis-testing, in the adoption of sophisticated statistical techniques, and in causal modeling of social processes.

There were, finally, the movements of the day (and the recent past) that seemed to invite explanations based on strain and deprivation. Fascism abroad and right-wing movements at home still attracted attention, and their grievances seemed to fit the logic. Political movements, including the labor movement and the nascent civil rights movement, were also seen as fueled by grievances that were understandable in terms of social strain and relative deprivation. A final impetus came from overseas. As anticolonial and national liberation movements emerged, and as television projected images of first world affluence around the globe, the notion of relative deprivation acquired new resonance. As these disciplinary, intellectual, and movement influences coalesced, strain and deprivation theories acquired new prominence within sociology.

There were at least three versions of these theories that derived from the distinct theoretical assumptions of symbolic interactionism, social psychology, and structural-functionalism. The first of these had the longest history; thus we return to the Chicago School for a brief look at the role of strain and breakdown in their explanations of collective behavior.

CHICAGO REVISITED

From the beginning, the Chicago School defined collective behavior in contrast with institutional behavior and routine social functioning. Crowds and other forms of collective behavior were seen as existing apart from established routines, normal patterns, normative guidelines, and group traditions. The lack of such patterns links strain to collective behavior almost by definition.

In the absence of such controls, the basic mechanisms of collective behavior acquire their particular potency. Milling, circular reaction, and interstimulation proceed with few limits or restrictions, heightening suggestibility and the rapid transmission of moods and sentiments. The resulting social unrest is a further form of strain or breakdown and the proximate cause of collective behavior, which emerges "under conditions of unrest or disturbance in the usual forms of living or routines of life" (Blumer 1951: 171).

It is not just that collective behavior occurs outside of routine social processes; it often occurs because they break down and malfunction. One interpreter of the Chicago School thereby claims that "[a]ll these writers would no doubt agree with Park and Burgess in identifying collective behavior as the result of failed social control" (Rule 1988: 98). These failed controls involve both moral constraint and coercive state power, but the former was probably more important to Park and Burgess and reflects a Durkheimian influence in their thought (Rule 1988: 98).

Rule (1988) links the early Chicago School with European crowd theorists that he designates "irrationalists." For them, the cause of collective behavior in general and civil violence in particular "was the breakdown of rational control over human behavior through the spread of what one might call 'crowd mentality'" (Rule 1988: 93). For the early Chicago School, strain and breakdown were crucial triggers for collective behavior.

As we have seen, the later or second Chicago School broke with the premise of irrationality and developed a more complex theory of collective behavior. The role of strain and breakdown remained central, however. Recall that Turner and Killian begin with a similar understanding of collective behavior as existing outside of usual social conventions and as bypassing established institutional patterns.

They then offer a more detailed portrait of the social order whose strains and breakdowns set the stage for collective behavior. It consists of a normative order, a social structure, and communication channels; all aspects of the social order are also underwritten by the taken-for-granted basis of everyday life.

With these specifications, one can identify a range of events that may trigger collective behavior. These include ambiguities or conflicts in normative expectations, strains and stresses in the social structure, and events that undermine the predictability and "naturalness" of everyday life. Although covering a lot of ground, these triggers describe different forms of strain and breakdown as precipitators of collective behavior.

Having said that, Turner and Killian add an important specification to this causal logic. They claim that although they may be necessary, "value conflicts, normative ambiguities, failures of role performance, and other 'breakdowns,' 'strains,' or 'dysfunctions' are not themselves sufficient to lead to collective behavior" (Turner and Killian 1987: 50). Several other factors must also come into play, as specified in their larger model of collective behavior (feasibility, timeliness, group formation, and so on).

Other work in this tradition also enlists strain and breakdown in accounting for collective behavior. Recall Kornhauser's (1959/2008) study of the politics of mass society. In such societies, people are atomized, and intermediate social groups that might provide social control and normative anchors are weak or absent. These conditions can be exacerbated by what Kornhauser calls discontinuities in authority, community, and society that increase the likelihood of collective behavior in general and extremist mass movements in particular.

A final example is Gusfield's (1963/1986) study of the temperance movement. In this and other symbolic crusades, the fuel is often strains and ambiguities surrounding norms, values, and status. Gusfield argues that it was status anxiety in a period of rapid social change that prompted white, native-born Protestants to rally around the cause of temperance as an expression of their values and a defense of their status.

This brief reprise of the Chicago School suggests three conclusions. First, the concepts of strain and breakdown are extremely broad; for better or worse, they link a highly diverse and varied set of conditions that can prompt collective behavior. Second, one or another version of strain or breakdown is consistently present in the Chicago School, from the early work of Park, Burgess, and Blumer; through the later contributions of Turner and Killian; and in the more empirical work of Kornhauser, Gusfield, and others. Finally, strain and breakdown alone cannot carry the whole burden of explaining collective behavior. As Turner and Killian argue, they may be necessary but are not sufficient by themselves to fully understand instances of collective behavior. The Chicago School thereby provides one version of strain and breakdown theories.

RELATIVE DEPRIVATION

If strain is necessary but not sufficient to explain collective action, we need to identify other causes or facilitators of that outcome. As Turner and Killian note, intersubjective interpretations always work in tandem with objective realities. This reasoning brings us to the notion of relative deprivation as a particular type of strain that arises when people make certain judgments about the circumstances they face. It is at the heart of a second group of strain-based theories of collective action.

The most straightforward way to link deprivation with collective action involves absolute deprivation and the hypothesis that the more deprived people become, the more likely they are to take action. This hypothesis, however, is suspect on at least two grounds. First, under conditions of absolute deprivation, the sheer struggle for survival often monopolizes people's time and energy so that despite having the motive, they lack the capacity to engage in collective action. Second, many of the groups that do engage in collective action are not the worst off, but rather have some resources already at their disposal. Both circumstances suggest the limits of explanations based on absolute deprivation and the plausibility of a more relative form of deprivation as a better explanation.

The concept of relative deprivation may also reconcile otherwise conflicting views of the origins of collective action in general and revolution in particular. James Davies (1962) finds this dilemma within Marx's work. On one hand, Marx suggested that "progressive degradation of the industrial working class would finally reach the point of despair and inevitable revolt" (Davies 1962: 5). On the other hand, Marx suggested that revolutionary aspirations would arise when workers' circumstances were improving but not as quickly as those of their capitalist overlords: "[O]ur desires and pleasures spring from society ... [b]ecause they are of a social nature, they are of a relative nature" (quoted in Davies 1962: 5).

Both views have partial validity and fit selected situations. Tocqueville, for example, identified the improving conditions of French society as an impetus to its revolution. A more rigorous and scientific theory of revolution, however, must resolve such contradictions and encompass a broader range of cases.

Davies seeks such a resolution by combining the two ideas in a specific sequence. "Revolutions are most likely to occur when a prolonged period of objective economic and social development is followed by a short period of sharp reversal" (Davies 1962: 6). This sequence is crucial because "[p]olitical stability and instability are ultimately dependent on a state of mind, a mood, in a society" (Davies 1962: 6). The combination of steady improvement followed by a sharp reversal thereby creates a protorebellious mood.

The role of expectations is central to this dynamic. Just as the low expectations of absolutely deprived groups can reinforce passivity, the rising expectations of better-off groups can spark action. Improving conditions create rising expectations. As long as conditions keep rough pace with expectations, people will be satisfied. If conditions deteriorate while expectations continue to rise, a tolerable gap between the two eventually becomes intolerable. People feel deprived relative to what they have come to expect; the "crucial factor is the vague or specific fear that ground gained over a long period of time will be quickly lost" (Davies 1962: 8).

Davies supports this "J-curve" theory of revolution by examining three cases in some detail: Dorr's rebellion (1842), the Russian Revolution (1917), and the Egyptian Revolution (1952). He notes that all of these were progressive revolutions and that the theory may not apply to retrogressive ones. Although claiming explanatory value, Davies is cautious about the predictive value of the theory.

Prediction is difficult because the theory so explicitly directs attention away from objective circumstances and toward subjective judgments, moods, and feelings. Data on these conditions is notoriously elusive and unreliable, but without it the theory cannot be tested. This difficulty has often plagued explanations based on relative deprivation; analysts can more readily assess objective data so they infer relative deprivation based on objective trends, thereby undermining the logic of the theory. Despite this hurdle, the relative deprivation model became a major variant of strain theories of collective action and revolution in the 1960s.

Shortly after Davies's work appeared, James Geschwender (1968/1997) proposed a broader model that incorporated the J-curve hypothesis along with several alternatives. Geschwender's model is meant to apply to both movements and revolutions, and to include both progressive and reactionary forms of collective action.

This model begins by reiterating Davies's J-curve argument, now renamed the rise and drop hypothesis. In this scenario, sustained improvement triggers expectations of continued improvement so that when there is a reversal in people's situation, there is an intolerable gap between what people expect and what they actually receive.

Alternative scenarios might produce similar outcomes. One is the rising expectations hypothesis. This is a "softer" version of the J-curve hypothesis, in which there is no actual decline in people's objective situation but merely a declining rate of improvement. Even this may suffice to create a gap between expectations and conditions, and Geschwender applies this reading to the civil rights movement of the mid-1960s.

In a third scenario termed the relative deprivation hypothesis, Marx's observation about the social and relative nature of our desires is revisited. In this case, a group's conditions may have actually improved, but done so more slowly than the conditions of another group. If more rapidly improving groups are taken as a reference group for comparison, yet another gap between expectations and conditions is created.

Downward mobility provides a fourth scenario. In this case, a sense of dissatisfaction is created when people compare their current situation with a previous one when they were better off. Such downward mobility may take an absolute form, exemplified by the loss of a job or a substantial pay cut. It may also take a relative form, as when a formerly subordinate group makes substantial gains and narrows the gap between its status and that of one's own group.

The final version involves status inconsistency. Given that people occupy multiple statuses in complex societies, it is likely that some of their statuses will be inconsistent (higher or lower) with others. If a higher status becomes a point of reference for judging a lower status, dissatisfaction will arise that may compel people into collective action to improve their lower status and resolve the inconsistency.

The distinctions among different types of relative deprivation suggest hypotheses about the intensity and direction of collective action. Thus, the rise and drop of the J-curve situation produces a bigger gap between what people expect and what they get than the rising expectations scenario. This may translate into a revolutionary movement in the former case and a reform movement in the latter.

The direction of collective action refers to its political orientation. The hypothesis is that the first three forms of dissatisfaction will produce forward-looking, progressive movements to improve a group's situation. Downward mobility, on the other hand, will produce a backward-looking, reactionary movement heavily reliant on scapegoating others. Status inconsistency cases could move in either direction.

Having explored different types of relative deprivation, Geschwender then proposes a basic mechanism that translates deprivation into action. That mechanism is cognitive dissonance. Thus, when people envision a possible state of affairs, believe they are entitled to it, and know they are not currently enjoying it, cognitive dissonance occurs. Altering one's environment and condition is one way of resolving dissonance. "Therefore, dissonance-reducing activities often take the form of social protest or revolutionary behavior" (Geschwender 1997: 104). Because these activities can take other forms as well, a basic challenge to this logic is to specify when cognitive dissonance leads to collective, politicized action rather than some other response.

Perhaps the most ambitious use of the concept of relative deprivation is Ted Gurr's analysis of *Why Men Rebel* (1970). He seeks to explain political violence by isolating factors that create the potential for collective violence, factors that politicize this potential, and factors that determine the magnitude and forms of political violence. He proposes almost one hundred distinct hypotheses about these variables; in appendices and asides about theory and method, Gurr endorses a rigorous, positivist approach to developing a genuinely scientific explanation of political violence.

Despite this complexity, Gurr claims that the "primary causal sequence in political violence is first the development of discontent, second the politicization of that discontent, and finally its actualization in violent action against political objects and actors" (Gurr 1970: 12–13). If violence originates in discontent, the latter originates in relative deprivation, which Gurr sees as "the basic, instigating condition for participants in collective action" (Gurr 1970: 13).

Relative deprivation is defined as a perceived discrepancy between value expectations and value capabilities; the former refers to what people believe they are entitled to, and the latter refers to what they believe they are capable of attaining. A perception of relative deprivation can thus take three forms. Decremental relative deprivation means that expectations remain constant while capabilities are perceived to decline. Aspirational relative deprivation means that capabilities remain constant while expectations increase. Finally, progressive relative deprivation occurs when expectations increase alongside decreasing capabilities.

Gurr emphasizes that people's perceptions are much more central than objective indicators when analyzing relative deprivation. Perceptions, in turn, rest upon values and beliefs that shape how people form expectations about what they are due and how they evaluate their capacity to get it. Like Geschwender, the argument acknowledges complexity and variation, but then identifies a basic causal mechanism common to all these variations.

In this instance, the question is what translates relative deprivation (whatever its causes) into the potential for collective violence. Gurr's answer is not cognitive dissonance, but rather Dollard's postulation "that the occurrence of aggressive behavior always presupposes the existence of frustration and, contrariwise, that the existence of frustration always leads to some form of aggression" (quoted in Gurr 1970: 33). Gurr adds the notion of threat to that of frustration, concluding that "frustration—aggression and the related threat—aggression mechanisms provide the basic motivational link between [relative deprivation] and the potential for collective violence" (Gurr 1970: 36). The degree of frustration or threat is thus the primary determinant of the intensity of relative deprivation.

Having placed a psychological mechanism at the heart of his theory, Gurr then explores some social origins of relative deprivation. Rising expectations may be caused by a "demonstration effect" whereby a new reference group or a new ideology provides a standard for comparison. Perceptions of declining capabilities also have social origins in the changing economic status of a group, a loss of its ideational coherence, and the impact of regime power on a group's interests.

These factors condition the potential for collective violence; a related set of social forces may politicize that potential. These include cultural processes of socialization, tradition, and legitimation as well as group ideologies, utilities, and communication channels. Finally, the magnitude and form of political violence will vary as a function of the coercive balance between a regime and its challengers as well as the balance of institutional support for each side in a conflict.

Although Gurr offers the most extensive treatment of relative deprivation, his analysis—like so many examined to this point—remains somewhat tangential to social movements. Most episodes of political violence do not emerge from social movements, and most social movements do not engage in political violence. Moreover, Gurr's orientation as a political scientist and his propensity for psychologically reductionistic explanations did not sit well with many seeking a more sociological explanation.

Relative deprivation nonetheless provides a second example of strain-based theories alongside the Chicago School. The concept speaks most directly to the social psychology of individual motivation and grievance formation, and more tangentially to issues of recruitment and mobilization. Although attending to these micro-level issues, macro-issues and structural factors were less explored. The third example of strain-based theories addresses precisely this structural level.

SMELSER'S FUNCTIONALIST APPROACH

Neil Smelser's *Theory of Collective Behavior* appeared in 1962. The most distinctive aspect of this version of strain theory was its link to Talcott Parsons's more general, structural-functionalist theory of social action on the premise that "[c]ollective behavior is analyzable by the same categories as conventional behavior" (Smelser 1962: 23). This heritage reflects not only Smelser's own training but also the broader conceptual hegemony enjoyed by Parsonian sociology in the 1950s and early 1960s.

Needless to say, this involved a complex, conceptual scaffolding as Smelser constructed his theory. The broader theory of action from which it was derived identified four basic components of social action. Values provide broad guides to action. Norms govern the pursuit of goals specified by values. Motivation of individual energy compels people to act and organizes them into roles. Finally, situational facilities provide knowledge and resources for action. Values are the most general component of action, with each succeeding component bringing greater specificity.

Each of these four components has its own hierarchy of seven levels, moving from the most general values, norms, motivations, and facilities to increasingly more specific ones. Picture a grid of social action with twenty-eight cells consisting of seven levels of specificity for each of the four components of action. Against this backdrop, strain is defined as "an impairment of the relations among and consequently inadequate functioning of the components of action" (Smelser 1962: 47).

Although strain could appear anywhere, it tends to emerge at the more specific levels of each component of action. It is the response to strain that distinguishes conventional from collective behavior. Conventional behavior responds to strain by moving to a higher level of generalization, reconstituting the meaning of strain at that level, formulating new principles or solutions, and then moving back down to the original level and instituting a response appropriate to the level where the strain originated.

Collective behavior initially responds the same way by moving to a higher level of generalization. However, "[h]aving redefined the high-level component, people do not proceed to respecify, step by step, down the line to reconstitute social action. Rather, they develop a belief which 'short-circuits' from a very generalized component *directly* to the focus of strain" (Smelser 1962: 71; italics in original). This is also referred to as a "compressed" response to strain that jumps across intermediate levels of social action.

Smelser's reliance on Parsons's functionalism smuggled in a conservative or managerial bias. A close reading makes it hard to deny that this theory regards collective behavior as an inappropriate if not deviant response to strain *by definition*. The conception of collective behavior as a short-circuited, compressed response to strain carries an inherently negative judgment that later attracted fierce criticism.

There are other distinctive elements to the theory as well. It is presented as a "value-added" analysis, borrowing the concept from economics. In industrial production, commodities are produced through a sequence of activities in which each adds a distinct value to the final product. Smelser proposes that collective behavior emerges through a similar value-added process of cumulative determinants. Each step is necessary but not sufficient to produce collective behavior; taken together the steps are collectively sufficient. Moreover, the manner in which each step combines with previous ones narrows the range of possible outcomes, excluding some and increasing the likelihood of other forms of collective behavior.

Smelser then identifies six determinants of collective behavior. The first is structural conduciveness; it refers to whether a social order facilitates or is permissive of some form of collective behavior. Thus, financial markets are conducive to panics due to the rapid transmission of rumor and quick convertibility of assets. Highly authoritarian regimes are not conducive to most forms of collective behavior due to highly centralized social control.

The second determinant is social strain, generically understood as "ambiguities, deprivations, conflicts, and discrepancies" (Smelser 1962: 16) in the social order. It is when strain occurs in a conducive context that the combination increases the likelihood of collective behavior.

The third determinant is the growth and spread of a generalized belief. This makes the strain meaningful to people, identifying a supposed cause and possible solutions. These beliefs also partake of the short-circuiting and compression discussed earlier, jumping over levels of social action to apply a broad solution to a specific strain. Such beliefs can exist for a long time without provoking collective behavior; again, they become causally effective in the context of prior conduciveness and strain.

The fourth determinant is a precipitating factor that increases the likelihood that the potential for collective behavior will be realized in a particular time and place. These factors are thus triggers for action that provoke people to act in a context of preexisting conduciveness, strain, and beliefs.

The fifth determinant is the actual mobilization of people into action. "This point marks the onset of panic, the outbreak of hostility, or the beginning of agitation for reform or revolution" (Smelser 1962: 17).

The final determinant is the operation of social control, and it "arches over all the others" (Smelser 1962: 17). Social control is really a counterdeterminant that is relevant in two ways. Some controls operate from the beginning to reduce conduciveness and strain and thereby abort the value-added process. Others commence once collective behavior emerges. In either case, the relevant controls must be absent or ineffective if an episode of collective behavior is to fully develop. If and only if all six determinants combine, collective behavior is certain to occur.

Close attention to the determinants may predict not only that collective behavior will occur but also what form it will take. Generalized beliefs are especially important here. In conjunction with other factors, hysterical beliefs will give rise to panics, positive wish-fulfillment beliefs will give rise to crazes, and hostile beliefs will provoke hostile outbursts.

Two types of movements are distinguished. Norm-oriented movements tend to be reformist or ameliorative in nature, whereas value-oriented movements tend to be revolutionary or transformative. Other determinants also predict the type of movement that emerges. For example, societies that are conducive to political protest are likely to see norm-oriented movements; those that are less conducive are likely to see either no movements at all or revolutionary, transformative challenges when they do occur.

Smelser's theory attracted considerable criticism, partly for its Parsonian heritage and partly on its own terms. Some thought it unfortunate that just when the field was recognizing continuities between conventional and collective behavior, this theory underscored their differences (Oberschall 1973: 22). Turner and Killian—no strangers to misguided accusations about imputing irrationality to collective behavior—ruefully noted that "Smelser's 'generalized belief' does sound very much like some of Le Bon's ideas" (1987: 5).

Many critics challenged the equation of generalized beliefs with short-circuited, compressed, or exaggerated responses to strain. For these critics, this depiction of generalized beliefs dovetailed with "an administrative or managerial perspective on collective behavior, in which unacknowledged evaluations take the place of forthright assertions of the social values underlying the study of collective action" (Currie and Skolnick 1970: 37). Criticisms that had long been made of functionalism in general thereby found a more specific target in Smelser's theory of collective behavior.

LATER EXEMPLARS

The 1960s brought a "cascade of social movements" (Zald 2007) that radically altered understandings about what movements were and how to study them. There was, however, a time lag in the theoretical response to these developments. As late as 1975, an authoritative review of the collective behavior literature featured a lengthy discussion of social strains as the major cause of social movements (G. Marx and Wood 1975). Less than a decade later, a parallel article about resource mobilization theory failed to mention strain in any significant way (Jenkins 1983).

The reasons for this remarkable change will be considered in the conclusion of this chapter. For now, suffice it to say that strain explanations moved from the center to the margins of the field of social movements, but they did not disappear altogether. The following examples document the persistence of certain uses of strain or breakdown even as a generalized, explanatory notion of strain fell into disfavor.

In the last third of the twentieth century, work on social movements and theories of revolutions progressed on almost parallel paths that rarely intersected. Ironically enough, some theories of revolution did retain the notion of breakdown even as it was becoming marginalized in social movement theory. One example is Goldstone's (1991a) argument that revolutions follow similar causal processes involving state breakdown, revolutionary contention, and state rebuilding.

The origin of state breakdown involves a conjunction of state fiscal distress, elite alienation and conflict, and a high mobilization potential among the general populace. In this interactive model, all three elements must be present if a full revolutionary challenge is to unfold. The background causes of this conjunctural model of state breakdown are historically specific, though they often involve demographic growth and population shifts which put new pressure on state resources (Goldstone 1991b). Ideological and cultural factors enter into the revolutionary process, but play only a secondary role in the collapse of existing social structures (Goldstone 1991b).

In his most definitive statement, Goldstone concludes that state breakdowns from 1500 to 1850 resulted from a single basic process of population growth that overwhelmed agrarian bureaucratic states and prompted fiscal instability, intraelite conflicts, popular unrest, and revolutionary ideology. This pattern triggered state breakdowns in the sixteenth and early seventeenth centuries as well as the late eighteenth and early nineteenth centuries when the population grew significantly in the early modern world (Goldstone 1991b).

Breakdown notions also appear in Piven and Cloward's (1979) work on poor people's movements. They emphasize the extent to which social structures limit opportunities for protest and diminish its force when it does occur. If social institutions typically preclude opportunities for protest, then it is only under rare and exceptional circumstances that deprived groups will be in a position to pursue their grievances.

Thus, major social dislocations are necessary before longstanding grievances can find expression in collective defiance. It is here that they point to social breakdowns in society's regulatory capacity and everyday routines as providing rare but potent opportunities for mass defiance. But breakdown is not enough; people must also see their deprivations and problems as unjust, mutable, and subject to their action.

Such insights are likely only when the scale of distress is high or when the dominant institutions are obviously malfunctioning. Societal breakdown thus not only disrupts regulatory capacity and everyday routines; it also opens a cognitive space in which people can begin to consider and pursue alternative social arrangements.

When protest happens, it is shaped by the institutional structures in which it occurs as people choose targets, strategies, and tactics. Mass defiance will be effective to the extent that it disrupts institutions that are important to elites. Defiance is thus best seen as a negative sanction imposed by protesters to extract concessions.

Whereas the logic of strikes or boycotts involves withholding valuable resources such as labor or purchasing power, the only thing deprived groups may be able to withhold is their acquiescence in social order. Mass defiance is the only true leverage that poor people's movements possess, and some significant societal breakdown is required for this resource to be unleashed.

In an interesting twist, breakdown is not just a background causal factor in protest but also a deliberate strategy as protesters seek to exacerbate institutional disruption to the point where they win concessions they would not otherwise realize.

In a subsequent programmatic statement, Piven and Cloward (1992) offer an explicit defense of breakdown theories that rests on a distinction between normative and non-normative forms of protest. They claim that non-normative protest is a more basic challenge to power because it not only pursues a specific agenda but also does so in a way that challenges elite power and rule-making.

The distinction is critical to the debate: "[Malintegration] analysts do not claim that breakdown is a necessary precondition of normative forms of group action. What they emphasize instead is that breakdown is a precondition of collective protest and violence, of riot and rebellion.... In effect, the [malintegration] tradition is being dismissed for an argument it never made" (Piven and Cloward 1992: 306).

They claim that the lateral integration of movement organization is less important than (breakdowns in) the vertical integration of social structure in explaining mass protest. Hierarchical social structures normally constrain opportunities for protest, but it is when those linkages are weakened and when grievances intensify that defiance is likely to emerge. Studies of both revolution and poor people's movements thus illustrate the persistence of strain and breakdown theories even as they moved to the margins of social movement theory.

A more recent reformulation of breakdown theories questions a false dichotomy between breakdown theories emphasizing external social strain and solidarity approaches stressing internal group cohesion. Snow et al. (1998) suggest that although the terms "strain" and "breakdown" are often used interchangeably, breakdown is a specific form of the broader concept of strain. Traditional breakdown theories viewed collective action as rooted in rapid social change and disintegration, which weaken social cohesion and exacerbate tensions and frustrations.

Snow et al. (1998) acknowledge that breakdown theories fell out of favor in the last third of the twentieth century because of conceptual vagueness, empirical weakness, and theoretical fads. However, they argue that their rejection was premature, and that a revised version of breakdown theory can be formulated that is compatible with the role of solidarity in generating collective action, and that empirically fits with a wide range of collective action.

The core of their argument is that the link between social breakdown and collective action is the disruption of the quotidian nature of social life. The latter refers to all the taken-for-granted aspects of everyday life; more specifically, the quotidian consists of daily practices and routines that comprise habitual social action, alongside the natural attitude of routinized expectations and the suspension of doubt about the organization of the social world and one's role within it. "When the quotidian is disrupted, then, routinized patterns of action are rendered problematic and the natural attitude is fractured" (Snow et al. 1998: 5).

In this way, a specific type of breakdown is seen as the impetus to collective action. As with all forms of breakdown theory, there are many ways in which people might respond to disruptions of the quotidian, so it remains to specify which disruptions are most likely to provoke collective action rather than social withdrawal, individual coping, or anti-social behavior. At a minimum, the disruption must be experienced collectively and it must not have a normal, institutional resolution if it is to provoke collective action (Snow et al. 1998: 6).

Four categories of events fit these guidelines. First, accidents that disrupt a community's routines or threaten its existence through "suddenly imposed grievances" are likely to spark collective action; Walsh's (1981) study of the community response to the nuclear accident at Three Mile Island is the classic example. Second, intrusions into or violations of community space by strangers or outsiders can provoke such responses; the cases of anti–drunk driving movements; antibusing movements; or neighborhood movements that resist halfway houses, group homes, or toxic waste dumps provide examples here. Third, changes in taken-for-granted subsistence routines can provoke collective action; the response of homeless people to disruptions in habituated survival routines provides examples of this type. Finally, and perhaps most evidently, dramatic changes in structures of social control can disrupt quotidian routines and provoke collective action; research on prison riots provides examples here.

Snow et al. thus challenge the presumed dichotomy between breakdown and solidarity by specifying that breakdown involves patterns and expectancies of everyday life rather than associational ties between individuals. It is the combination of a breakdown in everyday routines alongside strong ties within groups that may be most likely to promote collective action.

Even in a time of harsh criticism, the work of Goldstone on revolution, Piven and Cloward on poor people's movements, and Snow et al. on the quotidian nature of social life illustrate the persistence of strain and breakdown explanations of particular types of collective action.

CONCLUSION

Strain, breakdown, and deprivation models have a long history. Building on Durkheim, they rose to prominence with the Chicago School, relative deprivation, and Smelser's theory. More recently, somewhat more carefully specified versions of these theories have exhibited a dogged persistence in the face of criticism and alternatives.

The career of breakdown theories has an even stranger turn. There is a sense in which these explanations did not disappear as much as they were rebranded. Consider how the resource mobilization and political process models—discussed in the next two chapters—dismissed breakdown but emphasized opportunity as a cause of collective action. Upon closer examination, there is considerable conceptual overlap between what prior theorists meant by strain or breakdown and what later theorists mean by opportunity. Where they differ is their valuational bias.

The terms "strain" and "breakdown" inherently connote negative, problematic conditions to be prevented, avoided, or repaired. As these terms functioned in classical breakdown theories, they cast a negative light on the appropriateness of collective behavior. That is why breakdown theorists have been more likely to see social control in a positive light and protester aggression in a negative light (Useem 1998). Thus, it was not just breakdown as a neutral causal mechanism that provoked critics; it was also the negative value judgments implicit in the concept that drew their fire.

The concept of opportunity was tailor-made for this situation. On the one hand, it allowed resource mobilization and political process theorists to paint collective action in a positive light. In contrast with "strain," "opportunity" inherently signifies something to be sought, desired, seized, enjoyed, valued, and maximized. On the other hand, it preserves a way of talking about structural change that facilitates collective action.

Although opportunity and breakdown are not the same thing, they do the same work in each theoretical tradition. Both refer to external, variable processes that increase the likelihood of collective behavior. To the extent that opportunity has become a stand-in for strain and breakdown, the latter never really disappeared from social movement theory (Buechler 2004).

The rebranding and decentering of strain theories occurred because of critiques that emerged in the 1970s in conjunction with the emergence of new paradigms. The very same criticisms that marginalized strain theories were also the gateway to resource mobilization and political process theories.

One of the earliest criticisms was part of Jerome Skolnick's (1969) report to a national commission on violence. It identified two prevailing explanations of collective violence: social strain leading to frustration and hostility, and breakdown of social control. Either way, the outcome is seen as unstable, disorderly, deviant behavior. Moreover, participants are portrayed as destructive and irrational, whereas authorities are seen as normal and reasonable.

Skolnick's evidence suggested that such explanations were deeply flawed. First, the concepts of frustration and tension are too vague and psychologistic to explain the urban riots of the 1960s. Moreover, they obscure the political nature of those riots and the fact that otherwise normal, rational people participated in them. Finally, the violence was less a quality of the rioters than an emergent product of the interactions between protesters and authorities. Skolnick's critique thus challenged several assumptions of traditional strain and breakdown explanations.

A second challenge came from the Tillys (Tilly, Tilly, and Tilly 1975), and it was based on evidence from a century of collective action in Europe. Like Skolnick, they challenged stereotypical accounts of violent crowds and irrational masses by recasting violence as an interactive product of protesters and authorities and pointing to the group interests and reflective calculations that often motivate protesters.

More broadly, they challenged breakdown theories because they "suffer from irreparable logical and empirical difficulties. Some sort of solidarity theory should work better everywhere. No matter where we look, we should rarely find uprooted, marginal, disorganized people heavily involved in collective violence. All over the world we should expect collective violence to flow out of routine collective action and continuing struggles for power" (Tilly, Tilly, and Tilly 1975: 290).

These critiques eventually targeted the entire "classical model" of social movements, including "mass society, collective behavior, status inconsistency, rising expectations, relative deprivation, and Davies' J-curve theory of revolution" (McAdam 1982: 6). Despite variations, they all rest on a general causal sequence in which some background condition of structural strain provokes a disruptive psychological state that leads to a social movement (McAdam 1982).

There are several problems with this model. The claim that social movements are a response to social strain ignores the larger political context in which movements arise, and assumes a mechanistic and linear relationship between macro-level strain and micro-level behavior. The identification of individual discontent as the proximate cause of social movements presumes an abnormal psychological profile that sharply distinguishes participants from nonparticipants in collective behavior. The individual level of analysis also ignores how individual mental states are translated into genuinely collective phenomena. Finally, the individualistic emphasis denies the political dimension of collective behavior by implying that it is nothing more than a "convenient justification for what is at root a psychological phenomenon" (McAdam

1982: 17). When such assumptions guide the analysis, collective behavior is more likely to be perceived as deviant behavior than political contention.

The work of Goldstone, Piven and Cloward, and Snow et al. discussed previously demonstrates that there were creative ways to sustain more carefully specified versions of strain and breakdown explanations. But the criticisms just reviewed were sufficient to move such theories to the margins as fundamentally new approaches took their place. By the mid- to late 1970s, social movement theory was undergoing a major paradigm shift.

Part III
Paradigm Shifts

Chapter Seven

Resource Mobilization Approaches

The phrase "the '60s" has become a cultural cliché and a free-floating signifier. For our purposes, two points are important. First, "the '60s" refers chronologically to a "long decade" stretching almost twenty years from the late 1950s to the mid-1970s. Second, this period witnessed one of the most significant waves of social, economic, political, and cultural protest in the entire history of the United States. It is not surprising that these events fundamentally changed sociological approaches to social movements. What is surprising is that almost no one saw it coming.

THE CONTEXT

While the 1960s evoke images of protest, the 1950s connote tranquility. On the surface of American society, there was economic prosperity, steady employment, affordable education, stable families, and burgeoning suburbs. Having survived the Great Depression and a world war, it seemed that a society of material affluence, political stability, and cultural consensus was in the offing.

These expectations remained strong despite countervailing trends such as the Cold War, McCarthyism, the military-industrial complex, racial tensions at home, and anticolonial stirrings abroad. Prominent intellectuals opined that we had reached the end of ideology (Bell 1960) and that the greatest challenges in the future revolved around how to deal with the problems of abundance, leisure, and affluence (Galbraith 1958). There were, to be sure, some intellectual dissidents (Mills 1959; Riesman 1950), but their critical voices were hard to hear above the celebratory atmosphere of the times.

If things seemed quiet on the home front, they were not so abroad. In a time before "globalization" was a household word, anticolonial struggles and national liberation movements were emerging overseas and providing one of many sparks that would ignite the civil rights movement in the United States. The domestic movement took inspiration from the global ones, providing leverage against a political system whose lofty rhetoric had never matched its actual treatment of so many of its citizens.

The localized protests of poor Southern blacks in the 1950s gradually became a national movement as Northern liberals took up the cause and white students went south to join the movement. Although the movement for African American liberation would take many permutations, perhaps few were as significant as the early struggles that shattered the tranquil and complacent world of white America.

Among many other consequences, the early civil rights movement helped turn the state from a repressive agent or indifferent observer into a reluctant facilitator of movement activism. The Kennedy/Johnson administrations gave rise to the War on Poverty, the Great Society agenda, and other initiatives whereby the federal government actually facilitated activities such as community organizing, local activism, and legal representation for the poor.

It was this early civil rights movement that also triggered the "cascade of social movements" (Zald 2007) now evoked by the phrase "the '60s." White students took their cues from this early mobilization and organized the Free Speech Movement and the Students for a Democratic Society, which then morphed into an antiwar movement that thoroughly disrupted "business as usual" on the nation's campuses (and the broader society) by 1970. These actions, in turn, spurred countercultural and environmental movements, and added momentum to, and provocations for, a nascent feminist movement and a subsequent mobilization for gay and lesbian liberation. Although movements often come in cycles, it is difficult to overestimate the impact of this cycle on society in general and the study of social movements in particular.

The societal transition from tranquility to turmoil was mirrored in a theoretical shift from consensus to conflict. The 1950s were the apogee of functionalist theory in sociology, with its vision of society as a social system of integrated parts fulfilling functions, maintaining equilibrium, and managing tensions. A theory that seemed persuasive to many in the 1950s appeared increasingly irrelevant to many more in the 1960s. Even by the late 1950s, some sociologists were developing the alternative approach of conflict theory (Coser 1956; Dahrendorf 1959); within a decade, devastating (if sometimes overstated) criticisms of functionalism had created space for alternative theories of power, conflict, and domination (Mills 1959; Gouldner 1970).

These sociohistorical events changed sociology in other ways as well. The discipline became academically popular and its rapid expansion dovetailed with a more politicized, leftward drift among many of the baby boomer generation who entered sociology (McAdam 2007: 414–418ff). The upshot was that "[b]y 1970, many younger sociologists, students and new faculty had come to think of sociology as a sociological imagination that would remake the world, while the older generation had thought of it as a profession that would help manage the world" (Lemert 2008: 100).

In the study of social movements, a paradigm shift that no one foresaw in the early 1960s appeared almost predestined by the late 1970s. Under the weight of social change, political protest, cultural conflict, theoretical shifts, and activist biographies, the older collective behavior tradition was seen by many as ill-suited to studying new forms of collective action.

The newer paradigm challenged the accepted wisdom about collective behavior in several ways. First, it rejected the subsumption of social movements under collective behavior, claiming that the former were different enough from the latter to warrant their own mode of analysis (McAdam 2007: 421). Second, social movements were seen as enduring, patterned, and quasi-institutionalized, thereby challenging the traditional classification of them as noninstitutional behavior. Third, newer approaches viewed participants in social movements as "at least as rational as those who study them" (Schwartz 1976: 135), reversing the premise of irrationality that still lingered over the collective behavior tradition.

Finally, the psychological readings of collective behavior were displaced by a political interpretation of social movements as power struggles over conflicting interests that shared many organizational dynamics with more institutionalized forms of conflict (Oberschall 1973; McCarthy and Zald 1973, 1977; Tilly 1978). In sharp contrast with the collective behavior tradition, the new paradigm viewed social movements as normal, rational, political challenges by aggrieved groups, thereby recasting the study of collective action from an instance of deviance and social disorganization to a topic for political and organizational sociology.

The various strands of this new approach were initially designated by the generic name "resource mobilization." Although this diverse congeries of ideas would soon be differentiated into separate approaches, the rise of resource mobilization in the mid- to late 1970s was the first paradigm in the history of the discipline to place social movements at the center of the analysis. After almost a century of being ontological orphans of collective behavior or foster children of political sociology, movements came into their own in the politics of the 1960s and in the theories of the 1970s.

EARLY STRANDS OF RESOURCE MOBILIZATION

Alongside conflict theory, another theoretical challenger to the hegemony of functionalist theory that emerged in the 1960s was exchange or rational choice theory (Homans 1974; Blau 1964). If functionalism saw people as motivated by common values, rational choice theory saw them as driven by self-interest, leading them to choose courses of action that maximized benefits and minimized costs.

This approach derived from economics, and it was one economist in particular whose work had a major impact on the study of social movements. Mancur Olson's (1965) *The Logic of Collective Action* began with the premise that people are rational actors and proceeded to explore the challenges this posed for mobilizing collective action. Olson's work was widely cited in the social movement literature because it was such a direct rebuttal to images of irrational masses that were still associated with the classical model of social movements.

Olson argued that self-interest motivates people to pursue private goods but not necessarily public ones. The latter refer to goods that are available to everyone regardless of their contribution (or lack thereof) to making them available. The dilemma for collective action is this: If the goal is a public good, it is individually rational for each actor to not participate in the action because that imposes a cost and because they can enjoy the benefit without the cost if the movement succeeds. The paradox is that if everyone thinks this way, no one will engage in the action, and the public good will not be forthcoming.

This is the "free-rider" problem; logic predisposes rational actors to ride free on the actions of others in the hopes of maximizing their benefits and minimizing their costs. Within Olson's economistic logic, there is only one solution to this dilemma. People must be offered "selective incentives" (available to participants but withheld from others) if they are to be rationally motivated to participate in collective action seeking public goods. These stark choices prompted considerable debate in social movement theory even as the premise of the rational actor became the new baseline assumption about collective action.

Alongside exchange theory, conflict theory also informed the newly emerging paradigm. Oberschall (1973) was one strong advocate of Olson's rational choice premises who also explicitly linked the study of conflict and movements in an analysis that foreshadowed several key assumptions of resource mobilization theory (Oberschall 1973). His starting premise is that social movements and collective action are rational responses to self and group interests, and that they follow broader principles of political contention.

Oberschall then addressed the mobilization puzzle of why some people join movements whereas others do not. One classical answer to this question derived from mass society theory with its claim that the most alienated, isolated, or disengaged people were prime candidates for recruitment to social movements (especially extremist movements). Oberschall marshaled devastating logic and evidence to turn this assumption on its head by demonstrating that people who are socially connected are more likely to join movements, whereas more isolated individuals are less likely to do so.

Two forms of preexisting social organization facilitate mobilization into conflict groups. Communal organization involves long-standing, traditional ties with symbolic or moral overtones that link people together; it may arise on the basis of religion, culture, or ethnicity. Associational organization involves more formal, contractual ties that reflect common group interests; it may take the form of labor unions, political parties, or other voluntary associations.

In both cases, people are "preorganized" in ways that make them available for bloc recruitment and quick mobilization into collective action. If such ties are lacking (as in the mass society scenario), mobilization is less (rather than more) likely to occur. With such ties, it becomes easier for movements to put social pressure on individuals to join the movement, thereby overcoming the free-rider dilemma and increasing the likelihood of mass mobilization.

Reflecting another conflict principle, mobilization is more likely not only with horizontal integration but also with vertical segregation. If members of dominant and subordinate groups routinely interact with each other, it may create cross-cutting ties that militate against mobilization. If the groups are rigidly segregated, this will foster a stronger group identity and further contribute to mobilization for collective action (Oberschall 1973). Along with the premise of rationality, the importance of preexisting social organization became a bedrock assumption of the resource mobilization approach.

At the same time that Oberschall's work appeared, McCarthy and Zald (1973/1987) published a seminal essay on resource mobilization. They contrasted their model with the "hearts and minds" approach, noting that the latter "picture of movements composed of aggrieved individuals banding together to fight for their due seems to us seriously inadequate" (McCarthy and Zald 1987: 338).

One challenge they pose to the classical model of movements concerns the role of grievances. If movements are straightforward responses to grievances, then a society with increasing affluence and an expanding middle class should generate fewer grievances and hence fewer movements. In the 1960s and early 1970s, however, the United States experienced significant affluence and middle-class expansion alongside an explosion rather than a decrease in movement activism. This calls into question the causal importance of grievances in producing movements.

A contrary argument holds that educational attainment and socioeconomic status are positively correlated with sociopolitical participation. After a careful dissection of several intertwined trends, they conclude that it is not simply generalized affluence, increased education, or enhanced leisure that accounts for increased social movement activity. This is rather due to more specific factors deriving from these broader trends, including an enlarged pool of college students with discretionary time and an increase in professional occupations that allow their occupants the flexibility to participate in social movements as a corollary to their professional obligations.

They proceed to document how the 1960s was "a period in which institutionalized support for social movement organizations became increasingly available and in which life careers in movements were more and more likely to be combined with established professional roles" (McCarthy and Zald 1987: 358–359). With significant resources provided by churches, foundations, and government itself, an increasing number of professionals undertook part-time participation, temporary full-time positions, or full-time careers in the social movement sector.

They pose a second challenge to the classical model of movements concerning the functions of members. In their view, the significance of members has declined, particularly if funding comes from external sources and if grievances are framed by media-savvy professionals rather than rising up from a mass base. One result is a shift from intensive, exclusive membership to more partial, inclusive membership with relatively few obligations beyond signing petitions or sending checks to the organization.

They summarize these trends by contrasting the professional social movement with the classical model of movements. Professional movements are characterized by a full-time, entrepreneurial cadre of leaders who make careers out of such positions. They derive a large proportion of their resources from "outside the aggrieved group that the movement claims to represent" (McCarthy and Zald 1987: 375). The membership base may be small or virtually non-existent, amounting to little more than a mailing list of names. Nonetheless, such movements claim to speak for a given constituency and seek to shape policy in the name of that constituency.

Professional social movements may be both more durable and more vulnerable as a result. The durability emerges when the movement is diversified across several issues (such as conglomerate manufacturers) so that failure (or success) in one cause will not lead to the demise of the movement because it has other battles to pursue. The vulnerability derives from the movement's dependence on external resources and the need to mollify the churches, foundations, or government agencies that provide them lest those resources be withheld.

With some oversimplification, the argument of this essay might be summarized this way. The classical model of movements saw grievances and masses as independent variables leading to movements that then generated leaders and sought resources. The professional model reverses this logic, seeing entrepreneurial leaders and resource availability as independent variables leading to movements that then frame grievances and recruit membership to suit their purposes. Put more succinctly, "the definition of grievances will expand to meet the funds and support personnel available" (McCarthy and Zald 1987: 379). By reversing the classical logic, the argument sought to explain the seeming paradox of increased movement activity amidst relative affluence. "Whereas the classical model of social movements predicts less activity in prosperous times, our analysis predicts just the reverse" (McCarthy and Zald 1987: 387).

In this context, the early work of Charles Tilly and his collaborators (Tilly et al. 1975) merits further attention for its contributions to the emerging resource mobilization perspective. As noted at the end of Chapter Six, the Tillys argue for the superiority of solidarity theories indebted to the Marxist tradition over the breakdown theories deriving from Durkheim's legacy. Summarizing a wide-ranging body of persuasive historical studies, they claim that "at a minimum they share the assumption that the social base, the organizational form, the prior claims and grievances, the present mobilization of the ordinary actors in political conflicts provide a major part of the explanation for their actions" (Tilly et al. 1975: 273–274). The emphasis on solidarity over breakdown resonates with Oberschall's arguments about the importance of preexisting organization in fostering collective action.

The Tillys provide more specific evidence and logic about the "growth of complex organizations as vehicles of collective action" (Tilly et al. 1975: 276) that occurred in tandem with nationalized production, state-building, and electoral politics. The latter, in particular, "legitimized and promoted the growth of associations as vehicles for collective action. Religious associations, trade associations, friendly societies, and even social clubs whose everyday activities were drinking and talk flowered in the age of elections. They became the means by which ordinary people carried out their collective business" (Tilly et al. 1975: 277).

A third contribution of this work involves its challenge to conventional assumptions about the role of violence in collective action. The Tillys find that "the participants in European collective violence knew what they were doing" and that the fit between their grievances, actions, and demands "is far too good to justify thinking of participation in collective violence as impulsive, unreflective, spur-of-the-moment" (Tilly et al. 1975: 281). They proceed to question the very distinction between violent and nonviolent collective action, suggesting that violence is better seen as an interactive and emergent product than a fundamental type of action in its own right.

This discussion of the role of violence in collective action then comes full circle by endorsing a political interpretation of urban unrest in the 1960s, seeing it as rebellious protest expressing grievances rather than riotous mobs seeking catharsis. Like their European counterparts of previous centuries, these actors also "knew what they were doing." In emphasizing the role of solidarity over breakdown; the centrality of organizations and associations; and the political, rational character of protest and even many forms of violence, the Tillys helped lay the groundwork for the emerging resource mobilization perspective.

Although most research on social movements focused on case studies, William Gamson (1975, 1990) used a different methodology to examine a historical sample of fifty-three challenging groups in the United States between 1800 and 1945. The size of the sample gave Gamson a unique opportunity to explore some of the claims of the emerging resource mobilization approach. Like other thinkers in this paradigm, he sees collective action as a plausible response by outside groups in a political system that has never been as permeable or open to change as its pluralist defenders claim.

Gamson addresses the thorny question of measuring movement success by specifying two dimensions. One form of success involves winning acceptance from elites and recognition as a legitimate representative of a given constituency. Another form of success is indicated by winning new advantages for a movement constituency.

This creates four possible outcomes with the following frequencies in the sample: Full response means both acceptance and new advantages (roughly 40 percent); collapse means neither (roughly 40 percent); preemption means new advantages without acceptance (roughly 10 percent); and cooptation means acceptance without new advantages (roughly 10 percent).

Gamson tests the viability of "thinking small" or having relatively modest goals. The differences between multiple issue versus single issue challenges, limited versus radical goals, and small versus large movement constituencies do not have dramatic or consistent impacts on movement outcomes. The most significant finding here is that challenging groups that seek to displace their antagonists are notably less successful than those groups that do not seek such displacement.

The "free-rider" problem then comes in for scrutiny. Although persuasion and loyalty may be symbolically important in shoring up group solidarity, Gamson found clear evidence that groups using selective incentives (available to members but denied to outsiders) were notably more successful in gaining both acceptance and new advantages.

Gamson concurs with Tilly, Skolnick, and others in asserting that violence "should be viewed as an instrumental act, aimed at furthering the purposes of the group that uses it when they have some reason to think it will help their cause" (Gamson 1990: 81).

His data suggests that violence is related to success with an important proviso. "Unruly groups, those that use violence, strikes, and other constraints, have better than average success" (Gamson 1990: 87). Groups who are the recipients of violence, however, have worse than average success. Thus, "[w]ith respect to violence and success, it appears better to give than to receive" (Gamson 1990: 80).

Several strands of the emerging resource mobilization approach underscored the importance of organization in collective action. Such organization involves several dimensions that Gamson seeks to untangle in his data. He finds that bureaucratic organization can provide combat readiness, whereas centralized power can supply unified command. If bureaucratic, centralized movements can avoid factionalism, they have very high rates of success. Even nonbureaucratic, decentralized movements that avoid factionalism have "a modest possibility of success" (Gamson 1990: 108). Factionalism, however, is the death knell for nonbureaucratic, decentralized movements and a major challenge even for bureaucratic, centralized movements.

Gamson's final empirical contribution looks at the impact of what he calls the historical context on the success of challenging groups. What he finds is that a period of crisis (such as a war or economic downturn) is helpful to those challenging groups that do not seek to displace their opponents and that are able to persist over time so as to be ready to take advantage of opportunities presented by the crisis.

Gamson's timely, empirical contribution thus illuminated and largely supported several major arguments of the resource mobilization paradigm. When all these strands of work came together, that approach became institutionalized.

THE CONSOLIDATION (AND FRACTURING) OF A NEW PARADIGM

The year 1977 saw the consolidation of the resource mobilization paradigm. Two events were crucial. First, McCarthy and Zald (1977) published a seminal statement of the perspective that has become one of the most widely cited publications in the history of social movement theory. Second, they also sponsored a conference at Vanderbilt University that brought together a number of scholars and produced a collection of papers that illustrated the robust nature of the new paradigm (Zald and McCarthy 1979).

These scholars built on their previous work on the professionalization of social movements as well as the efforts of Tilly, Oberschall, Gamson, and others to articulate the resource mobilization perspective. In their words, this approach "emphasizes both societal support and constraint of social movement phenomena.

It examines the variety of resources that must be mobilized, the linkages of social movements to other groups, the dependence of movements upon external support for success, and the tactics used by authorities to control or incorporate movements" (McCarthy and Zald 1977: 1213).

Clarifying its distinctiveness, they note that the "new approach depends more upon political sociological and economic theories than upon the social psychology of collective behavior" (McCarthy and Zald 1977: 1213). Indeed, they challenge all previous approaches that cited grievances or deprivation as "causing" movements.

They question this linkage on empirical grounds, citing that studies have failed to find a strong connection between the two. They also question it on logical grounds, claiming that there is always sufficient discontent and grievances in a society to support a movement *if* organizational and resource challenges can be overcome. Finally, grievances should be seen as secondary because they are sometimes "defined, created and manipulated by issue entrepreneurs and organizations" rather than preceding and causing such organizations to emerge (McCarthy and Zald 1977: 1215).

McCarthy and Zald did not see themselves as orthodox rational choice theorists, but they did operate with a notion of bounded rationality (McCarthy and Zald 2002) in which actors calculate costs in terms of opportunities foregone, probabilities of repression, and the like. In response to Olson's free-rider problem, they used the resource mobilization perspective to understand how selective incentives, cost-reducing mechanisms, career incentives, and conscience constituents can produce movements despite the free-rider dilemma. This reasoning led them to examine how resources are aggregated to support movement activity and how organizations are structured to accomplish these tasks.

This perspective also explores the role of individuals and organizations outside the population the movement represents because the former often control the resources that determine movement success or failure. This suggests a "supply-and-demand" model for understanding the interaction between movements, resources, and the groups that control them. Finally, both individual and organizational behaviors are best understood through a "rational actor" model in which the calculation of costs and benefits is central to recruitment, mobilization, strategy, and tactics.

The theory defines the building blocks of collective action in a distinctive way. A social movement (SM) is defined as opinions and beliefs that represent preference structures for change. Such preferences, however, do not automatically translate into action. "In order to predict the likelihood of preferences being translated into collective action, the mobilization perspective focuses upon the preexisting organization and integration of those segments of a population which share preferences" (McCarthy and Zald 1977: 1218).

If SMs are preference structures, then social movement organizations (SMOs) are complex, formal organizations that seek to implement movement goals. Because more than one SMO can represent a given set of preference structures, they also distinguish social movement industries (SMIs) comprised of all the SMOs acting on behalf of a particular SM. Thus, there are multiple SMIs representing preference structures about civil rights, feminism, environmental protection, and the like; each industry contains multiple SMOs representing the industry's preference structures in somewhat different ways.

Finally, all the SMIs may collectively be referred to as the social movement sector (SMS) of society, which is set apart from more conventional sectors of mainstream society not pursuing social change through these strategies. These definitions are deliberately borrowed from economic studies of firms nested within larger industries. This conceptual borrowing suggests hypotheses about how competition between SMOs within the same industry and competition between industries for greater control of resources will affect the prospects for movement success or failure.

The mobilization of SMOs involves multiple challenges. These include turning nonadherents into adherents and then turning adherents into constituents who provide resources for the movement. Some movements attend more to their beneficiary constituency who will be better off if the movement succeeds, whereas others cater to conscience constituents who supply resources even though they do not stand to directly benefit from movement success. There is a method to the madness of these distinctions: "[t]he partitioning of groups into mass or elite and conscience or beneficiary bystander publics, adherents, constituents, and opponents allows us to describe more systematically the resource mobilization styles and dilemmas of specific SMOs" (McCarthy and Zald 1977: 1223).

The authors then propose a series of hypotheses about these various factors. Most broadly, they hypothesize that as more discretionary resources become available to various sectors of society, the amount available to the SMS will also increase, and that new movement industries and organizations will arise to compete for these resources. They also suggest that increases in resources controlled by conscience constituents are crucial to mobilization regardless of the resources available to beneficiary constituents.

These hypotheses reiterate the conclusion of their earlier work that increasing resource availability is a more critical determinant of movement activity than chronic (or even increasing) levels of deprivation and grievances. The article concludes with more specific hypotheses about the relations between resources, organization, and mobilization across a range of movement structures. This seminal article thereby combined a major theoretical statement with an ambitious research agenda for future work on social movements.

The new perspective outlined in this article was also advanced by the 1977 Vanderbilt conference that led to an important anthology (Zald and McCarthy 1979). These essays variously addressed the strengths and weaknesses of the rational choice model; the effectiveness of government repression against movements; the role of media in shaping perceptions of movements; changing repertoires of contention; and the relations between resources, strategy, and tactics in movements.

Although some of these essays could be read as elaborations of a unified resource mobilization perspective, one of them suggested something quite different. In a critical assessment of conventional accounts of 1960s movements, Charles Perrow notes that one "distinctively new approach, that of resource mobilization, threatens to supplant traditional collective behavior accounts, but I think it has immediately split into two wings" (Perrow 1979: 192–193).

What Perrow labels "RM I" derives from the work of Oberschall, Tilly, and Gamson; it sees protest as "the continuation of orderly politics by other (disorderly) means" (Perrow 1979: 199). Seen as political action, protest is thus a rational and ongoing expression of underlying grievances and interests that cannot find adequate resolution through conventional political solutions. Although the mobilization of resources is crucial in this model, such mobilization is seen as a form of political struggle. Thus, "RM I is a political process model; that is the central insight that distinguishes it from the traditional collective behavior and social movement literature" (Perrow 1979: 201).

"RM II" derives from McCarthy and Zald (1973); it is narrower in scope and draws its imagery more from economic models than political processes. "It is more rationalistic than RM I, is indifferent to ideology, and has little, even at times no, dependence upon grievances. Ideology, grievances and political power are the coin of RM I, but an economic-organizational, input-output model informs RM II" (Perrow 1979: 200).

In some respects, Perrow characterizes RM II as a very parsimonious approach in that "group solidarity is virtually dropped as a variable, along with grievances (which can be manufactured by issue-entrepreneurs if they do not exist and thus are not only secondary but, on occasion, unnecessary)" (Perrow 1979: 200–201). Put differently, "solidarity, guts, and even praxis, if you will, become irrelevant [and] political factors are only weak constraints, rather than possibly central factors" (Perrow 1979: 201).

Having deemphasized political factors, RM II substitutes an economic model in which the analysis turns upon "issue elasticity, substitutability of products, competition for resources, demand curves, advertising, vicarious consumption, product switching (brand changing) and product loyalty, product evaluation, product arousal value, slick packaging, entry costs into a social movement 'industry,' and so on" (Perrow 1979: 201). Although political factors are acknowledged, their role is more that of potential limits upon, rather than engines of, political protest.

The two approaches also differ in tone. The RM I, or political process model, invites a heroic and even romanticized image of valiant masses battling oppression. The RM II or economic-entrepreneurial model lends itself to a debunking stance that is skeptical about the legitimacy of a movement's agenda and cynical about its leaders' motives.

In the end, Perrow sees RM II as "a very striking formulation [that] constitutes a genuine insight" (Perrow 1979: 200). At the same time, it is able to explain only a limited number of specific movements in the 1960s protest cycle. Both the civil rights and student movements (which arguably sparked the entire protest cycle of the 1960s) predated the rise in prosperity and increased activity of churches and foundations that is so central to RM II explanations.

The latter fare better in explaining certain types of movements after 1965 or so. The hypotheses about prosperity, resource availability, conscience constituents, and external funding fit better in this time frame and correlate with the appearance of more moderate, bureaucratically structured, issue-oriented, professionally directed movement organizations that are at the heart of RM II. Even so, questions remain about whether the funding preceded the movements or not. "It seems possible that the foundations, churches, and liberal unions were pulled into the action by the movement" (Perrow 1979: 204).

Although the early strands of resource mobilization theory could be read as a unified challenge to collective behavior approaches, Perrow's scalpel slices this challenge into two separate components. The distinction between RM I and RM II would gradually become institutionalized as the difference between "political process" and "resource mobilization" models. Although bringing different emphases to their common subject matter, this division "was more like a fun sibling rivalry than a deep conflict that led one party or another to feel aggrieved" (Zald, personal communication). Indeed, proponents of both perspectives would continue to jointly publish anthologies and other collaborative work for decades thereafter.

At the risk of some confusion, this chapter has attempted to honor the chronology and evolution of ideas by referring to all the preceding contributions as elements of an (emerging) resource mobilization perspective united by its differences from, and criticisms of, earlier approaches. For the remainder of this chapter, "resource mobilization" will refer to the McCarthy and Zald–inspired RM II, whereas the next chapter will take up RM I in much more detail under the rubric of "political process" theory.

THE PARADIGM ELABORATED

The resource mobilization perspective quickly gained traction after the McCarthy and Zald (1977) article and Vanderbilt conference. The paradigm's maturation is evident in an edited volume appearing a decade later (Zald and McCarthy 1987a), whose contributions were about equally split between theoretical embellishments of the perspective and case studies of particular movements.

The more empirical contributions examined pro-life and pro-choice mobilization, religious groups, "organizational intellectuals," the transformation of the YMCA, the Methodist Church, and movements protesting nuclear power. The theoretical pieces had an equally wide range; the following discussion explores some of these contributions as illustrations of how the resource mobilization paradigm was developed and elaborated in its first decade.

The concept of SMIs consisting of multiple SMOs raises questions about how such organizations interact with each other (as well as how different industries interact within the SMS). The business imagery and market metaphor suggests hypotheses about whether and how SMOs will mimic the behavior of business firms that alternately compete and cooperate with one another.

On the competitive side, when there is a decline in overall resources available in a movement sector, movement organizations within that sector may be expected to engage in increased competition for those scarce resources. Such competition will be more intense among exclusive organizations that demand heavy commitment from their members than from inclusive organizations that demand less commitment (Zald and McCarthy 1987b).

Moreover, when multiple SMOs are appealing to similar audiences, the greater their ideological differences over the degree of change necessary and the tactics to achieve it, the more intense and rancorous the conflict between them will become. This competition will be especially intense if the SMOs have exclusive membership requirements and are competing for the same limited pool of potential members (Zald and McCarthy 1987b).

Other dynamics, however, may encourage cooperation rather than competition and conflict between SMOs. When different SMOs specialize in different tasks and tactics, they may be able to reach "domain agreements" and create a division of labor whereby each SMO makes a distinct but complementary contribution to achieving movement goals (Zald and McCarthy 1987b).

Cooperative relations between SMOs may also result when they face external social control that threatens their very existence, when there are extensive interlocks of leadership across SMOs, and when they have overlapping memberships and constituencies. Finally, when SMOs are faced with a significant countermovement challenge, they are more likely to downplay their differences and mobilize a cooperative alliance in response to the challenge (Zald and McCarthy 1987b).

While demonstrating the value of the market metaphor, the authors briefly acknowledge important differences between economic firms and SMOs. As they note, "competition for dominance among SMOs is often for symbolic dominance, for defining the terms of social movement action" (Zald and McCarthy 1987b: 180). A full accounting will thus require cultural and linguistic analysis to complement the entrepreneurial imagery.

Another instance of interorganizational relations involves interactions between movements and countermovements, in which the latter refers to the mobilization of sentiments in deliberate opposition to a movement. Indeed, such mobilization may give rise to a counter-countermovement that arises to oppose the countermovement but is distinct from the original movement. One can even envision entire countermovement industries, creating a mirror image of a given social movement industry devoted to resisting rather than fostering change.

Building on these insights, Zald and Useem (1987) analyze movement-countermovement relations as a type of loosely coupled conflict that resembles a debate in which both sides utilize the tactical repertoires provided by existing technology, social structure, and the historical moment. Countermovements are more likely to appear when a movement appears to be succeeding, when an appropriate ideology is available, and when resources and opportunities are available for such countermobilization.

Movements and countermovements may occasionally interact in tight spirals of reciprocal action, but their loosely coupled nature allows for periods of latency and contrasting or asynchronous cycles of mobilization and demobilization. The two sides may be joined in several ways: in a direct confrontation, in attempts to influence third parties, or simply in their efforts to neutralize or negate the other's effects.

A common strategy involves damaging actions that "raise the cost of mobilization for the other group" (Zald and Useem 1987: 260). This could involve restricting resource flows, engaging in surveillance or intimidation, or fostering a negative image of the movement and its members. Preemptive strategies attempt to "undercut the moral and political basis of a mobilization or countermobilization" (Zald and Useem 1987: 264). Finally, through persuasion and recruitment, movements and countermovements may seek to convert opponents to come over to their side of the conflict.

The dynamics between movements and countermovements unfold in a social context that involves other groups as well; the role of authorities can be especially relevant. In the simplest case, movements and countermovements battle one another with little involvement of outside parties. In another simple case, a movement confronts an authority who functions as a countermovement.

In more complicated or triangular models, both a movement and a countermovement may seek to influence the same authority structure while having little direct interaction. More typically, movements and countermovements seek both to influence authorities and carry on a campaign against each other, requiring a two-front strategy and a careful allocation of movement resources.

In still more complex cases of dual sovereignty, movements and countermovements may appeal to distinct authorities in separate regions, laying the groundwork for rebellion or full-scale revolution. In still other instances, movements may appeal to national authorities while countermovements court local authorities while also battling the movement directly. Thus, there are multiple ways in which the dance between movements, countermovements, and authorities may unfold.

Zald and Useem conclude by emphasizing that "movements and countermovements are nested in long waves of ideology and counterideology" (1987: 270). Movements emphasize what can (and should) be changed; their challenge is to find ideologies or values that make the change they seek seem desirable, possible, logical, or natural.

Countermovements (like conservative politics more generally) confront a distinct problem because they must "'remember the answers'. Often their leaders and cadre are in the position of defending policies whose justifications have receded into the routine grounds" (Zald and Useem 1987: 270). Although facing distinct challenges, movements and countermovements meet them in a mutual dance whose rhythm and dynamics often determine the success or failure of each contestant.

The multiple movement and countermovement organizations and industries comprise the social movement sector of a society. This sector, in turn, is shaped if not determined by still larger dynamics of political economy. Thus, a social movement sector can emerge only in a society with a distinct political system. It is especially likely to emerge in capitalist societies with rational-legal procedures and dense networks of formal organizations. But such sectors can vary across societies in terms of size, degree of organization, social location, ideological alignment, and degree of autonomy from mainstream political organizations and parties (Garner and Zald 1987).

A political economy perspective thereby helps identify the systemic constraints on social movements. These include major social categories (race, ethnicity, religion, gender, and so on) that can potentially be mobilized in a given society. They obviously include social class categories, but with interesting permutations. For instance, a society with many contradictory class locations may see a volatile movement sector as contradictory interests are redefined and rebundled into various configurations of movements.

In societies with a highly developed dual economy, movements may become bifurcated with relatively privileged workers opting for corporatist forms of union activism, whereas less privileged workers engage in sporadic, relatively unorganized protests. With such bifurcation, the prospects for an all-inclusive and unified workers' movement markedly recede (Garner and Zald 1987).

In late-industrial, consumer-oriented societies, the reproduction of relations of production is partially divorced from economic production and becomes mediated through consumption, community, education, and family. In such societies, there is considerable "space" for identity, status, cultural, and lifestyle movements to flourish. Other theorists would subsequently identify these as "new social movements" in advanced capitalism that have gradually displaced the "old" working-class movement of industrial capitalism.

In capitalist societies, the political and ideological systems attain at least a relative degree of autonomy from the economy, so they pose their own constraints and influences on social movement activity. For example, localized movements will have a particularly difficult challenge when they confront highly centralized political and ideological systems because the movement's ultimate target is so remote from its context of action.

State laws, policies, and practices shape the context of movement activism as well. States can repress and criminalize, accept and tolerate, or encourage and facilitate various forms of movement organization, strategy, and tactics. States can also sponsor quasi-movements or countermovements, foster clientelism, or coopt movements. States can even redefine the categorical identities that comprise the membership of existing or potential movements, as occurred with changing U.S. policy over Native American tribal identity and membership (Garner and Zald 1987: 312).

As a final example, the party system and structure "is probably the single most important variable for understanding the pattern of social movements" (Garner and Zald 1987: 312). The ease of starting parties, their organizational features, and the rules of the electoral system have profound implications for whether people will pursue their goals through movements or parties and the likelihood that one can transform into, or align with, the other.

These explorations into the relations between social movement organizations, the dance between movements and countermovements, and the impact of political economy on the social movement sector illustrate some of the implications of the core premises of the resource mobilization paradigm.

CONCLUSION

Just as the social movements of the 1960s shattered the tranquil façade of American life in the 1950s, the resource mobilization approach that followed in their wake transcended a half century of work on collective behavior and moved social movements to the center of the analytical stage for the very first time.

The impetus for this new paradigm was a seeming paradox. If movements respond to grievances, then why do we find not fewer but more movements in a society of increasing affluence? The answer seems obvious in retrospect, but was a genuine breakthrough at the time: Affluence made new resources available, and movements respond as much or more to availability of resources than to proliferation of grievances.

As this chapter has chronicled, there were many different strands that made up this paradigm shift and this challenge to the classical model of collective behavior in the early to mid-1970s. By the end of the decade, a clear distinction was emerging between the entrepreneurial approach of McCarthy and Zald and the political process model of Tilly and others.

The entrepreneurial approach got maximum mileage out of the metaphor that movement organizations could be analyzed like business firms organized into industries and sectors. This was also one way of bringing rationality back into the analysis of movements because this economistic imagery lent itself nicely to the premise that both individuals and organizations must not only secure resources but also calculate the costs and benefits of alternative courses of action. It also set this approach apart from the "hearts and minds" emphasis of earlier work.

This entrepreneurial approach that retained the label of resource mobilization had some important scope conditions. It was meant to apply to a historically specific type of modern, affluent, organizational society whose relative abundance of resources and associations fostered a densely populated social movement sector with permeable boundaries between movement organizations, interest groups, lobbying associations, political parties, labor unions, church groups, government agencies, and philanthropic foundations.

The political process model that gradually disentangled itself from the resource mobilization approach painted on a broader canvas. It traced social movements back to origins that were intertwined with capitalism, industrialization, urbanization, and state formation. But it also found plenty of contemporary applications as well. We turn now to an examination of this perspective.

Chapter Eight

Political Process Theory

The distinction between resource mobilization and political process theories evolved at the end of the 1970s. It was initiated by Perrow's (1979) contrast between RM I and RM II, and solidified in McAdam's (1982) critique of resource mobilization theory and articulation of the political process alternative. The turn of this decade was thus a crucial period. Before then, various challenging ideas, generically termed "resource mobilization," were linked by their opposition to earlier approaches such as collective behavior, relative deprivation, and social strain. When the challenge succeeded in displacing the older paradigms by 1980 or so, increasingly clear lines of division emerged between a more narrowly defined resource mobilization approach and political process theory.

THE CONTEXT

Given their intertwined history, resource mobilization and political process theories may be seen as twin responses to the same social, political, cultural, and intellectual context of the 1960s. As noted in the previous chapter, the seemingly tranquil surface of American life in the 1950s was soon to be shattered by a cascade of social movements at home and tumultuous interventions and entanglements abroad.

These broad social changes triggered a parallel change in sociological thinking. Concerns about integration and equilibrium gave way to questions about conflict and domination. Sociology also questioned its own role as part of the establishment, sparked by Gouldner's (1970) pronouncement of the "coming crisis of Western sociology," which led to a more reflexive and self-critical sociology of sociology (Friedrichs 1970; Halmos 1970). As rapid change occurred in the broader society, the discipline of sociology cultivated a more critical tone toward its own ideas as well as the power structure of American society.

Because the newly critical tone of much sociology echoed the political activism and social upheaval on so many campuses, sociology became newly popular as an academic home for a generation of politicized students (McAdam 2007). The result, as noted in the previous chapter, was that "[b]y 1970, many younger sociologists, students and new faculty had come to think of sociology as a sociological imagination that would remake the world, while the older generation had thought of it as a profession that would help manage the world" (Lemert 2008: 100).

It was this generation that helped carry out the paradigm shift from collective behavior, relative deprivation, and strain theories to the resource mobilization and political process approaches. At the same time, however, this shift had "elite" sponsorship by somewhat older and well-established academic sociologists. This is true for McCarthy and Zald's advocacy of resource mobilization ideas as well as Tilly and Oberschall's articulation of the political process model.

These social, political, intellectual, disciplinary, and generational processes reoriented social movement theory from psychologically rooted, grievance-driven, strain-induced explanations of collective behavior to rationally grounded, resource-based, political interpretations of collective action.

Despite this shared sociohistorical context, there was a slight difference in timing between these rivals. Resource mobilization theory captured the high ground early with the Vanderbilt conference and the seminal paper by McCarthy and Zald, both in 1977. This theory thereby became a foil against which the political process model could distinguish itself. Early critiques and rethinking of resource mobilization assumptions thus helped solidify the alternative political process model.

As noted earlier, Perrow's (1979) distinction between RM I and RM II is one of the first delineations of the differences between these approaches. Although not always couched as criticisms, the core assumptions of RM II (resource mobilization) that he identified frequently became points of criticism as political process advocates disentangled their approach from resource mobilization.

Thus, Perrow describes resource mobilization as downplaying politics and political interests, being indifferent to ideology, having a highly (and perhaps overly) rationalistic image of movement actors, downplaying (and occasionally dismissing) the role of grievances, all but ignoring group solidarity, and adopting a "cynical tone" toward its subject matter. These assumptions are the vectors along which political process theory would depart from resource mobilization by emphasizing politics, ideology, grievances, and solidarity, while also advocating a more nuanced view of the rationality of movement participants.

The latter issue was addressed head on with the injunction that sociologists should "[b]eware of economists bearing gifts" (Fireman and Gamson 1979: 8). The reference is to Mancur Olson's *Logic of Collective Action* (1965), which these critics saw as underpinning McCarthy and Zald's conception of movement participants as rational actors. According to Olson, rational actors will ride free on the efforts of others, posing a huge mobilization problem unless selective incentives can be deployed for some portion of the mobilization pool to recruit at least some participants.

The authors concede that these utilitarian assumptions are useful when "relevant interests are given, concrete, and selfish" (Fireman and Gamson 1979: 8). In movements, however, interests, opportunities, and threats are constantly in flux, rendering Olson's logic rather misleading for the study of collective action. Rather than applying broadly to collective action, these critics assert that "only in special circumstances is it both possible and worthwhile to use 'selective incentives' to get people to struggle for common interests" (Fireman and Gamson 1979: 9).

A more plausible way to account for successful mobilization is to recognize that movements operate with a collective logic rather than the individual logic of self-interest. This means that the creation of solidarity, the recognition of common interests, and the identification of opportunities loom much larger than selective incentives. With the cultivation of solidarity, mechanisms such as loyalty to the group and responsibility to principles can become powerful spurs to participation in collective action.

It is no coincidence that this critical analysis of the utilitarian rational actor led back to questions of group solidarity, political interests, and group consciousness. It suggests that the assumptions Perrow identified as distinguishing RM I and RM II have some internal consistency that further sharpens the contrast between them. It is now time to focus more directly on the establishment of the political process model.

TILLY'S ANALYSIS

Tilly's early work provided a sociologically informed history of collective action in Europe, with a particular focus on France (Tilly, Tilly, and Tilly 1975). In the late 1970s, the balance shifted as he published a historically informed, sociological treatise titled *From Mobilization to Revolution* (1978). While eschewing any grand theory of social movements, this work summarized the analytical principles that had informed his earlier work and provided a guide to the study of a broad range of social movements and collective action. If McCarthy and Zald's (1977) "partial theory" was the founding statement of what would become the more narrowly defined resource mobilization approach, Tilly's text (1978) did much the same for what would become known as the "rival" political process model.

Tilly identifies four classical traditions in the study of collective action. The Marxian tradition stresses conflicting interests, the ubiquity of conflict, and the importance of organization. The Durkheimian tradition emphasizes disintegration and anomie and sharply distinguishes between routine and nonroutine forms of collective action. John Stuart Mill's tradition sees collective action as arising out of aggregated calculations of individual interests that shape rational choices that lead to strategic interaction. Finally, the Weberian tradition stresses commitment to belief systems as well as movement organization and group interests; like Durkheim, it sharply distinguishes between routine and nonroutine forms of collective action.

Against this backdrop, Tilly characterizes his own approach as "doggedly anti-Durkheimian, resolutely pro-Marxian, but sometimes indulgent to Weber and sometimes reliant on Mill" (Tilly 1978:48). This emphasis is consistent with his earlier polemics favoring (Marxian) solidarity explanations over (Durkheimian) breakdown interpretations. At the same time, it acknowledges the (Millian) rationality of collective actors even in nonroutine and violent interactions while also recognizing the (Weberian) role of beliefs, ideas, and ideologies in shaping interests and facilitating mobilization.

As a first step in the analysis of collective action, Tilly offers a "polity model" that provides an admittedly static picture of standard interest-group politics. In this model, an outer set of boundaries identifies some population under the jurisdiction of some governmental authority. Within this population is another set of boundaries that defines the polity. Within the polity, one finds both the government and a number of other groups that are well-established members of the polity. Outside the polity but within the population, there are a number of challenging groups.

This seemingly simple model has several important implications. First, it rejects a pluralist image of power in which every member of the population is also a member of the polity. For Tilly, polity members have routine, low-cost access to power holders and decision makers and they are able to pursue their interests through normal political strategies. Challengers outside the polity, by contrast, lack such access so that normal political strategies are ineffective. It is challengers outside the polity who must resort to collective action if their interests are to be represented and their voices heard.

Although challengers sometimes win on their own, they often seek coalitions or alliances with established polity members to increase their chances of success. Such alliances may impose costs, however, because polity members may be less supportive of militant strategies and counsel more moderate appeals. This insight recalls McCarthy and Zald's (1977) analysis of how movements that rely on external resources may have to sacrifice some autonomy in exchange for those resources.

Sometimes challengers embark on a more ambitious campaign that is not geared to a specific grievance but rather to gaining entry into the polity. This threatens to change the balance of power between different interests on a whole range of issues for an extended period of time. For this reason alone, conflicts that revolve around entrances to (or exits from) the polity may be especially volatile and bitterly fought.

The polity model thus provides a static overview of the arena of political contention. The mobilization model analyzes the actual process of conflict from the perspective of a single contender. It examines relationships between group interests, organizational networks, mobilization processes, and several different dimensions of opportunity as they bear on each other and shape the resulting "dependent variable" of collective action itself.

If there is a "first cause" in this dialectical model, it would be group interests. These concern how a group experiences either gains or losses in its interactions with other groups. The thorny question is how to identify such interests. Tilly offers two rules of thumb. In the long run and on average, he advocates the Marxian logic that group interests can be inferred from their position in the relations of production.

In the short run, however, we must respect "people's own articulation of their interests as an explanation of their behavior" (Tilly 1978: 61). Although Tilly recognizes that this solution is not entirely satisfactory, it avoids presumptuous declarations of "false consciousness" when short-term expressions of interests are inconsistent with inferred interests based on a group's structural location.

Group interests have a direct bearing on organization, mobilization, and different aspects of opportunity. Concerning organization, Tilly identifies two dimensions. Categories refer to broad social identities based on shared characteristics such as race, religion, locality, gender, and the like. Networks refer to people who are linked by some direct or indirect interpersonal bond. Organization arises from the intersection of categories and networks. A genuine sociological group thus emerges "to the extent that it comprises both a category and a network" (Tilly 1978: 63).

This notion of organization emphasizes the inclusiveness of a group, meaning that highly organized groups absorb a large portion of their members' lives. Although Tilly regards it as an unproven hypothesis, logic and intuition suggest that the inclusiveness of a group (based on the degree of overlap between categories and networks) will have a major impact on its mobilization potential.

Articulation of interests and inclusiveness of organization have a direct bearing on a group's potential for mobilization. The latter is a process that turns passive individuals into active participants in public life and political struggle. A group's mobilization level is defined by two factors. The first is the quantity of resources under the group's control; the second is the probability that those resources will be delivered for the sake of collective action.

Given these two dimensions, effective mobilization requires two things. Groups must obviously accumulate as many resources as possible. At the same time, they must maximize their collective claims on those resources by reducing competing claims on them, enhancing the intrinsic satisfaction of group membership, and increasing the willingness of members to make their resources available to the group.

These general principles apply to several different types of mobilization. For instance, defensive mobilization (perhaps the most common form) occurs when a group experiences an external threat to its well-being and responds accordingly. Offensive mobilization means a pooling of resources in response to a newfound opportunity. Preparatory mobilization occurs with a longer-term view that anticipates future threats or opportunities and amasses resources now for battles to be fought later.

Although group interests and organizational inclusiveness both shape mobilization, Tilly emphasizes the latter. Consistent with Oberschall's work and in contradiction to Durkheim's breakdown imagery and mass society theory's emphasis on social isolation, mobilization for Tilly is a function of preexisting organization. Groups with a high degree of such organization are poised for action and can be mobilized quickly and effectively. Groups with weak internal links, on the other hand, rarely act collectively even in the face of major threats, new opportunities, or long-standing grievances and deprivations.

Mobilization is also influenced by different aspects of opportunity. To understand these influences, several starting assumptions are helpful. First, collective action always costs something for contenders, and contenders count costs as best they can. Second, because collective action also offers benefits, contenders weigh the potential benefits of action against its potential costs; logically enough, they act collectively when the balance is favorable, and pursue other options when it is not. Finally, however, logic is never enough because the calculation of costs and benefits occurs with imperfect information and can drastically shift as a result of strategic interaction (Tilly 1978: 99).

Opportunity involves several dimensions. One is repression/facilitation, referring to actions that raise or lower the costs of collective action. Although many actors can affect a group's opportunities, governments are often central because their policies, laws, and social control capacities so directly shape the context of collective action. Government responses to a group may thus range from repression to tolerance to facilitation.

Several propositions follow from these distinctions. For instance, large groups are more likely to face repression whereas powerful groups are less likely to meet that fate. Thus, strong groups engaged in small-scale actions are likely to be facilitated or tolerated, whereas weaker groups engaged in large-scale actions tend to meet repression. Although there are dramatic cases of repression provoking greater resistance and even revolution, Tilly reminds us that repression often works. More broadly, changes in government policies and actions can raise or depress the overall level of collective action as well as alter the relative attractiveness of different forms of action.

A second dimension of opportunity is power, or the likelihood that a group's interests will prevail over others in a conflict. Group power is thus always relative to specific parties, interests, and interactions. Some minimum threshold of power is a prerequisite for collective action; extremely weak groups may never be in a position to make gains relative to the costs of collective action. It is contention for power that links the static polity model with the dynamic mobilization model. Polity members have a built-in power advantage, but it may be neutralized when challengers forge coalitions with polity members or other challengers. Challenger-member coalitions may be especially important in limiting violent repression directed at a challenger.

The third dimension of opportunity is another tandem of opportunity/threat. In this dualism, opportunity refers specifically to the vulnerability of other groups to actions favoring a contender's interests, whereas threats are others' claims that can be damaging to a contender's interests. Although both can provoke mobilization, collective action typically responds more rapidly to threats than to opportunities (Tilly 1978: Ch. 4).

The mobilization model thereby suggests that group interests shape organization, mobilization, opportunity/threat, and repression/facilitation. Mobilization is also a function of organization, repression/facilitation, and opportunity/threat. Although these factors interact and codetermine each other, in the end it is mobilization, opportunity/threat, and power that directly bear on the emergence of collective action.

Returning to a more historical perspective, Tilly traces changing forms and repertoires of collective action over several centuries of European history. Thus, in the fifteenth and sixteenth centuries, collective actors tended to make competitive claims over resources also claimed by rival groups. From the seventeenth to the nineteenth century, reactive claims became more common as groups reasserted established claims that had been challenged, particularly by expanding state power and control over a population. From the nineteenth to the twentieth century, proactive claims emerged whereby groups claimed rights and resources they had not previously enjoyed.

This broad historical survey suggests that over time, the intrinsic costs of mobilization and organization have decreased, whereas the extrinsic cost of governmental repression has gone up. It also suggests that contenders operate with standardized repertoires of contention and use only a small number of the possible strategies and tactics that could be deployed. Major social changes also affect these repertoires. Thus, the proletarianization of the labor force gave rise to the strike as an initially reactive and now proactive tactic, just as the growth of electoral politics promoted the demonstration as a form of collective action (Tilly 1978: Ch. 5).

The same historical record sheds new light on the issue of violence in collective action. The main lesson is that collective violence arises out of the strategic interaction between groups rather than being an intrinsic characteristic of a challenging group. This suggests that most collective violence emerges out of actions that are not intrinsically violent and that closely resemble nonviolent forms of collective action in their origins.

When collective action becomes collective violence, state agents are heavily involved; they are the most consistent initiators and performers of such violence. Moreover, "[t]here is a division of labor: repressive forces do the largest part of the killing and wounding, whereas the groups they are seeking to control do most of the damage to objects" (Tilly 1978: 177). Collective violence often accompanies entries into, and exits from the polity, with governments directing it against new contenders and declining members in particular. These broad claims find empirical support in everything from nineteenth century brawls to 1960s urban "riots" (Tilly 1978: Ch. 6).

The same concepts and logic apply to rebellions and revolutions. To understand the latter, Tilly follows Trotsky's distinction between a revolutionary situation and a revolutionary outcome. "A revolutionary situation begins when a government previously under the control of a single, sovereign polity becomes the object of effective, competing, mutually exclusive claims on the part of two or more distinct polities. It ends when a single sovereign polity regains control over the government" (Tilly 1978: 191).

Not all revolutionary situations lead to revolutionary outcomes, but when they do it means that there is a significant displacement of former leaders by challengers. Depending on the extent of population splits and leader displacement, we can distinguish between coups, insurrections, civil wars, and full-scale revolutions.

With these distinctions, some patterns become evident. Revolutionary situations often emerge when contenders make exclusive, alternative claims; they intensify when such claims are widely accepted; and they intensify further when governments make no effective response. Revolutionary outcomes are more likely when the revolutionary situation is widespread, when there are coalitions between members and challengers, and when challengers control substantial force (Tilly 1978: Ch. 7).

Tilly's models thereby apply to everything from brief outbursts to sustained revolutions. Depending on the time frame, different explanatory logics apply. For a short-term analysis of collective action, the mobilization model and its purposive logic are crucial. For a longer-term analysis, the polity model and its causal logic offer the best insights. And for a truly long-term understanding of historical causation, a social change model attuned to proletarianization, urbanization, state-building, and industrialization provides the broadest explanations.

MCADAM'S MODEL

Although Tilly (1978) offered the richest early statement of what came to be known as the political process model, he made only passing reference to McCarthy and Zald's (1977) resource mobilization approach, suggesting that these had yet to be framed as rival alternatives. A mere four years later, McAdam (1982) explicitly used McCarthy and Zald (1977) as a critical foil against which to articulate political process theory.

McAdam begins with a critique of the "classical model" of social movements exemplified by collective behavior theory. This earlier approach rested upon a pluralist image of power in which all groups have potential access to institutionalized political power and none need recourse to collective action. Collective behavior was thereby seen as a psychological expression of discontent triggered by strain rather than a rational response to political grievances deriving from group interests.

McAdam acknowledges challenges to the pluralist image of power, including Tilly's polity model with its distinction between polity members and challengers. If pluralism is not plausible, then the equation of collective behavior with psychological discontent also becomes less tenable, and new understandings are required.

The early strands of the generic resource mobilization approach provided such understandings, and McAdam credits it with changing the "ontological status" of social movements, now seen as the rational, political expression of group interests. He further credits it with recognizing the role of external groups and the interaction between formal and informal groups in securing resources for collective action (McAdam 1982: 22–23).

At the same time, McAdam identifies weaknesses in the later, more narrowly defined resource mobilization model that are so fundamental as to require an alternative paradigm. His argument thereby shifts from deficiencies in earlier collective behavior approaches to differences between two recent alternatives in the form of resource mobilization and political process theories.

A first critical observation is that resource mobilization theory tends to blur the distinction between excluded groups and established polity members. Its subject matter, illustrative examples, and case studies are often closer to normal, interest group politics and lobbying organizations than to genuine social movement challenges. The latter are excluded from normal politics, use noninstitutional means, and often seek extensive change. Thus, resource mobilization theory may be least relevant precisely where social movements differentiate themselves most clearly from routine forms of political contention.

A second criticism concerns elite funding sources, which resource mobilization theory implies "are willing, even aggressive, sponsors of social insurgency" (McAdam 1982: 25). Given the change orientation of genuine social movements, it is doubtful that elites would routinely invest resources in such efforts. It is more likely that they do so only under pressure, and even then with the intent or consequence of undermining movement efforts rather than promoting them. Resource mobilization theory thus overstates the importance of elite sponsorship of movements and minimizes how it can contribute to the cooptation or demise of movements.

A third criticism is that resource mobilization neglects or minimizes the role of the mass base of movements. Although masses may be poor in some resources, they always have "negative inducements" (strikes, disruptions) at their disposal that are undervalued by resource mobilization theory. Such resources are especially important when there are preexisting forms of organization in the indigenous group that collectivize their resources and increase the probability that they will be made available for collective action. Resource mobilization theory therefore exaggerates the importance of elites and minimizes the role of the mass base; political process theory challenges and seeks to reverse both emphases.

A fourth criticism concerns the concept of resources, which is often used in such a vague, elastic fashion as to become meaningless. This problem opens the door to tautological reasoning because virtually every mobilization is "preceded by *some* increase in *some* type of 'resource'" (McAdam 1982: 33; italics in original). The larger danger with this ill-defined notion of resources is that it is "as vague and problematic as those—strain and discontent—underlying the classical theory" (McAdam 1982: 33).

A final criticism concerns grievances. In their efforts to move away from a "hearts and minds" approach, McCarthy and Zald imply that grievances are a constant background factor that cannot explain the variable appearance of movements. McAdam observes, however, that grievances always have a subjective side; they must be interpreted in certain ways if they are to motivate collective action. Even if "objective grievances" are persistent and widespread, the subjective process of interpreting them is a variable one that in turn is crucial in explaining episodic collective action.

Based on these criticisms, McAdam concludes that "resource mobilization affords a useful perspective for analyzing organized reform efforts initiated by established polity members. It is less convincing, however, as an account of social movements" (McAdam 1982: 34). McAdam thus offers the earliest systematic distinction between McCarthy and Zald's more narrowly defined resource mobilization theory and the political process alternative that had always been implicit in the work of Oberschall, Gamson, and Tilly. From this point forward, the classical model of collective behavior had at least two challengers (with others to appear shortly).

Whereas the classical model rested on an image of power as dispersed and pluralistic, the political process model assumes concentrated elite power. This power is substantial enough that elites don't need to resort to social movements to pursue their objectives. Even so, elite power is not so monolithic as to be beyond challenge. It is vulnerable to social movements under the right circumstances. The political process model seeks to identify those circumstances.

One factor is the structure of political opportunities. This variable factor can facilitate collective action whenever the stability of the entire political system is undermined or when the leverage of a particular political group is increased relative to its rivals. The former may invite multiple challenges by any and all groups sufficiently organized to do so, whereas the latter may provoke specific challenges by newly empowered groups.

Changing political opportunities facilitate collective action in at least two ways. First, they reduce the power discrepancy between challengers and elites so that a mobilization that may have appeared merely fanciful before becomes newly feasible. Second, when new opportunities improve the bargaining position of any particular contender, the costs to elites of trying to repress them goes up significantly. Although the theory does not delineate all the scenarios under which the structure of political opportunities might change, it makes a convincing case that when it does change, challenges to the status quo become much more likely and their prospects for success are significantly improved (McAdam 1982: 42–43).

A second factor concerns indigenous organizational strength. Opportunities mean nothing if groups are not organized to take advantage of them (or can quickly become so). McAdam endorses previous work underscoring the importance of preexisting organization within potential social movement constituencies and proceeds to identify four central resources that affect such organization.

Members are crucial to successful movements, and preexisting forms of both formal and informal indigenous organization help recruit members and build organization. This is particularly so in the case of bloc recruitment, in which entire segments of highly organized people are recruited *en masse* to join in collective action.

Such groups often provide another crucial resource in the form of solidarity incentives that aid in recruitment and foster cohesion. Without such incentives, the free-rider dilemma threatens to preclude collective action, but with preestablished interpersonal rewards or incentive structures deriving from group solidarity, such obstacles can be overcome.

Communication networks also arise in the context of indigenous organization among aggrieved populations. Consistent with broader studies of cultural diffusion, the presence or absence of such communication networks can mean the difference between successful mobilization and missed opportunities, just as their degree of development can crucially affect the pace and scope of mobilization.

Leaders are a final feature of group organization. When groups are already organized, they are likely to have established leadership cadres who can also help direct collective action. Thus, when members, incentives, communication, and leaders all coalesce, movements attain a level of indigenous organizational strength that allows them to take advantage of whatever political opportunities become available.

Alongside opportunity and organization, McAdam identifies cognitive liberation as a third crucial mechanism in the generation of insurgency. This process of collective attribution is lacking in the resource mobilization paradigm but central to the political process model. Both opportunity and organization can stimulate cognitive liberation, but the latter is presented as a third causal factor in the generation of collective action.

Borrowing from the work of Piven and Cloward (1979), cognitive liberation involves three dimensions. First, people must have the subjective perception that relevant aspects of the social order have lost legitimacy so that policies, actions, and leaders are seen as wrong or unjust. Second, people must overcome fatalism by demanding rights, implying a belief that the social order can actually change. Finally, people must acquire a sense of efficacy that their participation in social struggles can actually affect the outcome.

Preexisting organizational ties and cognitive liberation are thus likely to reinforce one another. People who are socially isolated from others (as in the mass society imagery) are unlikely to communicate with others in ways that suggest change is possible; fatalism is a more likely response. Social ties, however, create communication networks and social supports that are more likely to foster the cognitive liberation that is a necessary component for collective action.

Although movements may emerge from a favorable confluence of opportunity, organization, and cognitions, "the fortuitous combination of factors productive of insurgency is expected to be short-lived" (McAdam 1982: 52). Two additional factors become relevant when we seek to explain not just the emergence but the perpetuation of insurgency beyond its original phase.

One of these additional factors is already familiar. Just as movements need some form of organization to emerge in the first place, they need to sustain organizational strength if they are to survive over the long term. This is very often achieved by at least a relative shift from informal to more formal organization. As Gamson's (1990) work suggests, centralization and bureaucratization appear to be related to success in the history of American movements, but such formalization poses its own dangers (as Gamson also recognized).

These dangers are at least threefold. First, formalization can sow the seeds of oligarchization as the leadership becomes more differentiated from the base and begins to pursue a more self-interested agenda. Second, cooptation is a looming danger, particularly if the movement becomes increasingly dependent on external resources as those of the mass base are stretched to the limit. Finally, movements may lose much of their indigenous support as they cultivate ties with resource-rich constituencies.

It is the ongoing need for resources that drives movements toward formalization, but such formalization poses new dangers to the maintenance of insurgency. McAdam does not fully agree with Piven and Cloward's (1979) pessimistic analysis of how organization is the death of insurgency, but he recognizes that sustaining organizational strength *and* effective insurgency poses a major challenge to movements and leaders.

The second factor that influences movement maintenance is the social control response to insurgency. In general, weak movements invite repression because the costs of doing so to elites are low. The stronger the movement, the more likely it can avoid this fate.

Beyond the movement's own strength or weakness is the fact that movements create both threats to, and opportunities for, other movements and elites, and this will also condition the social control response of elites. As broad generalizations, noninstitutionalized tactics and revolutionary goals are most likely to threaten elite interests and invite a repressive response. Conventional tactics and reformist goals will be less threatening, but may also be less effective in achieving insurgent goals. Thus, "insurgents must chart a course that avoids crippling repression on the one hand and tactical impotence on the other. Staking out this optimal middle ground is exceedingly difficult" (McAdam 1982: 58).

With this theoretical scaffolding, McAdam constructs an empirically rich analysis of the rise and fall of black insurgency in the 1950s and 1960s. The generation of this insurgency in the later 1950s was due to new opportunities, organizational strength, and a sense of political efficacy. It led to the heyday of black insurgency in the first half of the 1960s when the movement was widely seen as making legitimate claims. In the later 1960s, the movement shifted to tactics and goals that posed a greater threat to elite interests that in turn sparked more repressive social control measures that contributed to the demise of black insurgency.

In broader theoretical terms, McAdam concludes that the pluralist image of power is clearly discredited by this history, but that models of elite power may be overstated. Historical evidence suggests that elites are not all powerful; their control can be effectively challenged by indigenous groups under the right circumstances. Finally, McAdam claims that the pace and extent of black insurgency cannot be explained by changes in social strain as suggested by the classical model nor by changes in external support as claimed by resource mobilization theory. With this study, McAdam thereby solidified the political process model as a major contender to both previous paradigms.

TARROW'S EMBELLISHMENTS

Alongside Tilly and McAdam, Sidney Tarrow is a third major theorist closely associated with the political process model. About a decade after McAdam's version of the theory appeared, Tarrow published a programmatic synthesis of movement theory, history, and research that embellished and extended the paradigm, drew on his extensive research into Italian social movements, and explored movement cycles.

Tarrow defines movements as "collective challenges by people with common purposes and solidarity in sustained interaction with elites, opponents, and authorities" (Tarrow 1994: 3–4). He argues that all movements face a collective action problem, but it is not how to get individuals to act on behalf of collective goods but rather how to solve the social problem of "coordinating unorganized, autonomous and dispersed populations into common and sustained action" (Tarrow 1994: 9).

With this formulation, Tarrow reiterates the limitations of Olson's utilitarian logic (initially criticized by Fireman and Gamson [1979]) for understanding social movements. He also echoes McAdams's delineation of the boundary between political process and resource mobilization approaches: "McCarthy and Zald seem not to have been worried about the fact that Olson was not primarily concerned with social movements but with interest groups" (Tarrow 1994: 15).

Tarrow devotes a major portion of his work to examining the birth of the national social movement. Following Tilly, he provides numerous examples of how the national social movement emerged when movement repertoires shifted from local and patronized to national and autonomous. He also traces how this newly modular form of collective action was made possible by increases in literacy, new forms of association, and patterns of diffusion. Cross-national comparisons also suggest how the rise of the modern state provided the resources, grievances, targets, and opportunities for people to engage in collective action.

The focus then shifts to "the powers of movement," beginning with opportunity structures. In a major historical example, this variable is crucial in explaining labor activism in France and the United States in the 1930s and its relative absence in Britain and Germany in the same time period: "[I]t was the political opportunities opened by the French Popular Front and the American New Deal that caused the upsurge of labor insurgency in a poor labor market, and not the depth of workers' grievances or the extent of their resources" (Tarrow 1994: 84).

Some forms of political opportunity emerge because of changing conditions. Thus, any process or event that increases access to participation improves opportunities for groups to mobilize. Second, any process or event that alters or destabilizes ruling alignments can create new opportunities. A third aspect of variable opportunity structures involves influential allies who can be partners in a larger coalition against a common opponent. A final type arises through divisions between elites; challengers can often exploit such divisions to gain concessions that would not otherwise be forthcoming.

Although some forms of opportunity are thus variable over time in the same place, other forms may be institutionally stable over time but variable across place, as revealed by cross-national comparisons. The possibilities are complex, however. Weak states would appear to provide more opportunity than strong states, but the latter may provide a clearer target and greater capacity to effectively implement reforms when movements are successful. Repression can also have counterintuitive effects. It would appear to reduce opportunity almost by definition, but repression can also radicalize opposition and encourage a type of "unobtrusive mobilization" (Tarrow 1994: 93) that creates solidarity and opposition just below the surface of a seemingly tranquil polity.

The powers of movement also reside in a diverse repertoire of contention. Here Tarrow makes a distinctive claim that the "power of collective action results from three possible characteristics—challenge, uncertainty, and solidarity" (Tarrow 1994:

102). Although challenge and solidarity are somewhat familiar, uncertainty is a wild card for all participants because no one knows the duration, cost, or "diffusability" of a particular action until it runs it course. Good organizers thereby seek to maximize both challenge and uncertainty while relying on solidarity to achieve both.

Challenge, uncertainty, and solidarity combine in different ways to yield three basic forms of contention: violence, disruption, and convention. There is a seeming paradox: Whereas violence is easy to initiate and disruption may be the most potent form of challenge, most modern protests are more conventional. At the same time, today's conventions (strikes, demonstrations, and so on) were yesterday's disruptive tactics, suggesting how the repertoire of contention "has evolved through the absorption of the innovations that work and the rejection of the ones that do not" (Tarrow 1994: 116).

Alongside opportunity structures and the dynamics of acting collectively, the powers of movement also involve framing processes. Here, Tarrow acknowledges the role of symbolic discourse and political culture, leading him to argue for "a strategic approach to the construction of meaning, based on the concepts of collective action frames, consensus formation and mobilization and political opportunity" (Tarrow 1994: 119). Many of these concepts rose to prominence as a separate perspective in the later 1980s and will be examined in the next chapter. Suffice it to say here that Tarrow was among the first to recognize the need to bring cultural processes of interpretation more fully into the political process model while also insisting that cultural symbols "require concrete agency to turn them into collective action frames' (Tarrow 1994: 133).

The final power of movement resides in mobilizing structures. Here, Tarrow distinguishes three levels of organization: the formal organization of McCarthy and Zald's (1977) social movement organization, the broad but often informal organization of collective action in a particular confrontation, and mobilizing structures. The latter are perhaps most crucial for linking leaders to organization and center to periphery. Mobilizing structures solve the "coordination problem," especially when they "are sufficiently robust to stand up to opponents, but flexible enough to change with new circumstances and draw on energies at the base" (Tarrow 1994: 136).

Indeed, his argument is that "the most effective forms of organization are based on autonomous and interdependent social networks linked by loosely coordinated mobilizing structures" (Tarrow 1994: 136). This is supported by wide-ranging historical evidence, as well as more contemporary emphases on cultivating internal democracy and free spaces within movements.

Having reviewed several powers of movement, the concluding emphasis falls on opportunity: "The major power of movement is exerted when opportunities are widening, elites are divided and realignments are occurring. On such occasions, even movements that are poorly organized can take advantage of generalized opportunities" (Tarrow 1994: 150).

Tarrow's most distinctive contribution to the political process model is his research on cycles of protest. In such cycles, there is heightened conflict throughout the society, a rapid diffusion of contention across different groups, a quickened pace of innovation, and new or transformed collective action frames (Tarrow 1994: 154). It is the structure of the cycle that is highlighted. "What is most important about this structure is the broadening of political opportunities by early risers in the cycle, the externalities that lower the social transaction costs of contention for even weak actors, the high degree of interdependence among the actors in the cycle and the closure of political opportunities at the end" (Tarrow 1994: 154).

Cycles are initiated by early risers who demonstrate the vulnerability of authorities to movement demands and alter the interests of other contenders who may either benefit or suffer from the early riser's challenge. Either way, "the demonstration effect of collective action on the part of . . . 'early risers' triggers a variety of processes of diffusion, extension, imitation and reaction among groups that are normally quiescent" (Tarrow 1994: 156). Because of this heightened activism across the social landscape, cycles often expand repertoires of contention, introduce new forms of organization, and increase interaction among contending groups.

These dynamics are richly illustrated in at least four cycles of protest: the rebellions of 1848 in Europe, the French Popular Front and American New Deal in the 1930s, the movements of the 1960s in Western Europe and the United States, and the wave of democratization in Eastern Europe during the 1980s. The examples suggest that cycles are more similar in their origins than in their outcomes.

The diverse outcomes of different cycles of protest, in turn, may be explained by returning to the issue of opportunity: "It is the changing structure of opportunity emerging from a protest cycle that determines who wins and who loses, and when struggle will lead to reform" (Tarrow 1994: 177). Although cycles can end with different types and degrees of success, their greatest impact is often in incremental changes in political culture, as evidenced by changing collective action frames, repertoires of contention, and policy agendas (Tarrow 1994: 184).

Tarrow concludes with more speculative observations about the trajectory of collective action. After 200 years, the national social movement and its episodic cycles may be fundamentally changing. We may be entering a permanent movement society in which global communication and rapid diffusion make collective action the norm rather than the exception.

Moreover, those same forces may render movements "ex-prisoners" of the state; they are less likely to be contained, controlled, or channeled by state actors because they are increasingly transnational. Finally—and more ominously—the relatively peaceful and nonviolent repertoire of collective action that evolved alongside the state may be giving way to more violent and terrorist forms of collective action. Even so, Tarrow's analysis (based on opportunities, repertoires, framing, and mobilization) will remain relevant to understanding collective action.

CONCLUSION

This chapter has chronicled three major figures in the establishment of the political process model. This approach was implicit in the work of various scholars since the early 1970s, was systematized by Tilly in the late 1970s, was explicitly contrasted with McCarthy and Zald's resource mobilization approach by McAdam in the early 1980s, and was conceptually embellished and elaborated by Tarrow and others thereafter.

The work reviewed in the last two chapters may be seen from at least two frames of reference. A "high-altitude" view reveals a major fault line between the classical model of collective behavior on the one hand and the resource mobilization/ political process alternatives on the other hand. Whereas the former analyzed collective behavior as an initially fragmented, amorphous, apolitical, and psychological response to social strains and deprivations, the latter studied collective action as an organized, rational, political response to shifting opportunities.

A "low-altitude" view reveals fault lines between resource mobilization and political process theories. The former emphasizes formal organization, elite sponsorship, external resources, rational actors, interest group constituencies, entrepreneurial leadership, and manufactured grievances. The latter underscores diverse organizational forms, informal mobilizing structures, solidarity and group consciousness within the mass base, indigenous resources, a more nuanced image of rationality, challengers outside the polity, shifting repertoires of contention, and the central role of opportunity.

A final difference between these rivals concerns grievances. Resource mobilization advocates made the polemical claim that grievances were all but irrelevant for explaining collective action, and that they sometimes emerged in response to resource availability rather than the other way around. Among political process theorists, McAdam acknowledged a larger role for grievances with his concept of cognitive liberation, but they clearly remained secondary to organization, mobilization, resources, and opportunity in the political process model.

It was the explicit repudiation or implicit marginalization of grievances that helped pave the way for the next major paradigm in the study of social movements.

Chapter Nine

Framing and Social Construction

Resource mobilization and political process approaches were not the only new paradigms to emerge in the 1970s and 1980s. The same limitations of the classical model of social movements and the same super-charged sociopolitical climate of the 1960s that sparked these meso-level paradigms also encouraged approaches that were both "smaller" and "bigger" in scope.

The "smaller" approach attentive to micro-level dynamics focused on framing, signification, media, and the social psychology of protest. The "larger" approach attentive to macro-level processes examined new movement forms that corresponded to a new type of society. Hence this chapter explores social constructionist alternatives; the next takes up new social movement theory.

THE CONTEXT

These developments in social movement theory reflected larger trends in sociological theory as a whole. We have seen how theoretical shifts from the functionalist concern with integration and order in the 1950s to conflict theory's preoccupation with power and domination in the 1960s opened the door to a more political interpretation of social movements in the 1970s. Although resource mobilization and political process approaches are meso-level theories, they also resonated with macro-level premises about domination and social order.

With their characteristic focus on resources, organization, mobilization, and opportunity, however, resource mobilization and political process approaches marginalized the social psychology of protest. Questions about grievances, motivations, recruitment, and interpersonal dynamics within social movements received significantly less attention with the rise of these approaches. Finally, although the "rational actor" model was crucial in challenging the classical model, it appeared increasingly inadequate as a means of addressing the social psychology of social movements.

These gaps were an open invitation for new ways of understanding the micro-level dynamics of social movements. Simplistic notions of psychological strain, relative deprivation, or frustration-aggression soon gave way to more complex interpretations of how interpersonal dynamics generated meso-level collective action.

The symbolic interactionist tradition within sociology was particularly well-positioned to provide such understandings. In part, this was because this approach underwent a revival in the fertile theoretical soil of the 1960s and 1970s. Within a relatively short span of time, Blumer (1969) codified the core premises of inter-actionist theory, Berger and Luckmann (1966) analyzed the social construction of reality, Garfinkel (1967) established an ethnomethodological variant of the approach, and Goffman (1959, 1974) developed a dramaturgical sociology attentive to how performers in encounters frame meanings for themselves and others.

Although Turner and Killian (1957, 1972, 1989) had long sought to preserve the links between interactionist theory and collective behavior, these new develop-ments in interactionist theory provided a plethora of novel insights into the social psychology of collective action.

Beyond sociology itself, there was a broader "cultural turn" occurring in social theory more generally. Ironically enough, it was structuralist theory that paved the way for the cultural turn by identifying the arbitrary relation between the signifier and the signified, and tracing meanings to dualistic contrasts between opposing signs.

Once meanings were relativized in this way, poststructuralism challenged the idea that any solid, fixed meanings exist. As the analysis shifted from essential un-derlying meanings to multiple discursive texts, the new goal became deconstructing all authoritative meanings and interpretations by revealing their partial, positional, fragmentary, and fluid status.

Although sociology tended to hold poststructuralism at arm's length, broader themes of meanings, texts, and significations found numerous expressions in sociol-ogy. Giddens (1986), Sewell (2005), Bourdieu (1977), and their followers explored structuration processes, cognitive schemas, discourse analysis, and cultural capital. There was a revival of Weberian and Durkheimian variants of cultural sociology, and a new section on the sociology of culture appeared within the American Socio-logical Association.

Theoretical trends both within and beyond sociology thus thematized cultural questions of meaning and signification. As this filtered into the study of social move-ments, new attention was paid to the social construction of meaning, grievances, motivation, recruitment, and identity in the context of collective action.

The social movement arena was also ripe for this kind of analysis by the 1980s. Having focused on the obvious political dimensions of the earliest movements in the 1960s protest cycle, new questions subsequently arose about the cultural components of these movements as well as a broader category of movements sometimes seen as "cultural" rather than "political" in orientation.

In the first category, questions arose about how political movements frame grievances, discontent, and deprivation as a kind of injustice that is illegitimate and necessitates a collective challenge. In the second category, a belated recognition of movements oriented to countercultural themes, status politics, identity politics, religious motivations, lifestyle interests, and environmental concerns called out for new understandings attentive to the role of meaning and signification. When all these forces coalesced, the emergence of new paradigms attuned to framing and the social construction of protest was all but overdetermined.

POLITICIZING DISCONTENT

The classical model of social movements identified strain, breakdown, deprivations, ambiguities, discontent, cognitive dissonance, or psychological frustrations as underlying causes of collective behavior. Smelser (1962) even sought to link different types of "generalized beliefs" to different forms of collective behavior.

One difficulty with these explanations is that such conditions can foster a wide range of reactions, including social withdrawal or isolation, antisocial behavior, various forms of deviance, vigilante justice, and the like. Hence, the translation of these conditions into participation in collective action is hardly automatic. What is lacking in standard strain or deprivation explanations is some account of the factors that politicize discontent and lead to collective action rather than some other response.

Although social constructionist approaches would tackle these issues from a variety of angles, Piven and Cloward (1979) offered one of the earliest and clearest statements of this process. As students of mass insurgency, defiance, and protest, they underscored how rare such episodes are because social structures normally preclude such responses. In their view, protest movements emerge only when there is a dual transformation of consciousness and behavior.

In terms of the former, the key issue is the perception that existing social arrangements have lost legitimacy. In their words, "[l]arge numbers of men and women who ordinarily accept the authority of their rulers and the legitimacy of institutional arrangements come to believe in some measure that these rulers and these arrangements are unjust and wrong" (Piven and Cloward 1979: 4).

Participation in mass defiance is most likely when people also come to believe that change is possible and that their own participation will make a difference in the outcome. Although important, these additional changes in consciousness make sense only if there is an initial perception of the injustice or illegitimacy of existing arrangements.

It was these transformations in belief that McAdam (1982: 50) identified as "cognitive liberation," noting that this process rests more on interactive definitions of the situation than personal observation or empirical evidence. When combined with other causal factors such as opportunity and organization, cognitive liberation played an important role in the political process model of collective action. Despite this early recognition, most political process theorists subsequently emphasized the structural factors of opportunity and organization over the "subjective" process of cognitive liberation.

William Gamson is a notable exception. Where he differed from many other resource mobilization and political process theorists was in his training as a social psychologist. This led him to pay particular attention to micromobilization, interaction, and meanings. Indeed, he claimed that resource mobilization "has not been particularly strong on the role of ideas and political consciousness in shaping collective action. Nor has it paid much attention to how long-term mobilization processes are mediated and altered in face-to-face interaction. Resource mobilization has neglected social psychology" (Gamson et al., 1982: 8–9). In response, Gamson and his associates proposed that social psychology "is an indispensable component of an adequate theory of resource mobilization, not an antagonist of it" (Gamson et al. 1982: 9).

A crucial issue is that challengers often face belief systems that legitimize existing authorities. "To succeed, challengers must loosen the bonds by delegitimizing the authority that is the target of their challenge" (Gamson et al. 1982: 6). Claiming that there are significant parallels between macro- and micromobilization, the authors examine micro-level challenges as encounters (Goffman 1961) with a single focus, heightened awareness, and definite beginning and end.

In such authority encounters, people are initially compliant. Challenges to authority emerge when at least some people adopt an injustice frame, or "a belief that *the unimpeded operation of the authority system ... would result in an injustice*" (Gamson et al. 1982: 14; italics in original). Such challenges become stronger if they break the bonds of authority and coalesce into an oppositional force.

While intermittently citing historical cases, the heart of this study involves fabricated encounters in which volunteers in focus groups face increasing evidence that their participation is being manipulated to support a private interest. The key questions are at what point, and through which processes, do initially compliant participants reject the prevailing definition of the situation by mounting a challenge to authority?

In their sample, roughly half of thirty-three groups achieved an operational definition of collective resistance by unanimously refusing to sign an affidavit at the end of the focus group. Some went further by mobilizing for future action or seizing other documents, but about half the groups failed to achieve a significant degree of resistance. The variation in outcomes across the sample gives the study its analytical leverage.

Gamson et al. acknowledge that resources are essential for long-term mobilization. In micromobilization encounters, however, they propose a threshold hypothesis: Some resources are necessary, but beyond a certain threshold additional resources do not matter a great deal. In micromobilization, it is know-how that looms large. This includes a repertoire of knowledge about how to do collective action along with the skills to apply that knowledge. In their sample, groups with know-how were more likely to mount successful challenges to authority.

Successful challenges also require organizational development, especially because challengers typically begin with organizational deficits compared with the authorities they challenge. Organizing acts must build loyalty to the challenger, manage the logistics of collective action, and mediate internal conflict. In their sample, the "most important loyalty-building act ... was speaking for the group and, in particular, the development of multiple spokespersons" (Gamson et al. 1982: 107). Thus, for micromobilization, formal organization is less important than a degree of cohesion, consensus, and shared response that allows spokespersons to represent the group.

People often comply with authority because of self-interest, obligation, facework, and a reified sense of authority. Breaking out of such compliance requires "divesting acts." One of the most important of such acts in the sample was "rim talk" that questioned the rationale for following the procedures of the focus group. By challenging the prevailing definition of the situation, rim talk undermined authority, fostered a collective orientation, and challenged the taken-for-granted quality of the legitimating frame (Gamson et al. 1982: 116). Such talk was a gateway to various forms of "contract voiding" among successful challenging groups.

Although rim talk can problematize the taken-for-granted quality of a legitimating frame, further steps are required to produce noncompliance. Specifically, an injustice frame must at least partially displace the legitimating frame. Injustice frames define what is happening as a violation of shared moral principles and provide a rationale for challenging authority. Such reframing can take two forms. Attention calling points out questionable acts by authority figures; context setting defines what is wrong by applying an injustice frame to unfolding events (Gamson et al. 1982: 125–126). In the sample, successful challengers reframed events earlier than other groups, but the injustice frame had to be accompanied by a collective orientation that undermined the bonds of authority if challengers were to succeed.

In general, successful challengers must achieve adequate organization (indicated by multiple spokespersons), adequate framing (indicated by early context setting), and adequate breaking out (indicated by early contract voiding). Accomplishing these tasks was sufficient but not necessary for successful challenges because even groups that failed to achieve some of them could succeed in a favorable climate. On the other hand, lack of know-how was a major handicap that could undermine all three tasks; it posed a severe obstacle to successful challenges.

In reaching broader conclusions, the authors distinguish between fixed elements (climate and assets) and dynamic ones (micromobilization processes). Concerning the former, a favorable climate and adequate threshold of resources facilitates chances for success. Concerning the latter, challengers are more likely to be successful if they engage in organizing acts that build cohesion, divesting acts that weaken bonds of authority, and reframing acts that support an injustice frame.

With this study, Gamson et al. began to remedy the social-psychological shortcomings of resource mobilization theory by analyzing multiple micromobilization processes, including framing. Subsequent work delved more deeply into the variety of framing tasks undertaken by social movements.

FRAMING TASKS

Although Gamson et al. (1982) sparked a reconsideration of social-psychological dynamics in social movements, David Snow, Robert Benford, and their associates are perhaps best known for studying framing in social movements. Like Gamson, their roots in social psychology and symbolic interactionism led them to focus on the social construction of protest, grievances, and micromobilization.

Resource mobilization theory can be faulted for "assuming the ubiquity and constancy of mobilizing grievances" (Snow et al. 1986: 465). Even more troublesome is the meta-assumption that if grievances are ubiquitous, there is no further role for social-psychological analysis. On a more positive note, Snow et al. credit Piven and Cloward (1979), McAdam (1982), and Gamson et al. (1982) with restoring social psychology and grievance formulation to their rightful place in the study of collective action.

Building on this work, they argue that "what is at issue is not merely the presence or absence of grievances, but the manner in which grievances are interpreted and the generation and diffusion of those interpretations" (Snow et al. 1986: 466). This requires Goffman's (1974) notion of frames as interpretive schemata that people use to identify, label, and render meaningful events in their lives. Frames allow people to organize experiences and guide actions, both in everyday life and in social movements.

A central task confronting movements is frame alignment, or the linkage between individual interests, values, and beliefs on the one hand and social movement activities, goals, and ideology on the other (Snow et al. 1986: 464). When congruent and complementary, movements should be able to recruit a committed membership with relative ease. Frame alignment is thus a crucial movement task affecting prospects for successful micromobilization.

Four different frame alignment processes are identified. The first is frame bridging, which involves the linkage of two or more preexisting frames that are ideologically congruent but structurally unconnected. Such bridging occurs when movements work at outreach, education, promotion, and diffusion of their goals to some audience already sympathetic with (if uninformed about) movement goals.

Put somewhat differently, frame bridging activates unmobilized sentiment pools or public opinion clusters; it recruits people by demonstrating that there already is a movement representing their views. One example is a mass mailing from a movement organization noting that many Americans are concerned about the dangers of the arms race and that the recipient may well be among that group. Frame bridging essentially says "We're already on the same page; why not join us?"

A second process is frame amplification. This involves the "clarification and invigoration of an interpretive frame that bears on a particular issue, problem or set of events" (Snow et al. 1986: 469). What amplification does is to underscore linkages between preexisting values or beliefs in the population and a movement's goals. In essence, frame amplification says "If you really believe in this general principle, then you should support our movement goal because it is consistent with that principle."

Two subtypes are distinguished. Value amplification appeals to broad goals or preferences in the population. For example, by "framing their mobilization appeals in the language of cherished democratic principles, peace activists ... seek to redefine their public image as a movements serving the best interests of their country ..." (Snow et al. 1986: 469).

Belief amplification addresses ideas that may either support or impede action about a problem. Such beliefs concern the seriousness of a problem, the cause of a problem, the nature of antagonists, the probability of change, or the necessity of resistance. Whether values or beliefs, such ideas often atrophy; frame amplification revivifies them, restores their salience, and links them to movement goals.

A third frame alignment process is frame extension. When there is no preexisting fit between a movement and those it seeks to recruit, it may have to modify its frame to encompass concerns of those not directly committed to the movement's original goals.

A local peace and justice group illustrated several frame extension strategies. These strategies included having rock and punk bands at rallies to attract the bands' followers to the cause, illustrating how scaling back the defense budget could help fund community needs, and incorporating issues of interest to racial and ethnic minorities under the broad banner of "peace and justice." Frame extension thus says "We'll acknowledge and work on your concerns; why not help us work on ours as well?"

The final and most elaborate frame alignment process is frame transformation. Here, a lack of any preexisting resonance means that "new values may have to be planted and nurtured, old meanings or understandings jettisoned, and erroneous beliefs or 'misframings' reframed" (Snow et al. 1986: 473).

With frame transformation, the objective situation may not change, but its intersubjective interpretation does. Frame transformation may redefine a condition "previously seen as unfortunate but tolerable ... as inexcusable, unjust, or immoral" (Snow et al. 1986: 474). It may also change attributions of the problem by shifting the focus from fatalistic self-blaming to system-blaming interpretations.

Frame transformation can vary in scope between domain-specific and global interpretive frames. The former refer to slices of life that are bracketed off from others so change is limited to that domain; the latter refer to holistic conversions evidenced in statements such as "I am an entirely different person now" (Snow et al. 1986: 475). Frame transformation invites people to look at a familiar world through radically different lenses, leading to different conclusions about how they should act in the world.

In all these ways, frame alignment challenges the facile assumption that grievances are constant, transparent, ubiquitous, and unproblematic features of social movements. Frame alignment is not an ideological given but rather a movement accomplishment. Moreover, it is one that "once achieved, cannot be taken for granted because it is temporally variable and subject to reassessment and renegotiation" (Snow et al. 1986: 476). Framing is thus an ongoing feature of successful mobilization.

In subsequent work, Snow and Benford (1988) argue that ideational elements in social movements must be recognized in analytical and not merely descriptive terms. After criticizing new social movement theory for downplaying ideology, they note that "[i]n the case of the resource mobilization perspective, even less attention is devoted to ideological considerations" (Snow and Benford 1988: 198). Both paradigms treat ideas as unproblematic givens rather than movement accomplishments. Differential success in framing may thus be able to explain differential movement outcomes.

Klandermans (1984) had previously claimed that movements must engage in both consensus mobilization to garner support and action mobilization to activate supporters. Snow and Benford build on this by distinguishing three types of framing.

"*Diagnostic framing* identifies a problem and attributes blame or causality" (Snow and Benford 1988: 200; italics in original). Of the two, problem identification is often more straightforward than attributional consensus. For example, research on the peace movement illustrates that the identification of threats posed by nuclear weapons was rarely challenged. Even within this movement, however, there was considerable dispute over underlying causes, ranging across technological, political, economic, or moral factors. Such competing attributions imply different targets and strategies. A movement that cannot achieve consensus on both processes is less likely to succeed.

A second framing task is prognostic framing. Here, movements address the classic Leninist question of what is to be done by framing solutions and the tactics and strategies to implement those solutions. Prognostic framing also identifies the targets of change; not surprisingly, targets vary with the attributions of diagnostic framing.

Thus, peace movement advocates who attributed the problem to technology tended to advocate technological solutions by preventing deployment of the most dangerous or destabilizing weapons. Those favoring a more political diagnosis of the problem favored political solutions that would shift power from nation-states to international institutions that might contain the arms race. Thus, competing diagnoses generate conflicting prognoses that may undermine movement effectiveness.

A third movement task is motivational framing. This provides a rationale for action, a call to arms, and vocabularies of motive supporting that action. This is an independent framing challenge, evidenced by numerous cases in which people agree on a problem, an attribution, and even a solution, but still fail to act. Motivational framing is thus needed for cognitive liberation by convincing people that change is possible and that their participation will make a difference.

The efficacy of frames rests on other factors as well. Cognitively, the ideas comprising a belief system may be more or less persuasive depending on their centrality, range, and interrelatedness. Phenomenologically, frames may be more or less effective depending on their empirical credibility, experiential commensurability, and narrative fidelity.

Mobilization thus depends not only on resources, organization, and opportunity "but also on the way these variables are framed and the degree to which they resonate with the targets of mobilization" (Snow and Benford 1988: 213). Without effective framing, "objective conditions" will not generate collective action.

Framing has a natural affinity with social-psychological approaches and micromobilization processes. With the concept of master frames, however, the framing paradigm demonstrates its capacity to address larger patterns and longer time frames.

Snow and Benford (1992) explore this potential in examining cycles of protest. This level of analysis is more commonly associated with the political process model illustrated by Tarrow's studies of protest cycles and the emphasis he placed on various forms of opportunity in explaining such cycles.

Compared with political process explanations, the "treatment of ideological factors in relation to the course and character of movements has been far from satisfactory" (Snow and Benford 1992:135). In correcting this shortcoming, the concept of master frames provides another means of explaining both the temporal clustering and cyclicity of collective action from a social constructionist perspective.

Master frames operate much like ordinary frames, but on a larger scale applicable to multiple movements. They have several variable features. In terms of attribution, they can locate causes in either internal or external factors. In terms of scope, they can be relatively restricted and closed or elaborated and inclusive. In terms of potency, they can resonate more or less strongly in terms of empirical credibility, experiential commensurability, and narrative fidelity. The most powerful master frames thus combine external attributions, elaborated codes, and high potency.

Adding master frames to the other processes that are used to explain movement clustering and cyclicity suggests a number of hypotheses. First, the emergence of a protest cycle may derive from the appearance of a new master frame. On the other hand, the lack of mass mobilization when structural conditions are otherwise favorable may be due to the absence of a resonant master frame.

Concerning movement sequence, earlier movements are likely to foster master frames that are then adopted by later movements in the cycle. By the same token, later movements may find their own framing efforts hampered by the existence of an established master frame to which they must somehow adapt.

A similar dual logic applies to tactics. New master frames may promote tactical innovation for "early risers" in a cycle of protest, but they may also constrain exploration of novel tactics for later movements in the cycle that adopt the same master frame.

The shape and duration of a cycle of protest is also affected by its master frame. The greater the potency of the frame and the more it lends itself to extension and amplification, the broader the shape and longer the duration of the protest cycle. Finally, the decline of a protest cycle may be due "in part to changes in the prevailing cultural climate that render the anchoring master frame impotent" (Snow and

Benford 1992: 149), or to the emergence of competing frames that undermine the initial frame's resonance.

The study of framing thus "complements and supplements resource mobilization and other structuralist perspectives in at least three ways" (Snow and Benford 1992: 151). It reveals the inspiration for and legitimation of collective action, it allows for an empirical examination of the politics of signification in movements, and it illustrates how framing processes can affect political opportunity and re-source availability. In all these ways, the framing approach sought not to displace structural approaches but to strengthen and complement them precisely where they were weakest.

MOVEMENTS AND MEDIA

Movement frames often challenge rival frames of dominant interests. Indeed, "[e]very regime has a legitimating frame that provides the citizenry with a reason to be quiescent. It is a constant, uphill struggle for those who would sustain collective action in the face of official myths and metaphors" (Gamson 1988: 219). Such struggles inevitably involve the broader political culture and the mass media.

Political culture consists of broad themes (e.g., technological progress) and counterthemes ("technology will run amok and destroy us"). Movements operate in this broader political culture, but they also develop issue cultures, interpretive pack-ages, and frames assigning meanings to particular topics the movement confronts. Successful frames create persuasive meanings and incorporate new or unexpected events.

Mass media and media discourse are part of the broader political culture as well as the issue cultures surrounding particular topics. The institutional power and sheer volume of media discourse make them central players in political and cultural conflict. Frames achieve media prominence through several value-added steps (Gamson 1988).

First, sponsoring activities contribute to the prominence of a package. Political and organizational authorities are often effective sponsors because they know how to manipulate the journalistic practices and condensing symbols that are central to media discourse. Movement organizations are sponsors for an alternative inter-pretive package as they seek to frame grievances, garner support, and neutralize opposition.

Second, media practices are a crucial part of the mix. Media professionals tend to "unconsciously give official packages the benefit of the doubt" and to "make official packages the starting point for discussing an issue" (Gamson 1988: 226). Moreover, media professionals often have long-standing, routinized access to official sources that they are reluctant to jeopardize by questioning them. The "balance norm" provides some counterweight to these tendencies, but even here "balance" is more typically provided by opposing authority figures than by movement challengers.

Third, cultural resonance between a package and the broader political culture is central to achieving media prominence. Once again, official authorities are often highly skilled at framing messages to resonate with broad cultural themes and thereby acquire media prominence.

Movements are often at a disadvantage on all three steps. Despite these obstacles, challengers are sometimes able to take actions that provoke new discourses and challenge dominant frames. Thus, "[c]ollective action is a vehicle for creating a contested discourse ... [that] exposes frame vulnerabilities in the official package" (Gamson 1988: 228). When unexpected events occur that undermine official definitions and reinforce challenger frames, movements can reorient media discourse.

A potent example may be found in discourses about nuclear power. In the 1950s and 1960s, there was a dualistic package of faith in progress regarding nuclear energy and fears of destruction concerning nuclear weapons. Aside from movements against atmospheric testing, the relatively small amount of collective action around these issues did not produce frames with much media resonance.

The paucity of antinuclear frames led to the "dog that didn't bark." In October of 1966, the Fermi nuclear reactor outside Detroit underwent a partial meltdown that "was extremely serious. The mystery of Fermi, then, is why it didn't become the center of media discourse and the symbol that [Three Mile Island] became" (Gamson 1988: 231). The answer is that "there was no significant antinuclear-power discourse during this era. Nuclear power was, in general a nonissue" (Gamson 1988: 232).

During the 1970s, by contrast, antinuclear activism in general and direct action at the Seabrook nuclear reactor significantly altered the issue culture of nuclear power and sponsored several antinuclear frames that gained media prominence. When the accident at Three Mile Island occurred in 1979, the event resonated with and reinforced these frames. When this dog barked, it put the nuclear power industry on the defensive for decades. In this case, collective action altered the issue culture, undermined official frames, capitalized on counterframes and supporting events, and thereby contributed to future mobilization efforts around this and related topics.

The political consciousness required for collective action thus has a complex relationship to media discourse. Gamson (1992) explored this nexus in greater detail by assembling focus groups to discuss the issues of troubled industry, affirmative action, nuclear power, and the Arab-Israeli conflict.

Each issue has a corresponding media discourse. This raises at least two questions. First, what role does this discourse play in shaping people's understanding of events? Second, under what circumstances do these understandings promote the political consciousness necessary to sustain collective action?

The study examined three components of collective action frames: injustice, agency, and identity. The injustice component involves a "hot" or emotion-laden cognition of moral indignation about harm done to others. Media discourse often adopts a narrative form that lends itself to injustice frames. At the same time, it tends to personalize blame and treat issues episodically so it is difficult for people to formulate coherent understandings about systemic causes of such injustice.

In the focus groups, there was plenty of working-class anger over various issues, but "the targets for indignation ... were limited to those with visibility in media discourse" (Gamson 1992: 58). Gamson cautions against a simplistic interpretation, suggesting that people don't just parrot the media but rather forge their own cognitive links in developing injustice frames. Such frames, in turn, are a "critical catalyst for the appearance of other elements of a collective action frame" (Gamson 1992: 58).

The agency component of such frames means a sense of efficacy that problems are not immutable but rather subject to change through people's own efforts. Agency is a big challenge for any movement given structural impediments to citizen participation and a political culture that encourages apathy, quiescence, passivity, and cynicism.

Agency varied by issue. It was more evident for issues "close to home," such as industrial problems and affirmative action; and less so for "distant" issues, such as conflict in the Middle East (unless respondents had a direct ethnic identification). Official sympathy for an issue fostered media portrayals that favored agency. In the case of nuclear power, however, media portrayed the movement as a viable actor despite official discouragement. Under the right circumstances, then, people acquired agency on certain issues when media portrayals granted some standing to collective actors.

The identity component of collective action frames refers to definitions of "we" and "they" that recast abstract problems as caused by an adversary that "we" can challenge. Whereas agency requires overcoming passivity and quiescence, identity requires transcending the deeply rooted individualism of American culture.

Most groups did invoke an adversarial frame on at least one issue. Not surprisingly, it was less likely in heterogeneous groups with social cleavages and more likely in homogenous groups. Black groups in particular were more likely to use adversarial frames, and this occurred in terms of class as well as race.

Considering the three components together, it appears that the "injustice component of a collective action frame facilitates adoption of the other elements" (Gamson 1992: 114). It increases attention to and sympathy for movements and promotes identification with victimized groups. When agents of injustice are identified, it fosters collective identity as well.

More generally, people understand events by combining experiential knowledge, popular wisdom, and media discourse. The balance between these elements varies by issue. Frames based on all three sources are especially robust, whereas those short on experiential knowledge are more subject to the influence of media discourse.

Among the working-class people in this study, counterthemes resonated with their worldview on a majority of issues. Their popular wisdom often contradicted official frames; this in turn provided "an entry point for collective action frames with the same resonances" (Gamson 1992: 162). The likelihood of such frames emerging also depended on the degree of proximity to, and engagement with, an issue.

In contrast with conventional wisdom, this research revealed a highly deliberative quality to how ordinary people blend diverse sources of information to construct meaning about complex issues. When this process supports a collective action frame, it is typically because an injustice theme pervades the conversation. Such a theme, in turn, is more likely when it is reinforced by all three sources of information (media discourse, popular wisdom, and experiential knowledge).

These results call for a more complex understanding of the links between media and political consciousness. Although media are rarely supportive of collective action frames, people are rarely passive recipients of media discourse. Media are better seen as tools in a multicausal relationship that includes popular wisdom, experiential knowledge, and the particular strategy people use to make sense of an issue.

Movements and media may also be seen as interacting systems (Gamson and Wolfsfeld 1993). In structural terms, this involves a mutual relationship of power and dependency; in cultural terms, it "focuses attention on the more subtle contest over meaning" (Gamson and Wolfsfeld 1993: 115).

There is a mutual but asymmetrical dependency between movements and media. Because movements need the media more than the media need movements, the media have greater power in this dynamic. Movements need media for mobilization, validation, and scope enlargement. Media need movements as one of many sources of good copy. Compared with official sources, however, movements are less powerful and more dependent in their dealings with media outlets.

In cultural terms, the "movement-media transaction is characterized by a struggle over framing" (Gamson and Wolfsfeld 1993: 118). In this struggle, media have the dual role of being the target as well as the medium of communication. Because they often convey dominant, taken-for-granted frames and assumptions, media are often the target of movement efforts to problematize those frames and move them from the realm of uncontested to contested ideas.

Ideally, movements seek standing, preferred framing, and sympathy from the media. This is more likely when movements have the resources, organization, planning, and division of labor to pursue these objectives. A sympathetic reception is also more likely when the movement's goals are narrowly defined.

From the media side, elite audiences will have a greater impact on movement framing strategies. If the media favor entertainment value or visual depictions, this may influence leadership choices within the movement and promote "action strategies that emphasize spectacle, drama, and confrontation" (Gamson and Wolfsfeld 1993: 124).

When Gamson (1990: Ch. 10) updated his historical study of social protest to include movements after 1945, he noted two major changes in American society: the rise of the national security state and "the rise of television and, with it, the much more central role for the mass media, affecting the strategies of both challengers and authorities" (Gamson 1990: 146). Since 1990, both movements and media have become more sophisticated about their roles in the mutual dance between them. Hence, it is fitting that this dance has become more central to social movement theory.

THE SOCIAL CONSTRUCTION OF PROTEST

Although the social constructionist approach to social movements is often equated with framing, it applies to other aspects of movements as well. This brief section draws upon several examples to illustrate the broader applicability of social constructionist premises to collective action.

Mobilization is one example of a socially constructed process. It can be divided into two subprocesses: Consensus mobilization involves efforts to obtain support for a movement's viewpoint, whereas action mobilization motivates people to actually participate (Klandermans 1984). These categories correspond closely to processes of frame alignment and motivational framing discussed earlier.

Whereas resource mobilization theory falls back on the rational actor model (and encounters the free-rider dilemma) to address participation, a social constructionist approach recognizes a more subtle element shaping participation. Put succinctly, *"persons have to decide to participate at a point when they do not know whether others will participate"* (Klandermans 1984: 585; italics in original).

Although people may not have knowledge, they do have expectations about the participation of others and its bearing on movement success. Hence, movements often try to shape these expectations by choosing goals, strategies, and tactics that minimize costs, maximize benefits, and foster beliefs about a high likelihood of widespread participation. "The expectation that others will participate works as a self-fulfilling prophecy" (Klandermans 1984: 597). Thus, in addition to beliefs or frames, mobilization itself is a socially constructed process.

A dramatic example is provided by a study of the Dutch peace movement of the early 1980s (Klandermans and Oegema 1987). In October 1983, 4 percent of the entire population of the Netherlands participated in a massive demonstration. Although this is an astounding figure, it represents only a fraction of the people who supported the goals of the movement. The gap between support and participation illuminates key obstacles in the social construction of protest.

Four aspects of mobilization may be distinguished. First, the mobilization potential of a movement represents the broadest pool of people who support a movement's goals. Recruitment networks are a second stage in the construction of mobilization whereby deliberate efforts are made to inform and entice people to join through new or preexisting communication channels.

A third stage concerns motivation to participate. As noted earlier, this is not just a function of costs and benefits, but of perceptions of costs and benefits as well as expectations about the participation of others. Finally, there are barriers to participation that arise at the last minute even among people who intend to participate.

These aspects of mobilization may be conceptualized as a funnel that is broad at the top and progressively narrower at each stage. Thus, not everyone is sympathetic, not everyone who is sympathetic is recruited, not everyone who is recruited is motivated, and not everyone who is motivated overcomes participatory barriers.

The evidence from this study is dramatic: 74 percent of the population agreed with movement goals, 59 percent were the target of a mobilization attempt, 10 percent intended to participate, and 4 percent overcame barriers and actually did so. More generally, this suggests that successful movements construct the mobilization process to maintain as wide a funnel as possible; movements that fail to do so are likely to fail in reaching their larger goals as well.

Alongside mobilization, collective identities are also socially constructed in at least two ways. First, framing often identifies the major actors in a conflict and imputes characteristics, motives, and consciousness to them. Such framing typically identifies protagonists, antagonists, and audiences (Hunt, Benford, and Snow 1994).

Protagonist identity fields define the people and groups who are participants in, supporters of, or presumed beneficiaries of a movement. Such framing makes fundamental distinctions and attributions between in-groups and out-groups and uses boundary maintenance activities to sustain these definitions. It helps create and sustain a sense of "we" in social movements.

Antagonist identity fields define the opponents of the movement; such frames include "claims about countermovements, countermovement organizations, hostile institutions, inimical publics, and social control agents" (Hunt, Benford, and Snow 1994: 197). Such framing identifies targets for the movement that in turn shape strategies and tactics; it concretizes the "they" that "we" oppose.

Audience framing defines neutral or uncommitted observers of the movement. Such framing has a dialectical relationship to strategy, depending on whether audiences are seen as potential sympathizers to be recruited, potential opponents to be neutralized, or power brokers who will influence the outcome of a conflict.

Movement identities are also socially constructed through interactional dynamics and accomplishments. "From this standpoint, collective political actors do not exist *de facto* by virtue of individuals sharing a common structural location; they are created in the course of social movement activity" (Taylor and Whittier 1992: 109–110).

In lesbian feminist communities, the establishment of group boundaries, the raising of oppositional consciousness and the negotiation of symbolic meanings all contributed to the construction of collective identities. By affirming femaleness, politicizing sexuality, and valorizing experience, lesbian feminists created a movement abeyance structure in which they could survive even as their radical politics became more marginal to the mass women's movement (Taylor and Whittier 1992: 121–122).

A final example of the social construction of protest concerns the role of opportunity that features so prominently in the political process model. In that perspective, opportunity is often treated as a straightforward political or structural variable affecting movement origins, trajectories, and endings.

There is, however, a cultural side to opportunity as well, so that "[p]olitical opportunities are subject to framing processes" (Gamson and Meyer 1996: 276). This is often most evident in internal struggles within movements over how to interpret and assign meaning to external events.

Thus, the same "objective" event may be framed by some adherents as a major setback and by others as a newfound opportunity. If, as W. I. Thomas noted long ago, situational definitions are real in their consequences, the victor in such internal framing contests over opportunity will define the terrain upon which movements subsequently mobilize resources, formulate strategies, and devise tactics.

These brief examples suggest that the social construction of protest is not just about the framing of grievances. The dynamics of mobilization, the formation of identity, and the definition of opportunity also rely heavily on social-psychological dynamics of interaction and negotiation as well as social constructionist processes of meaning and signification.

CONCLUSION

Although the framing approach of Snow, Benford, and their colleagues has arguably become more prominent than some other variants, the social constructionist paradigm as a whole has become central to the analysis of social movements.

The emergence and prominence of this perspective may be viewed from several angles. First, like the resource mobilization and political process approaches, social constructionist theory was a response to the cycle of social movements of the 1960s, 1970s, and 1980s. These movements were ripe for analysis not just in terms of resources and strategies but also in terms of framing and signifying practices.

Second, these approaches revived and revised the symbolic interactionist strain of the classical model of collective behavior associated with Park and Burgess, Herbert Blumer, and Turner and Killian. Modern constructionist approaches, however, adopted a more favorable view of movements. Indeed, in contrast with the negative bias of the early Chicago School or the detached objectivity of Turner and Killian, contemporary constructionists often take a sympathetic stance toward the movements they study. Finally, this revival of constructionist approaches took social movements as objects of analysis in their own right rather than subsuming them under the broader category of collective behavior.

The third and most obvious impetus for constructionist approaches has been the shortcomings and gaps in resource mobilization and political process models of collective action. For all their strengths in analyzing resources, organization, and opportunity, the latter ignored or downplayed framing, signification, and culture more generally (Buechler 1993). Social constructionist approaches were tailor-made to remedy this shortcoming; when they did so, they became the third major paradigm in the contemporary analysis of social movements.

As it rose to prominence, advocates of social constructionism retained a certain modesty in their theoretical claims. Rather than a totalistic perspective that could replace rivals, social constructionism was presented as filling gaps, correcting biases, complementing existing work, and restoring a micro-level dimension to social movement theory. This tone helps account for the relatively wide acceptance and broad recognition of the importance of framing and social constructionist processes even by supposedly "rival" perspectives and practitioners.

Chapter Ten

New Social Movement Theories

The meso-level orientation of resource mobilization and political process theories left "space" for rivals addressing other levels of analysis. Thus, social constructionism addressed the micro-level of social psychology, whereas new social movement theory analyzed the macro-level of social structure and broad historical transformations between societal types. Both gained an initial hearing by addressing levels of analysis marginalized by prevailing theories.

Whereas social constructionism was a homegrown variant with symbolic interactionist roots, new social movement theory was a European import with a different heritage. Hence, in the latter case, explicit attempts were made in the late 1980s to bridge the gap and synthesize American and European approaches. In the end, however, these efforts met with rather limited success.

THE CONTEXT

Although sociological approaches to social movements can be traced back at least to the European "holy trinity" of Marx, Weber, and Durkheim, social movement theory in the United States has almost always had a distinctly American cast. This is certainly true of the Chicago School and collective behavior approach that dominated much of the twentieth century. European scholars informed the political sociology approach of the 1950s, but receded again as the major paradigm shift from collective behavior to resource mobilization and its competitors unfolded in the 1970s and 1980s.

If movement theory in the United States can be crudely summarized as a transition from collective behavior to resource mobilization/political process, European social movement theory was markedly different. As U.S. scholars were studying collective behavior, European theorists were still largely working within a Marxist tradition focused on class cleavages, industrial conflict, working-class mobilization, and the prospects for proletarian revolt.

When U.S. social movement theory underwent its paradigm shift from collective behavior to resource mobilization, European approaches underwent an equally basic paradigm shift from working-class mobilization to new social movements. Thus, both traditions underwent major transformations in the 1970s, but they neither started nor ended in the same place. Resource mobilization emerged through a critical dialogue with collective behavior in the United States while new social movement theory derived from an equally critical reexamination of orthodox Marxism on the European continent. The theoretical gulf between the later orientations was as great as that between the earlier ones (Crossley 2002: 10).

There are equally sharp contrasts in theoretical style on opposite sides of the Atlantic. Theorizing in the United States has largely followed a middle-range strategy that is analytical, empirical, and scientific; occasionally empiricist and positivist; and nominally neutral or objective even as it has focused on "good" movements with which the theorist sympathizes.

In sharp contrast, the "European trajectory has been more firmly framed by the Marxist/Hegelian tradition of the philosophy of history" (Crossley 2002:10). European analyses of collective action have been more likely to follow a "grand theory" strategy that is historical, philosophical, and speculative; occasionally metaphysical and teleological; and distinctly normative in blending ethical, political, and cultural issues.

This history is crucial to appreciating the term "new social movement(s)." The "newness" of these movements is at least two-fold. First, it derives from their contrast with the "old" social movement variously described as the labor movement, working-class mobilization, socialist challenges to capitalism, and the like. "Newness" is less a claim about unprecedented features of contemporary movements than an assertion that one type of movement rooted in the class cleavages of a capitalist society has given way to another type of movement with different roots in a postindustrial society.

Second, the "newness" at issue thus refers as much to prevailing social structures as the movements they foster. "European debates have typically been as much about the constitutive structure and type of society in which modern movements emerge, the relation of those movements to that society and their 'historical role' therein, as they have been about the movements themselves. There has been an assumption that societies centre upon certain key conflicts or contradictions and that these conflicts generate particular movements, perhaps even a singular key movement, which seeks to address them" (Crossley 2002: 10).

This focus on broad questions of societal types and corresponding movements reflects both the style of continental theorizing in general and its Marxist heritage in particular. It also underscores the gulf between European philosophical premises and the epistemology of American approaches that routinely eschew issues of this scope.

New social movement theorizing was most obviously stimulated by new forms of collective action. In this regard, it is difficult to overestimate the impact of the May 1968 uprising in France. One testimony to this impact is the sheer diversity of interpretations it provoked. Different observers and participants saw it as the leading edge of antisystemic movements, a symbol of antimodernism, an expression of postmaterialism, a reprise of generational rebellion, and even an entirely new type of revolution. Whatever the interpretation, the event spawned new forms of collective action whose cultural, spiritual, or symbolic elements displaced more conventional political struggles throughout the 1970s and 1980s.

Many of these movements both reflected and promoted not just a "cultural turn" but also an "identity turn" across many disciplines. Poststructuralist, postmodernist, multicultural, anticolonial, feminist, and queer theorists all called attention to the socially and politically constructed nature of diverse social identities, just as the movements associated with these labels challenged old identities and valorized new ones as part of these sociocultural struggles.

The conjuncture of grand European theorizing, fundamental structural transformations, and novel collective action thereby inspired visionary work that has collectively come to be identified as new social movement theory.

SOME MAJOR THEMES

Despite common usage, the term "new social movement theory" is misleading if it implies widespread agreement on core premises. It is more accurate to speak of a congeries of interrelated ideas and arguments that comprise new social movement theories with many variations on a general approach to the topic (Buechler 1995, 2000). As a first approximation, however, it is possible to identify several themes that are prominent in most if not all versions of new social movement theories.

First and foremost, these theories identify a distinct social formation that provides the context for the emergence of collective action. Although theorists may differ on specifics, the attempt to theorize a historically specific social formation as the structural backdrop for contemporary forms of collective action is perhaps the most distinctive feature of new social movement theories (as noted by Crossley previously). As a corollary, transitions between social formations change the context and hence the types of movements one is likely to see over time.

A second theme is a causal claim that links these new movements to the contemporary social formation; new social movements are direct responses to postindustrialism, late modernity, advanced capitalism, or postmodernity. If contemporary society is defined by capitalist markets, bureaucratic states, scientized relationships, and instrumental rationality, then new social movements are historically specific responses to these conditions. These depictions often emphasize the extent to which large, anonymous, institutional forces have become especially intrusive and invasive; these "colonizing efforts" (Habermas 1987, 1984) have prompted new collective responses to new forms of social control in late modernity.

A third theme concerns the diffuse social base of new social movements. Some analysts see these movements as rooted in a fraction of the (new) middle classes (Eder 1993; Kriesi 1989; Offe 1985). Others have argued that these movements are no longer rooted in the class structure, but rather in other statuses such as race, ethnicity, gender, sexual orientation, age, or citizenship that are central in mobilizing new social movements (Dalton, Kuechler, and Burklin 1990). Still others have argued that even these statuses are less important than ideological consensus over movement values and beliefs. For all these reasons, the social base of these movements is presumed to be more complex than in older and more conventional class-based activism.

This leads to a fourth theme concerning the centrality of collective identity in social protest (Hunt, Benford, and Snow 1994; Johnston, Larana, and Gusfield 1994; Klandermans 1994; Melucci 1996, 1989; Stoecker 1995). With the uncoupling of activism from the class structure as well as the fluidity and multiplicity of identities in late modernity, the ability of people to engage in collective action is increasingly tied to their ability to define an identity in the first place (Melucci 1996, 1989). This places a premium on the social construction of collective identity as an essential part of contemporary social activism, and it has led to a belated appreciation of how even "old" class-based movements were not structurally determined as much as they were socially constructed through mobilization itself (historians had appreciated this point well before social movement theorists explicitly recognized it [Thompson 1963]).

A fifth theme involves the politicization of everyday life as the "relation between the individual and the collective is blurred" (Johnston, Larana, and Gusfield 1994: 7) and formerly intimate and private aspects of social life become politicized. The equation of the personal and the political fosters not only identity politics but also lifestyle politics in which everyday life becomes a major arena of political action. Like many aspects of these movements, this characteristic cannot be understood apart from its social context. For new social movement activists (and theorists), it is late modernity with its invasive technologies that has blurred the lines between the political and the personal. Thus, movements are as much responses to the systemic politicization of life as initiators of it.

A sixth theme concerns the values advocated by new social movements. Although some have argued that the sheer pluralism of values and ideas is their defining hallmark (Johnston, Larana, and Gusfield 1994), others have focused on the centrality of postmaterialist values (Inglehart 1990; Dalton, Kuechler, and Burklin 1990) in such activism. Whereas materialist values involve redistributive struggles in the conventional political sphere, postmaterialist values emphasize the quality rather than the quantity of life (Habermas 1987, 1984). Rather than seeking power, control, or economic gain, postmaterialist movements are more inclined to seek autonomy and democratization (Rucht 1988). As a generalization about new social movements, the "postmaterialist" designation can be challenged. Where accurate, however, it means that such movements are resistant to conventional strategies of cooptation via material rewards.

A seventh theme involves cultural, symbolic forms of resistance alongside or in place of more conventional political strategies (Cohen 1985). For many movements, this signifies a philosophical or spiritual rejection of the instrumental rationality of advanced capitalist society and its systems of social control and cooptation. This cultural emphasis rejects conventional goals, tactics, and strategies in favor of the exploration of new identities, meanings, signs, and symbols. Although some have criticized this orientation as apolitical, such criticisms ignore the importance of cultural forms of social power. As Nancy Whittier (1995) has argued, if hegemony is an important form of such power, then the culturally oriented, antihegemonic politics of new movements is an important form of resistance. The very ability to envision and symbolically enact new and different ways of organizing social relationships can itself be a potent challenge to dominant social arrangements (Melucci 1996, 1989).

A final theme in new social movement activism is a preference for organizational forms that are decentralized, egalitarian, participatory, prefigurative, and ad hoc (Melucci 1989; Gusfield 1994; Mueller 1994). For these movements, organization is less a strategic tool than a symbolic expression of movement values and member identities. New social movements function less as standing armies than as cultural laboratories that vacillate between latency and visibility (Melucci 1996, 1989) as they episodically organize for specific battles and then revert to politicized subcultures that sustain movement visions and values for the next round of explicitly organized activism.

Although these themes distinguish new social movement theories from other approaches, they may also be used to identify two ideal types of such theories that we can loosely label "political" and "cultural." The political version draws upon neo-Marxist scholarship to identify the social formation of advanced capitalism and to trace links between this formation and the emergence of new social movements.

This version is macro-oriented in general and state-oriented in particular. It retains a concern with strategic questions and instrumental action as the ultimate goals of social movements while recognizing the importance of identity formation, grievance definition, and interest articulation as intermediate steps in the process of movement activism. It recognizes a role for new constituencies in social activism based on race, gender, nationality, or other characteristics, but it does not jettison the potential for class-based or worker-based movements alongside these groups.

This version thus emphasizes the potential for proactive, progressive change if appropriate alliances and coalitions between class-based and nonclass-based movements can be forged. The political version is wary of the "apolitical" nature of more culturally oriented new social movements as limiting their potential for producing meaningful social change. And finally, this perspective identifies the social base of new social movements in class terms by analyzing the complexity of contemporary class structure and its contradictory locations as the backdrop for social activism.

The cultural version of new social movement theory is post-Marxist in presuming a more radical break between past and present societal types and movement forms. The cultural version identifies the prevailing social formation in cultural or semiotic terms as an information society whose administrative codes conceal forms of domination. It emphasizes the decentralized nature of both power and resistance, so it is not particularly macro-oriented or state-centered, but rather focused on everyday life, civil society, and the creation of free spaces between state and civil society.

The cultural version eschews strategic questions and instrumental action as pitfalls to be avoided, while emphasizing symbolic expressions that challenge the instrumental logic of systemic domination. This version not only recognizes new social constituencies but also argues that the old worker-based constituencies for social activism have been transcended along with industrial capitalism. The cultural version views activism as a defensive reaction to domination that can potentially challenge systemic imperatives, but it rejects the language of "progressive" movements as invoking an unwarranted metaphysics of history.

This approach also rejects the apolitical label often attached to culturalist movements by arguing that political movements are the most easily coopted and that cultural movements fighting on symbolic terrain can do more to expose contemporary forms of power than more conventionally political movements. And finally, this version is more likely to identify the social base of new social movements in nonclass terms that identify other statuses or distinctive values and ideologies as defining movement constituencies. This typology is no more than an ideal-typical sensitizing device, but it helps to organize a variety of issues into two relatively coherent positions with a fair degree of internal consistency (Buechler 1995). We turn now to several theorists who have forged distinctive combinations of these themes and orientations.

EUROPEAN EXEMPLARS AND DEBATES

An overview of some major new social movement theorists will serve several purposes. First, it will illustrate the range of orientations in this area, as well as the distortion that is introduced when these diverse perspectives are referred to as a single paradigm. Second, it will illustrate how the core themes sketched previously can be combined in various ways. Third, it will provide examples of perspectives that approximate the "political" and "cultural" ideal types contrasted previously. Finally, it will illustrate central debates about the nature of new social movements and the societies that generate them. Four theorists best exemplify the range of new social movement theories in the context of their own national traditions: Manuel Castells (Spain), Alain Touraine (France), and Jürgen Habermas (Germany) are discussed in this section; Alberto Melucci (Italy) receives more extended treatment in the next section.

Castells's (1978, 1983) focus is the impact of capitalist dynamics on the transformation of urban space and the role of urban social movements in this process. He argues that urban issues have become central because of the growing importance of collective consumption and the necessity of the state to intervene to promote the production of nonprofitable but vitally needed public goods.

It is in this context that Castells sees the rise of urban social movements in a dialectical contest with the state and other political forces seeking to reorganize urban social life. He views the city as a social product that is a result of conflicting social interests and values. On the one hand, socially dominant interests seek to define urban space in keeping with the goals of capitalist commodification and bureaucratic domination; on the other hand, grassroots mobilizations and urban social movements seek to defend popular interests, establish political autonomy, and maintain cultural identity.

Although arguing that class relationships are fundamental, Castells recognizes that they exist alongside other identities and sources of change, including the state as well as group identities based on gender, ethnicity, nationality, and citizenship. For Castells, urban protest movements typically develop around three major themes.

First, some demands focus on collective consumption provided by the state, thereby challenging the capitalist logic of exchange value with an emphasis on the provision of use values in community contexts. Second, other demands focus on the importance of cultural identity and its links to territoriality, thereby resisting the standardization and homogenization associated with bureaucratic organization by establishing and defending genuine community. Finally, still other demands express the political mobilization of citizens seeking more decentralized government emphasizing self-management and autonomous decision making. For Castells, the goals of collective consumption, community culture, and political self-management are advocated by urban social movements in a wide variety of cross-cultural settings.

This analysis of urban social movements exemplifies several new social movement themes, including an emphasis on cultural identity, a recognition of nonclass-based constituencies, the theme of autonomous self-management, and the image of resistance to a systemic logic of commodification and bureaucratization.

At the same time, Castells remains closer to conventional Marxism than many other new social movement theorists by offering a "both/and" rather than an "either/or" stance toward familiar social movement dichotomies. Thus, rather than counterposing "old," class-based movements with "new," nonclass-based movements, the roles of both constituencies are recognized in urban social movements. Rather than contrasting "political" and "cultural" orientations, he recognizes that urban social movements contain a dialectical mixture of both orientations that finds expression in civil society and the state. Rather than dichotomizing between "instrumental" strategies and "expressive" identities, Castells acknowledges the mutual interplay between these themes in many urban social movements.

With this more catholic and inclusive approach, Castells's version of new social movement theory is more attentive to the role of the state than some other versions of the theory that appear to eschew instrumental action altogether. As a result, he is more likely to emphasize the role of political dynamics, such as changing political opportunity structures, than some other scholars of new social movement theory. Finally, Castells's approach suggests the compatibility of a certain style of neo-Marxist analysis with at least some versions of new social movement theory.

Alain Touraine (1977, 1981, 1985) argues that with the passing of metasocial guarantees of social order, more and more of society comes to be seen as the product of reflective social action. The growing capacity of social actors to construct both a system of knowledge and the technical tools that allow them to intervene in their own functioning—a capacity Touraine calls "historicity"—makes possible the increasing self-production of society, which becomes the defining hallmark of postindustrial or programmed society.

The control of historicity is the object of an ongoing struggle between classes defined by relations of domination. Such classes take the form of social movements as they enter into this struggle. In postindustrial society, the major social classes consist of a popular class of consumers and clients and a dominant class of managers and technocrats. The principal field of conflict for these classes is culture, and the central contest involves who will control society's growing capacity for self-management.

As the state becomes the repository of society's ever-increasing capacity to control historicity, there is reason to believe that the central conflict in postindustrial society will come to center around this institution. In a recent formulation, Touraine (1992) locates new social movements between two logics: that of a system seeking to maximize production, money, power, and information; and that of subjects seeking to defend and expand their individuality.

Touraine's work directly addresses the likely constituency for new social movements. In an empirical study of the workers' movement in France, Touraine and his associates (Touraine, Wieviorka, and Dubet 1987) reiterate his distinctive claim that there is one central conflict in every type of society. In industrial society, this conflict centered around material production, and the workers' movement posed the obvious challenge.

With the coming of postindustrial society, Touraine et al. still expect one principal adversarial movement, although they remain uncertain about whether new social movements will fill this role. In a subsequent work, Touraine (1988) suggested that there is no single class or group that represents a future social order and that different oppositional social movements are united simply by their oppositional attitude. Touraine's inability to define the constituency for collective action (despite his insistence that each societal type has a single central conflict) underscores the difficulties that new social movement theorists have in unambiguously identifying the constituency for such movements.

In Touraine's case, this uncertainty may derive from the seemingly apolitical nature of these movements. He sees contemporary social movements as evidence of a displacement of protest from the economic to the cultural realm, accompanied by the privatization of social problems. The typical result is an anxious search for identity and an individualism that may undermine genuinely collective action (1985).

Touraine (1985) further implies that movements based on difference, specificity, or identity too easily dismiss the analysis of social relations and the denunciation of power. In yet another work he (1988) suggests that appeals to identity are purely defensive unless they are linked with a counteroffensive that is directly political and that appeals to self-determination. This ambiguity about the political status of new social movements is a common thread within this paradigm.

Jürgen Habermas (1984, 1987) proposes the most elaborate theory of modern social structure by distinguishing between a politico-economic system governed by generalized media of power and money and a lifeworld still governed by normative consensus. Whereas the system follows an instrumental logic that detaches media like money and power from any responsibility or accountability, the lifeworld follows a communicative rationality requiring that norms be justifiable through discussion, debate, and consensus.

The problem for Habermas is that in modern society, system imperatives and logic intrude on the lifeworld in the form of colonization, so that money and power come to regulate not only economic and political transactions but also identity formation, normative regulation, and other forms of symbolic reproduction traditionally associated with the lifeworld. Habermas suggests that the relationship of clients to the welfare state is a model case for this colonization of the lifeworld, in that the welfare state monetarizes and bureaucratizes lifeworld relationships as it controls the extent and kind of spending on welfare policy to fit system imperatives.

More generally, Habermas argues that colonization alters each of the basic roles arising from the intersection of the politico-economic system and public and private lifeworld (employee, consumer, client, and citizen). In each case, these dynamics concentrate decision-making power in the hands of experts and administrative structures using instrumental rationality to make decisions that are correspondingly removed from contexts of justification and accountability within the lifeworld.

Given this conception of social structure, Habermas locates new social movements at the seams between system and lifeworld. In doing so, he implies that new social movements have a largely reactive character: At best, they can defend the lifeworld against the colonizing intrusion of the system and sustain the role of normative consensus rooted in communicative rationality that has been evolving within this sphere throughout the process of societal modernization.

Habermas thus offers little evidence that new social movements can contribute to any broader social transformation that challenges the dominance of the system and its generalized media of exchange over the lifeworld. Although few expect new social movements to achieve complete societal transformation, many envision a more extensive and progressive role for movements than simply defending the lifeworld. Another dimension of Habermas's argument, however, implies a larger role for such movements. This concerns the goals or demands associated with new movements. For Habermas, as for many others, these demands are less about material production and more about cultural reproduction, social integration, and socialization.

These new movements thus practice a new politics concerned with quality of life, projects of self-realization, and goals of participation and identity formation. Many of these movements are united around a critique of unlimited material growth and unfettered technocratic priorities, with environmental and peace movements playing central roles. Because these are not traditional distributional struggles, they are less likely to be coopted by political parties or allayed by material compensation. The implication is that under some circumstances, new social movements may contribute to the larger legitimation crisis that Habermas (1975, 1984, 1987) associates with advanced capitalism, and hence to opportunities for more substantive social transformation.

These sketches illustrate some of the main contours of new social movement approaches while also suggesting the diversity between the ideal types sketched above. This diversity derives from different national settings, protest histories, and theoretical traditions. As suggested earlier, this diversity warrants speaking of "new social movement theor*ies*" rather than a unitary "new social movement theory."

There remain, however, important points of agreement as well. Despite their differences, these analysts concur that their societies have arrived at a distinct social formation whose structural features shape contemporary collective action as decisively as liberal capitalism shaped proletarian protest. Their work has also given rise to several core debates about new social movements that further illustrate some of the core themes identified above (Buechler 1995).

Perhaps the most obvious debate concerns what is actually new about such social movements. Critics have dismissed "newness" as simply the early stages of conventional movements (Tarrow 1991) or the cyclical return of romantic, moral-idealistic critiques of modernity (Brand 1990). Defenders of the "newness" of such movements have found it in their postmaterialistic values, resistance to cooptation (Offe 1990), democratic formulation of collective needs (Eder 1993), or recognition of modernity's irreversible structural differentiation (Cohen 1983).

This debate suggests that the term "new" is less a definitive empirical claim and more a means of pointing to family resemblances in contemporary collective action. Rather than fetishizing the term or posing sharp dichotomies between new and old, we should recall the heuristic origin of the term to symbolize the transcendence of the "old" labor movement and the emergence of a new social formation with correspondingly different forms of collective action.

A second debate concerns whether new social movements are merely defensive (as Habermas's colonization thesis seems to imply) or potentially progressive and transformative. Rucht (1988) implies that system modernization may provoke defensive reactions that are antitechnological and even antimodern, whereas lifeworld rationalization may provoke more progressive outcomes of democratization and self-determination.

Some otherwise diverse theorists also locate the potentially progressive effects of new social movements less in their specific programs than in their democratizing potential. For Cohen (1982, 1983), this takes the form of an expansion and institutionalization of civil society. For Flacks (1988), it means the cultivation of a democratic consciousness that narrows the gap between "everyday life" and "making history." For Laclau and Mouffe (1985), it means the liberatory potential of expanded democratic discourse in postmodern social worlds.

A third debate concerns the desirability of political or cultural practices in new social movements. As we have seen, for more politically oriented theorists, the cultural aspects of new social movements may undermine their prospects for structural transformation (Boggs 1986; Epstein 1991). In the sharpest version of this critique, Kauffman (1990) argues that the "antipolitics" of identity encourages apolitical introspection, politically correct lifestyles, and personal transformation over political activity. Despite its radical veneer, such stances may actually mirror and promote the values of the marketplace.

More culturally oriented theorists tend to reverse these values. They see conventional political tactics as playing by the rules of a game controlled by elites and inevitably leading to cooptation, marginalization, or institutionalization. For them, an apolitical orientation is a strength, not a weakness, because it can pose more profound symbolic and cultural challenges to the instrumental rationality of a technocratically administered society (Melucci 1989).

A final debate concerns the social base of new social movements. As noted earlier, there are at least two positions that abandon talk of "class" altogether. One equates "old" movements with class movements and sees new movements as drawing on other identities rooted in race, ethnicity, gender, nationality, and so on. Another stance sees the base of new social movements in terms of a common ideological worldview rather than a homogeneous social base deriving from a common identity (Dalton, Kuechler, and Burklin 1990).

Having said this, the most common thread in new social movement theory is to link such movements to some type of middle-class base. As a "contradictory class location" (Wright 1989), the combination of privileges and restrictions that characterize new middle classes (and especially social and cultural specialists) may predispose them to the appeals of new social movements. At the same time, such movements may offer one vehicle for such amorphous social groups to formulate a collective class identity in the first place (Eder 1993; Kreisi 1989).

None of these debates lends itself to easy resolution. They are better seen as comprising a theoretical field of issues and concerns at the heart of new social movement theories. We turn now to the best navigator of this theoretical field.

MELUCCI'S ANALYSIS

The central insight of new social movement theories is that different social formations give rise to distinct types of social movements. Castells, Touraine, and Habermas, however, primarily address new features of contemporary society and only secondarily analyze new social movements. Alberto Melucci's work reverses this emphasis. While acknowledging a new type of information society, Melucci has made the analysis of new movements the primary focus of his extensive work. For this reason, it merits more detailed attention.

Melucci positions his work in relation to the limits or weaknesses of other theories of social movements. Thus, structural theories exemplified by Habermas may account for why but not how movements arise; resource mobilization theories may account for how but not why they arise; and political exchange theories exaggerate the instrumental nature of new movements and ignore their increasingly cultural and symbolic role.

For Melucci, collective action is less an effect of structure or an expression of values than it is the product of purposeful orientations that develop within a field of opportunities and constraints. He takes a constructivist view of collective action that sees whatever unity or cohesion a movement achieves as an ongoing accomplishment rather than a structural or ideological given.

Much the same may be said for collective identity. Prevailing theories like resource mobilization either presuppose or marginalize the importance of collective identity in social movements. For Melucci, the establishment and maintenance of such identity is a major movement accomplishment; indeed, in some cases it is the *raison d'être* of a movement. Even in movements with more conventional political ambitions, the establishment of collective identity precedes and profoundly shapes any meaningful calculation of costs and benefits on the part of movement participants.

In analytical terms, Melucci's conception of collective action has three dimensions. First, he contrasts solidarity with the aggregation of individual behavior. Second, he contrasts conflict with a consensual orientation to action. Third, he contrasts actions that transgress systemic norms and limitations to those that conform to them. These distinctions yield a three-dimensional definition of social movements as involving solidarity, conflict, and actions that break the limits of compatibility of a system.

In descriptive terms, contemporary collective action has several distinct features. First, its goals are often heterogeneous and relatively non-negotiable. Second, it largely ignores the political system and seems disinterested in seizing power. Third, such action challenges the modern divide between public and private. Fourth, there is a "certain *overlap between deviance and social movements*" (Melucci 1996: 103; italics in original). Fifth, solidarity is often a major movement objective in itself. Finally, such action rejects representation in favor of participation and direct action (Melucci 1996: 102–103).

In empirical terms, the most common examples of these analytical and descriptive features of contemporary collective action are movements "arising around youth, urban, women's, ecological and pacifist, ethnic and cultural issues" (Melucci 1996: 97). These movements best illustrate the cultural, symbolic, and spiritual aspects of recent collective action. Whether approached analytically, descriptively, or empirically, however, the key question remains how collective action reflects and derives from, as well as opposes and challenges, the broader social formation of which it is a part.

This leads Melucci to conceptualize modern complex societies as based on the production of signs and the processing of information in accordance with the instrumental logic of administrative systems. Given this, the search for meaning and the decoding of information is central to social life in general and to collective action in particular. Contemporary conflicts are thus likely to emerge at the intersection of information production, symbolic resources, and social control. Because power is increasingly embedded in the flow and control of information and accompanied by strong conformity pressures, movements that challenge prevailing cultural codes strike directly at this new form of power.

As the arena of collective action shifts from the political to the cultural, traditional approaches that reduce it to political struggle address only a symptom and miss the novel features of new social movements. "The area of movements is now a 'sector' or a 'subsystem' of the social. Recognizing this autonomy forces us to revise dichotomies like 'state' and 'civil society.' The notion of 'movement' itself, which originally stood for an entity acting against the political and governmental system, has now been rendered inadequate as a description of the reality of reticular and diffuse forms of collective action" (Melucci 1996: 3–4).

Another feature of contemporary society concerns the fracturing of traditional bases of identity. The pace of change, plurality of memberships, and abundance of messages all serve to weaken traditional points of reference and sources of identity rooted in religious affiliation, local neighborhoods, political parties, or social classes. The result is a homelessness of personal identity that turns people into nomads of the present (Melucci 1989).

The erosion of traditional forms of identity has at least two consequences. First, it fosters a quest for individual identity and a culture of individual needs that becomes central to modern social life. Such trends are underscored by social technologies that convert previously deterministic zones of life to areas of choice. Consider how medical intervention has turned birth and death into social facts rather than natural events, how the separation of sexuality and reproduction has created new erotic potentials, how psychotherapy underwrites the search for self-realization, and how bodily transformations allow people to create new selves and identities.

Paradoxically enough, this new emphasis on meeting personal needs also fuels participation in new social movements as people join movements on the basis of an individualist logic of what makes sense for them to do in a quest for personal fulfillment.

The paradox is at least partially resolved in the late modern linkage of personal and planetary concerns: Individual survival and fulfilling personal needs are increasingly and self-evidently contingent on successfully addressing global problems of ecological preservation, resource sustainability, and conflict resolution.

Given this linkage, the valorization of personal needs is less a retreat from larger concerns than a bridge to them by providing motivation and fostering recruitment into new social movements. The latter also fulfill needs for belonging and a sense of "we-ness" through contemporary collective identities that arise through purposeful choice rather than ascriptive accidents. Precisely because they are not structurally determined, however, the construction of collective identities is a central task of the new movements.

Such construction takes place in "networks composed of a multiplicity of groups that are dispersed, fragmented and submerged in everyday life, and which act as cultural laboratories" (Melucci 1989: 60). Such loosely organized movements in the form of submerged networks precisely allow people to meet expressive and personal needs through associations with like-minded individuals while also providing the skeletal framework for more intensive, if episodic periods of political mobilization and public action.

These organizational forms have a self-referential quality. They are not merely an instrumental means to a goal; "they are a goal in themselves. Since collective action is focused on cultural codes, the *form* of the movement is itself a message, a symbolic challenge to the dominant codes" (Melucci 1989: 60; italics in original). The mere existence of a form of social organization that contradicts the prevailing, technocratic, instrumental rationality of administrative systems thus poses a subtle challenge to such systems; when it also fulfills deeply felt personal needs, that challenge is likely to grow.

These organizational qualities mean that contemporary collective action vacillates between visibility and latency. The latter phase nourishes collective action by sustaining alternative frameworks of meaning embedded in alternative lifestyles and communities. It also accounts for some of the unconventional features of new social movements, including their unstable membership, self-reflexivity, collective identity, information resources, and an awareness of global interdependence.

Contending that movements now operate not as characters but rather as signs or messages, Melucci (1989: 75–76) identifies three forms of symbolic challenge. Through prophecy, movements announce that alternative forms of rationality are possible. Through paradox, dominant codes are exaggerated to the point where their underlying irrationality becomes evident. Through representation, movements separate form and content to reveal the contradictions in prevailing systemic logic.

The target of such challenges is the elusive power of modern complex systems, which is less visible but more widely dispersed through bureaucratic networks. The systemic effect of symbolic challenges is "rendering power visible. The function of contemporary conflicts is to render visible the power that hides behind the rationality of administrative or organizational procedures" (Melucci 1989: 76). By making power visible, movements reveal it as a social construction rather than a natural force. They make it recognizable and negotiable in ways that were previously impossible.

The promise of new social movements resides less in achieving a specific agenda than in promoting democratization in society and in everyday life. This becomes crucial in postindustrial society where the demands of decision making erode the traditional distinction between the state and civil society and threaten an expansion of technocratic decision making into all spheres of life.

New social movements pose a potential counterweight to this tendency because their symbolic challenges foster free spaces located between the political system and the networks of everyday life. In these free spaces, ordinary people can consolidate new collective identities, find myriad forms of participation, and establish new modes of representation for their needs and interests. Through such mechanisms, new social movements can also foster a reconsideration of ultimate ends so often obscured in conventional political disputes.

Melucci's work thereby offers the most comprehensive synthesis of various strands of new social movement theories that emerged in the last two decades of the twentieth century. Given this status, it is ironic that Melucci has also been extremely wary about the ontological status of social movements in general and new social movements in particular.

Thus, he cautions that a "social movement is an object created by analysis; it does not coincide with the empirical forms of collective action" (Melucci 1981: 173) that are inevitably diverse and heterogeneous rather than unified and homogeneous. He also contends that the concept of social movements is somewhat outdated and that we should speak of networks or areas of contention rather than social movements. Finally, he explicitly rejects any essentialist notion of movements as tragic figures or historical personages guided by a grand design or universal plan of history.

The same cautions apply to discourses about new social movements, which too often reify the category into a distinctive type rather than guiding research into similarities and differences across movements and eras. Melucci ruefully notes that as "one of those who introduced the term 'new social movements' to sociological literature ... I have observed with embarrassment the progressive ontologization of this expression, which in the course of the debate came to be characterized as a veritable 'paradigm'" (Melucci 1988: 335).

This has promoted a very misguided debate: "both the critics of the 'newness' of the 'new movements' and the proponents of the 'newness paradigm' commit the same epistemological mistake: they consider contemporary collective phenomena to constitute unitary empirical objects ... The controversy strikes one as futile" (Melucci 1996: 5). The real issue is whether there are new elements that can be attributed to a new social order that is distinct from the previous order of industrial capitalism.

These cautionary notes recur throughout Melucci's writings. Given his centrality to this approach, it is all the more striking that he holds the very concept of "new social movements" at arm's length. For Melucci, the phrase "new social movement" is less an ontological claim about empirical realities than a sensitizing concept to formulate research questions and guide investigations into contemporary collective action.

CONCLUSION

New social movement theories offer a robust alternative to resource mobilization, political process, and social constructionist approaches. Although they have dominated European theorizing for decades, their U.S. reception is a more convoluted story.

Melucci's (1980) writings became available in English three decades ago, alongside Habermas's (1981) early statement on the topic. In 1985, the journal *Social Research* published a special issue on new social movements featuring articles by Touraine, Melucci, and many others. By the late 1980s, international conferences and symposia were trumpeting the virtues of cross-fertilization and the prospect of a synthesis in which resource mobilization theory would explain the "how," whereas new social movement theory would explain the "why" of movements (Klandermans and Tarrow 1988).

These collaborations fostered stronger connections between the empirical research agendas of scholars on both sides of the Atlantic and led to some important conceptual refinements. Despite the promising rhetoric, however, virtually all U.S. interpreters rebuffed or misinterpreted crucial aspects of new social movement theory. One reason was clashing theoretical styles. It was always simplistic to think that diverse theories could be synthesized by combining "how and why" questions or integrating macro-, meso-, and micro-levels. This is only feasible if theories rest on compatible epistemological assumptions.

In reality, the historical, speculative, philosophical and normative dimensions of European social theory have remained foreign to the analytical, empirical, scientific, and sometimes positivist approach of U.S. sociological theory. As a result, U.S. theorists "cherry-picked" certain concepts out of new social movement theories, but they never confronted, much less accepted, the foundational assumptions and epistemological roots of such theories.

Rather than a synthesis, U.S. and European approaches look more like ships passing in the night. An example is the debate over the "newness" of these movements. In the European context, this debate was productive because it retained the idea that "newness" was as much an attribute of postindustrial society as it was a quality of movements; the concept was a sensitizing device to explore connections between the two.

In the U.S. context, "newness" was interpreted as a strictly empirical claim about movements in a certain chronological period, divorced from any larger analysis of the surrounding social context. This led to some devastating critiques demonstrating that "old" nineteenth century movements had many of the supposed features of late-twentieth century new social movements (Calhoun 1993; Tucker 1991). Although it is easy to show that "old" and "new" are not mutually exclusive categories, however, the debate is "futile," to use Melucci's (1996: 5) term, because this was never the claim nor the intent of new social movement theorists in the first place.

The most dramatic evidence of this mismatch concerns the central claim of new social movement theory: that different social formations foster distinct types of movements. It is precisely these connections that are lost in the American discussion. Thus, the introduction to a popular reader on new social movements (Larana, Johnston, and Gusfield 1994) identifies eight characteristics of such movements; none make substantive reference to the historically specific social formation these movements inhabit.

What seems lost on American theorists is more readily evident through European eyes. In the words of one practitioner, the "main focus of the European tradition is on broad social-structural changes ... Within the European debate, the concept of 'new social movements' occupies a central place. Typically, these movements are seen as carriers of a new political paradigm and heralds of a new era labeled postindustrial, postmaterialist, postmodern, or postfordist ... In the United States, on the other hand, not even the concept of 'new social movements' has been able to gain currency, and little attention has been paid to the macrodevelopments that are central to the European discussion" (Kriesi et al. 1995: 238).

The American interpretation of new social movement theories thereby filtered out their most distinctive claims and cherry-picked new "variables" such as identity to add to the empiricist approach. As we will see in the next chapter, the dubious quest for theoretical synthesis became a dominant theme in social movement theory at the end of the twentieth century.

Part IV
Recent Trends

Chapter Eleven

Alternatives, Critiques, and Synthesis?

The paradigms examined in the previous section comprised the main contours of social movement theory in the last three decades of the twentieth century. There were, however, other strands of work that coexisted alongside these perspectives. The major paradigms and alternative strands created a rich context for critical debates, conceptual cross-fertilization, and potential syntheses.

This chapter accordingly pursues three tasks. First, it briefly reviews some alternative strands of work that largely fell outside the major paradigms discussed so far. Second, it returns to those paradigms to identify major criticisms from rival perspectives as well as adherents. Finally, it sketches an attempted synthesis of perspectives, noting the emergent difficulties and subsequent criticisms of doing so.

THE CONTEXT

Compared with previous decades, the 1980s and 1990s brought theoretical eclecticism to sociology. Although this frustrated advocates of a rigorous, unified, positivist program of theoretical development, it encouraged revisiting older theories, developing newer ones, or combining diverse conceptual approaches.

This climate invited metatheoretical discussions that analyzed theories and ideas in terms of their foundational assumptions (Ritzer 1991; Collins 1994). It also focused attention on theoretical dichotomies such as structure versus agency or micro- versus macro-levels, inviting efforts to reconcile such dualisms (Giddens 1986; Bourdieu 1977).

This theoretical eclecticism was matched by methodological diversity. Although positivist and statistical approaches hardly disappeared, they were decentered as qualitative, critical, and narrative methods acquired new legitimacy.

These disciplinary developments reflected larger intellectual currents. The cultural turn in social theory had its counterpart in the revival of cultural sociology. More broadly, although postpositivism, poststructuralism, and postmodernism had arguably less influence on sociology than on some other disciplines, their concern with rethinking foundational assumptions and interrogating power dynamics inevitably shaped sociology in general and the study of movements in particular.

This was the context in which a new generation of graduate students and faculty entered the discipline of sociology. Although some traditional subfields languished, the areas of race and ethnicity, class and power, sex and gender, and peace and justice became particularly popular as reflected in the growth of American Sociological Association (ASA) sections in these areas. These also tended to be more politicized areas of study that eschewed "objectivity" in favor of a more partisan approach.

Similar growth swelled the ranks of the ASA section on collective behavior/social movements throughout the 1980s and 1990s. In this period, social movements went from a marginal subfield to a "hot" topic in much the same way that deviance had been "hot" in the 1960s and 1970s. Ironically, the study of movements heated up at the same time many movements were cooling down. The dramatic mass movements of the 1960s protest cycle had largely disappeared or been coopted, preempted, routinized, or institutionalized by the time social movements became a hot topic of study.

Despite the irony, there remained sufficient collective action to sustain this new interest. Even newer "new movements" appeared in the form of gay and lesbian mobilizations; anti-AIDS activism; antinuclear, peace, and justice movements; anti-intervention and antiapartheid mobilizations; animal rights campaigns; environmental justice campaigns; and many others.

On the international scene, Solidarity's challenge to Soviet domination in Poland provided a template for collective action throughout Eastern Europe that helped bring down the Soviet Union. Even these dramatic events were soon eclipsed by transnational campaigns opposing neoliberal globalization that continue to gain momentum.

Although not always resembling 1960s mass movements, collective action thereby continued at home and abroad. Indeed, this continuity could be seen as a further institutionalization of the social movement sector (McCarthy and Zald 1977) or a "movement society" (Tarrow 1994) as a permanent feature of contemporary social life.

There thus emerged an interesting parallelism between the institutionalization of at least some forms of collective action and a more institutionalized presence for those who studied them. It was in this context in which alternative approaches thrived, critical debates unfolded, and theoretical syntheses were proposed.

SOME ALTERNATIVE THEORETICAL THREADS

Describing social movement theory in terms of rival paradigms risks exaggerating the coherence within and exclusivity between them. In reality, many concepts, themes, and even theorists are linked to more than one paradigm, and some important ideas never found a congenial home within any of them.

This section discusses some of these threads. It is neither exhaustive nor representative. The more modest goal is to provide some illustrations of work at some tangent to the paradigms already discussed. In some cases, this was a deliberate response to the limitations or shortcomings of a dominant paradigm. This review thereby foreshadows some of the major criticisms of the leading paradigms.

One such thread underscored emotions in collective action. Because this gained even more momentum at the turn of the century, it will be discussed in a later chapter. Here, we explore four other strands: the theoretical significance of mass defiance; the analysis of revolutions; an emerging emphasis on cultural dimensions of movements; and examples of explicitly normative, politically progressive work on social movements.

Piven and Cloward's (1979) analysis of mass defiance put them at odds with both resource mobilization and political process theories in at least three ways. First (as discussed in Chapter Six), they take issue with Tilly's dismissal of breakdown explanations of collective action. For Piven and Cloward, protest is unusual because social structures and institutions routinely preclude opportunities for it. It is only on rare occasions that society's regulatory capacity and everyday routines loosen their grip and that meaningful protest becomes possible.

Second, these authors criticize attempts to "normalize" collective action. Although this may have originated in an attempt to rescue collective action from connotations of deviance and irrationality, it obscures the most distinctive elements of mass protest.

Collective action is "normalized" when it is seen as an extension of politics as usual. It is normalized when the distinction between normative and nonnormative tactics is minimized. It is further normalized when movements are operationalized as movement organizations similar to interest groups or lobbying associations. It is finally normalized when the tactical violence of protesters is downplayed.

For Piven and Cloward, the power of protest derives precisely from how it differs from conventional politics; thus, the distinction between normative and nonnormative protest is crucial. The former pursues its goals through widely accepted rules of the game; the latter challenges the rules themselves. Non-normative protest poses a much more basic challenge by "defying the legitimacy of prevailing norms themselves" (Piven and Cloward 1992: 303). Although acknowledging that this distinction is not always clear, "a riot is clearly not an electoral rally, and both authorities and participants know the difference" (Piven and Cloward 1992: 303).

The third and most basic issue concerns the role of organization in collective action. Although differing in their emphasis on formal organization or less formal networks, both resource mobilization and political process theory see organization as a vital resource and virtual prerequisite to movement success.

Piven and Cloward, by contrast, revive Michels's iron law of oligarchy and see formal organization as signaling the demise of effective protest. In their view, movement organizations seek self-preservation, divert scarce resources, and create cooptable leaders. Because organizational leaders are separated from the mass base, they discourage mass defiance and unruly protest in favor of more conventional and less threatening tactics. Although debatable as a broad generalization, they present evidence for these claims in the case of poor people's movements (even as the latter remain vaguely defined; Piven and Cloward 1979).

Although Piven and Cloward challenged dominant movement paradigms, the study of revolutions has been largely divorced from social movement theory. The point of departure for modern theories of revolution was Barrington Moore's (1966) survey of democratic, communist, and fascist paths to modernization where differing combinations of social classes sponsored and benefited from revolutions against the old order.

In a founding statement of the political process perspective, Tilly invited scholars to adopt a broad research agenda in *From Mobilization to Revolution* (1978) and offered a conceptual framework for analyzing how revolutionary situations led to various types of revolutionary outcomes. The invitation was largely ignored because movement scholars focused on more limited types of collective action, leaving a void concerning revolutions.

The void was filled by Skocpol's (1979) work that followed Barrington Moore's strategy of detailed case studies to advance a theoretical understanding of great revolutions. Reviewing previous theories, Skocpol finds some utility in both Marxist and political-conflict theories (exemplified by Tilly). Even so, she proposes an alternative structural perspective on the causes, courses, and consequences of great revolutions.

The first premise of this perspective is that revolutions are better explained in terms of broad structural forces than voluntaristic purposive agents. There are multiple problems with this voluntarist image. It implies that social order rests on consensus and that the loss of legitimacy is a major blow to regime stability. It obscures the actual causes of revolutions, including how challengers acquire the capacity (as opposed to the will) to rebel. It oversimplifies a more complex reality consisting of institutionally determined situations and relations (Skocpol 1979: 18).

The second premise is that these institutional structures include not just domestic but also international forces. In contrast with modernization theories that focus on the internal dynamics of social change, Skocpol emphasizes the international structure of competing states. As societies undergo modernization processes at different rates and engage in military conflict and economic competition with other states, it is often the international context that begins the destabilization that ultimately provokes revolution.

The third premise is that states have at least a potential autonomy that gives them a central role in revolutionary processes. States and their leaders are not reducible to society or economics; their leaders often stand in opposition to dominant classes or political elites in a complex power struggle. With the rise of an international state system, these elites have interests and agendas shaped by global pressures and competition as much as or more than by domestic political forces. With these premises "Skocpol's social-structural approach became the dominant theory of revolutions for the last two decades of the twentieth century" (Goldstone 2002: 211).

This dominance was short-lived, however, as other cases, new revolutions, and different factors were considered or reconsidered. Surveying a broader range of cases suggested that "international pressures would only create state crises if states were already weakened by fiscal strain" (Goldstone 2002: 213). When fiscal strain was accompanied by declining economic opportunities, a perception of regime vulnerability, and intra-elite conflicts, then revolutionary situations became more likely.

From an even broader perspective, sustained population growth in preindustrial economies with limited production capacity often triggers these more proximate causes. There is a striking correlation from 1500 to 1800 whereby revolutionary challenges waxed and waned in tandem with broader demographic trends of population growth and stability. Although this helps explain the causes of revolutions, Goldstone also restores a role for ideology in shaping "the outcome and trajectory of the postrevolutionary state" (Goldstone 2002: 214).

Whereas Piven and Cloward's work was at odds with dominant paradigms, Goldstone sees theories about revolutions and social movements as "converging on similar sets of conditions and process for protest and revolutions" (Goldstone 2002: 217), including political opportunities, mobilization networks, and cognitive framing.

Indeed, Goldstone proposes an evolutionary link between movements and revolutions whereby opposition deemed legitimate by authorities becomes a social movement, whereas opposition regarded as illegitimate may become a revolutionary challenge. It may well be that "[t]heories of revolution are thus making strong progress on the problem of integrating revolutionary theory with the analysis of other kinds of social protest" (Goldstone 2002: 218).

Although there may be convergence with mainstream movement theory on this issue, another area of divergence concerns the role of culture. With the partial exception of social constructionist approaches, the major movement paradigms have emphasized structural forces, organizational dynamics, and political contention. This has prompted a call to "bring culture back in" to the study of movements. Although nothing as coherent as a "cultural paradigm" has emerged, there has been a lot of work moving away from mainstream theory on a cultural tangent.

One early and somewhat idiosyncratic effort advocated a cognitive approach to social movements (Eyerman and Jamison 1991). This views movements as engaged in cognitive praxis or knowledge creation along with the cultivation of collective identity. Such cognitive praxis has been ignored in the both the voluntarist emphasis of U.S. theory and the deterministic orientation of European theory.

Better models of cognitive praxis are to be found in Habermas's account of communicative rationality, in which knowledge claims are justified through discourse, or in Melucci's view of movements as symbolic challenges whose cultural codes unmask dominant power. For Eyerman and Jamison, cognitive praxis is the core activity of a social movement; they are first and foremost laboratories of collective learning that develop new ways of understanding social processes.

These modes of understanding cannot be reduced to secondary frames or supporting ideologies; they are rather constitutive of movements themselves. Movements foster change when these practices transcend the movement to create new types of knowledge that become part of society's self-understanding.

Seeing movements as knowledge producers underscores the role of movement intellectuals who articulate the interests and cognitive praxis of the movement. Such activity creates "public intellectuals" who take society as an object of analysis and develop new understandings of that object for society as a whole. A sociology of knowledge approach is thus required to see how the cognitive praxis of movements makes a major contribution to the cultural transformation of social orders.

There are many ways to reintroduce culture into the study of social movements. Even a political process theorist such as McAdam (1994) acknowledged the structural bias of movement theory and the need to restore culture in at least three different senses.

First, movements often have important cultural roots alongside structural causes. This may occur through framing activities and the availability of master frames, through newly expanded cultural opportunities, or through the identification of ideological or cultural contradictions in dominant belief systems. Long-standing activist subcultures can also play a crucial role in sustaining movements and ideas through periods of abeyance until opportunities for activism improve.

Second, movements develop their own internal cultures that often become "worlds unto themselves that are characterized by distinctive ideologies, collective identities, behavioral routines, and material cultures" (McAdam 1994: 45–46). Over time, movement cultures change with the influx of new constituencies or generations, posing challenges to, and opportunities for, movement continuity and effectiveness.

Third, movements have cultural consequences for the larger society that often transcend their structural or political impacts. These may include new collective identities, alternative norms and values, or novel cultural artifacts. McAdam's admittedly sketchy overview thus identifies some effects of culture in movement origins, maintenance, transformation, and outcomes.

By the mid-1990s, the editors of an anthology on culture and social movements proclaimed that "we are headed toward a 'softer' set of factors than those of the past—ones that are at their heart mental and subjective" (Johnston and Klandermans 1995: 3). Although claiming that "we may well witness something close to paradigmatic changes" (Johnston and Klandermans 1995: 20), the authors advocate an integration of cultural factors with organization, mobilization, opportunity, and framing.

If the goal is to grasp the interaction of these factors, three types of research questions may advance that goal (Johnston and Klandermans 1995: 22–23). The first concerns how culture can act as both an opportunity and a constraint in relation to collective action. The second concerns how a deeper understanding of framing will reveal connections between mental life and outward behavior. Finally (echoing McAdam) there are questions about the creation of internal movement culture and the circumstances under which it becomes its own opportunity or constraint.

These are relatively early indications of renewed attention to cultural processes that had been marginalized by dominant perspectives on social movements. As we shall see, the attempt to restore a cultural emphasis to the study of social movements became an enduring theme into the twenty-first century.

A final example of work that unfolded at a tangent to mainstream movement theory is normatively oriented, politically progressive analyses of social movements. Eschewing any pretense of objectivity, these authors write not about movements but for and from movements. They advocate progressive politics and societal democratization.

Such approaches often presume a fundamental conflict between capitalism and democracy, in which the former threatens democratic participation by subordinating it to institutional, bureaucratic, and technocratic power and decision making. One antidote to such domination is the role of social movements in creating free spaces that foster democratic change in the United States (Evans and Boyte 1986).

In a delightfully jargon-free summary of the history of U.S. social movements, Evans and Boyte see progressive social movements as the major bulwark against capitalist domination. Movements have played this role by establishing and defending free spaces between private lives and institutional forces in which ordinary citizens can act with dignity, independence, and vision. Such spaces allow various constituencies to acquire new self-respect, group identity, and leadership skills.

These free spaces also have vital roots in strong communities and the dense networks of daily life. Although many movements initially emerge from such communities as a defensive response to some threat, the most effective ones create free spaces that empower ordinary people and foster democratic initiatives. It is the transformative potential of free spaces and the movements that create them that makes them vital to societal democratization.

A parallel argument notes that everyday life and "making history" are separate realms in American society (Flacks 1988). Elites can make history in the conduct of their everyday lives, whereas most people experience a gulf between the two. Indeed, Flacks suggests that people grudgingly accept powerlessness as an acceptable trade-off as long as elites maintain the material base and social conditions of everyday life.

This bargain was most evident in the post–World War II era, but it unraveled with the increased participation, social activism, legitimation crises, and conservative backlashes of the 1960s and 1970s. Although resistance and liberation movements have been vital, the most important movements promoted a democratic consciousness that narrows the gap between everyday life and making history so that the latter becomes a populist, participatory project.

For Flacks, this democratizing impulse links popular movements throughout U.S. history; each has narrowed the gap between daily life and making history by expanding the sphere of decision making for ordinary people. If one searches for a viable political left in the United States, it is not in major parties or organizations but rather in those social movements that have advanced democratization of the larger society (Flacks 1988).

These advocates criticize conventional academic work on social movements as "abstracted empiricism." The quest for variables, classification, hypotheses, and generalizations decontextualizes and reifies movements. The ironic result is that "the more systematic, theoretical, and coherent the field of social movement research has become, the less it seems able to tell us much about what is happening in the world we actually inhabit"(Darnovsky, Epstein, and Flacks 1995: xvi).

These strands selectively illustrate the vibrant work that has occurred outside of, on a tangent to, or in direct confrontation with prevailing movement paradigms. We turn now to the critical debates surrounding those paradigms.

PARADIGMATIC DEBATES AND CRITIQUES

The last decade of the twentieth century did not feature new paradigms; it instead was a time for the development, expansion, and modification of existing paradigms in response to critical debates from within, between, and outside them.

Earlier chapters noted that the resource mobilization and political process approaches are sibling rivals sharing some assumptions while differing on others. This duality is also evident in criticisms of this family. Some are aimed at common assumptions underlying both, whereas others target one or the other version of the theory.

Resource mobilization theory in particular attracted much critical fire. Although many of these criticisms were valid, their sheer volume and repetitiveness also reflected the status of the target. Resource mobilization had so thoroughly dethroned the collective behavior approach and so quickly became hegemonic that for a time almost no other work could be done without a ritualistic critique of these reigning ideas.

As noted earlier, the initial criticisms of resource mobilization theory were that it downplayed politics and political interests, was indifferent to ideology, had a highly rationalistic image of movement actors, minimized the role of grievances, ignored group solidarity, and adopted a "cynical tone" (Perrow 1979).

McAdams's articulation of the political process alternative also grew out of particular criticisms of resource mobilization theory. These included its tendency to blur the distinction between excluded groups and established polity members, its overemphasis on the importance and benign nature of elite funding sources, and its underemphasis on the importance of the mass base and indigenous resources.

The political process sibling stressed the political dimension of collective action that had been understated by resource mobilization. Indeed, its unrelenting focus on political struggle attracted criticisms that political process theory either reduced all collective action to state-centered, political challenges or simply ignored campaigns with different targets, logics, or goals. It was also seen as deterministic, thereby obscuring the role of agency in collective action.

Alongside these accusations, perhaps the most common criticism of political process theory was that its overly generalized concept of political opportunity was "in danger of becoming a sponge that soaks up virtually every aspect of the social movement environment ... Used to explain so much, it may ultimately explain nothing at all" (Gamson and Meyer 1996: 275).

By the early 1990s, both siblings were being criticized for minimizing discontent, grievances, and ideology. The privileging of formal social movement organization (especially in the resource mobilization version) was challenged and the role of alternative, informal social movement communities was suggested (Buechler 1993). The meso-level focus was also faulted for diverting attention from micro- and macro-levels of collective action.

Even more fundamentally, the model of the rational actor attracted persistent challenges as inadequate for explaining collective action (Fireman and Gamson 1979; Ferree 1992; Crossley 2002). This abstract, individualized, and decontextualized view of the social actor obscured the truly collective nature of action, identity, and interests in movements as well as their often diverse membership.

Most fundamentally, the resource mobilization and political process approaches were widely faulted for ignoring the multiple ways in which movements are embedded and engaged in cultural processes alongside political or instrumental ones. Although these cultural processes are multifaceted, perhaps most obvious are practices of meaning and signification that would become central in the social constructionist and framing alternatives to resource mobilization and political process theory.

McCarthy and Zald (2002) subsequently offered their own assessment and response to critics. They begin by clarifying the implicit and explicit scope conditions of the theory, which is best suited to societies with strong voluntary associations, freedom of speech and assembly, a relatively open mass media, and a political system receptive to political action outside the electoral arena. Despite these conditions, they note that the theory has been successfully applied to a broader range of societies and conditions.

On the issue of the rational actor, they claim that "we are not now and never have been orthodox rational choice theorists" (McCarthy and Zald 2002: 543). At the same time, they acknowledge that their work was "nested in a concept of rational action" (McCarthy and Zald 2002: 543) that made it difficult to account for the collective nature or "jointness" of social movement participation.

The authors also acknowledge that the concept of resources went largely unexamined even as it figured centrally in the theory. They accept the criticism that at least in some cases it is prior insurgency that shakes loose new resources rather than resource availability that sparks insurgency (as they originally claimed).

McCarthy and Zald further acknowledge taking "sentiment pools" or change preferences at face value rather than examining the historical, cultural, and political processes that shape them. They also concede at least a soft version of Piven and Cloward's critique by granting that the more formalized and professionalized social movement organizations become, the more they are likely to advocate routinized, normative forms of protest rather than nonnormative, mass defiance.

On broader issues, the authors acknowledge both "a blindness to the role of culture in social movement processes" and "an underdeveloped analysis of the role of political opportunity" (McCarthy and Zald 2002: 555). In the case of culture, they claim not to have denied such processes but rather to have assumed them as background parameters so as to "put in the foreground organizational and macroenvironmental processes" (McCarthy and Zald 2002: 555).

The authors recognize competing paradigms, noting that the political process approach has probably become more prominent than resource mobilization. They also concede that grievances are important, but claim that "the question is when and how do they matter?" (McCarthy and Zald 2002: 557). Most generally, they conclude that although culture is important, "[w]hat is not clear is how cultural analysis complements RMT. Or does it supplant and contain it?" (McCarthy and Zald 2002: 558).

Although graciously acknowledging their critics, the authors make a case for the past impact, enduring vitality, and future prospects of resource mobilization theory; those prospects are bright to the extent that the theory can accommodate its critics and incorporate their insights into a broader but still cohesive framework.

The tendency of resource mobilization and political process theories to downplay grievances, ideology, and culture opened the door to social constructionist and framing approaches. Compared with their predecessors, the latter have attracted relatively less criticism. In part, this is because social constructionism simply arose later in this cycle of social movement theorizing than resource mobilization and political process theory.

More fundamentally, framing approaches never sought the wholesale displacement of preceding theories in the way that resource mobilization/political process approaches appeared to do. Framing advocates consistently acknowledged the importance of organization, resources, and mobilization. They proceeded to argue, however, that such ideas were incomplete and needed to be complemented by a renewed focus on the cultural dimensions of collective action.

Although these factors may have led to relatively fewer and more muted criticisms of social constructionism, it did not escape criticism altogether. Perhaps the most common criticism is the tendency to see movement frames in purely instrumental terms.

Thus, framing approaches often presume active leaders who invent frames to recruit passive followers who have little to say about the process. In other words, the emphasis is "from the organization to the individual, not the other way around. We are never told how the potential audience reacts to the marketing pitch of social movement organizations, and how this reaction affects the interpretive process" (Aguirre 1994: 268).

From a somewhat different angle, this instrumental view of framing is problematic because it suggests frames are simply a cultural "resource" alongside material ones. This may obscure the more fundamental nature of frames; they "are not objects or utensils in the objective world, which agents can pick up and use like tools. They are constitutive aspects of the subjectivity of social agents" (Crossley 2002: 141).

This constitutive role includes emotion as well as cognition, but the "many definitions and applications of frames and framing processes deal almost entirely with their cognitive components" (Jasper 1998: 413). Although motivational framing would seem to include emotions, it is one of the least discussed aspects of framing processes. Because "[c]ognitive agreement alone does not result in action" (Jasper 1998: 413), this lack of attention to emotions prevents framing theory from convincingly explaining how people actually become motivated to act collectively (see also Goodwin and Jasper 2004).

Such criticisms hint at larger difficulties in using frame analysis to "complement" a resource mobilization/political process approach. A complementary relationship implies compatible, underlying assumptions. The instrumental, calculative worldview of resource mobilization/political process theory, however, is simply antithetical to the more fundamental, culturally constitutive role of signification processes. Put succinctly, "[a]gents' constructions of reality cannot strike them as constructions, or else they would lack the accent of reality ... " (Crossley 2002: 142).

Just as McCarthy and Zald provided unique insight into the status of the resource mobilization approach, Benford (1997) has offered an "insider's critique" of framing theory. For example, he notes that although the approach has inspired conceptual development and numerous case studies, it lacks systematic empirical work comparing cases so as to clarify ambiguities and resolve questions about framing processes.

Benford also faults framing work for a descriptive bias that has led to countless names for various frames at the expense of a more analytic focus. Frames have also been treated as overly static, with insufficient attention to how they evolve and change. This has fostered a certain monolithic tendency in which frames are taken to reflect a single reality rather than conflicting or interacting interpretations of multiple "realities."

Some framing work also suffers from reification or reductionism. The former treats frames as if they were things, with attendant dangers of anthropomorphizing frames or movements and thereby neglecting the role of agency and emotions. Problems of reductionism treat frames as purely cognitive properties of individual actors, again ignoring their collective, dynamic, and interactive nature.

Finally, Benford's critique acknowledges that "our analyses of framing processes often have a built-in, top-down bias" (Benford 1997: 421). This elite bias is fostered by the most common methods in use: sampling and interviewing movement leaders or key activists and treating them as representative of the broader movement. Based on these friendly criticisms, Benford offers an admittedly ambitious agenda for future work on framing that would transcend these problems and enrich the perspective.

New social movement theories have also received their share of critical attention. For those who equate movements with state-centered, political challenges, the pre-, post-, or antipolitical nature of new social movements all but disqualifies them from consideration as social movements in the first place (Tilly 2004).

For those advocating a politically progressive, anticapitalist challenge, the problem is less with the theory than with the movements, whose symbolic, spiritual, lifestyle, and identity-oriented dimensions are seen as a capitulation to modern marketing strategies rather than a challenge to the logic of commodification (Boggs 1986; Epstein 1991; Kauffman 1990).

Other critiques have challenged the fundamental "newness" of these movements. Tarrow (1991) suggested that theorists have jumped the gun by prematurely proposing an entirely new category of movements. In reality, "new" movements may merely be the early stages of activism that subsequently coalesces into something quite conventional; hence, there is no need for claims of "newness."

Another challenge to "newness" locates such activism in a much broader, cyclical time frame. Since the rise of modernity, there have been waves of romantic or moral-idealistic challenges to the utilitarian, instrumental quality of modern life. "New" social movements may thus not be new at all, but rather be the latest wave of such antimodern movements dating back to the eighteenth century (Brand 1990).

The most direct challenge to claims of newness was historical in nature. New social movement theorists liked to characterize the "old" labor movement as monolithic and exclusively political, but this is something of a "straw man." In fact, a variety of nineteenth-century labor movements (Calhoun 1993) and French syndicalism in particular (Tucker 1991) closely resemble "new" social movements in their blending of expressive, identity-oriented, life-politics with more conventional political challenges.

Melucci has offered the most cogent response to this criticism. Whereas he and other new social movement theorists used the term as a sensitizing concept to guide research, critics have "ontologized" the category (Melucci 1988: 335), leading to the epistemological mistake of considering "contemporary collective phenomena to constitute unitary empirical objects" and creating a "futile controversy" (Melucci 1996: 5).

In the context of these critical debates, Melucci's *Challenging Codes* (1996) is an interesting text. On the one hand, it summarizes almost two decades of theoretical development and empirical research on contemporary "information societies" and the new social movements they inspire. On the other hand, it incorporates opportunity, mobilization, and framing while insisting on the social constructionist origins of these factors. It may be read both as an acknowledgement of the weaknesses of new social movement theory and a reassertion of the ontologically fluid, socially constructed, interactively negotiated nature of contemporary collective action.

In this respect, Melucci did more to incorporate American ideas into his perspective than American theorists did with new social movement insights. This became evident in the proposed synthesis of the mid-1990s to which we now turn.

AN ATTEMPTED SYNTHESIS

From the mid-1980s to the mid-1990s, major international conferences on social movements were held almost annually. This cross-fertilization partially blurred the distinctions between American and European approaches, undercut theoretical provincialism, and encouraged a more comparative perspective in the analysis of social movements (McAdam, McCarthy, and Zald 1996a: xii).

These processes also led to proclamations of an emerging "synthetic, comparative perspective on social movements that transcends the limits of any single, theoretical approach to the topic" (McAdam, McCarthy, and Zald 1996b: 2). This synthesis sought to incorporate most if not all major theoretical approaches under the broad rubrics of political opportunities, mobilizing structures, and framing processes.

The concept of political opportunities was derived most directly from the political process approach of Tilly, McAdam, and Tarrow. It was also prominent, however, in some strands of new social movement theory. Whereas opportunity was treated in the United States as a variable over time that explained the emergence of particular movements, it was studied in the European context as involving variations across space that afforded greater or lesser openings for collective action in different societies.

The importance of mobilizing structures has become evident from work in both the resource mobilization and political process traditions. Although the former emphasized formal social movement organizations, political process theory recognized informal organizational networks and related settings such as churches or universities that facilitated mobilization. The concept of mobilizing structures is meant to transcend a sterile debate between these alternatives by recognizing the viability of both.

The role of framing processes was, of course, the contribution of social constructionist approaches. This emphasis on the role of ideas in refining vague discontent into collective grievances had important roots in the collective behavior tradition, but framing represents other theoretical traditions as well. It resonates with the emphasis among new social movement scholars on culture, meaning, and identity. It is also anticipated in political process theory's recognition of the role of cognitive liberation.

Concerning movement origins and emergence, the proponents of the synthesis emphasize political opportunity as the key variable accounting for the episodic appearance of movements. At the same time, they acknowledge that opportunity is necessary but not sufficient; without some initial organization and nascent frames, movements are not likely to arise even in response to opportunities. Once movements are underway, it is the interactive dynamics of all three factors that determine their course and outcome (McAdam, McCarthy, and Zald 1996b).

This proposed synthesis was a bold attempt to find a center that would hold together diverse strands of movement theory and research. It was a worthy effort if only for the dialogue it fostered and responses it provoked. Having said that, many found the proposed synthesis less than convincing.

It is worth noting that its advocates represent only two of the three perspectives in the synthesis; there is no comparable spokesperson for framing or a cultural analysis. More significantly, the synthesis could be construed as a "makeover" of the political process approach; the former's three dimensions mirror the latter's triad of political opportunity, indigenous organization, and cognitive liberation (standing in for "framing processes"). No other paradigm is represented in all three dimensions of the synthesis.

Although some paradigms are overrepresented, others are given short shrift. The synthesis claims to represent new social movement theory's interest in opportunity, culture, and identity, but this is a highly selective borrowing of ideas divorced from the organic context of the parent theory. The central claim about links between new societal types and corresponding movements is completely absent from the synthesis. No other paradigm in the synthesis underwent such radical conceptual surgery.

The third element of the triumvirate—framing processes—serves conflicting purposes. On the one hand, the initial discussion of its role in the synthesis is to "bring culture back in" by acknowledging a diverse grab bag of prior concepts and traditions, including collective attribution, social construction, social-psychological dynamics, the collective behavior tradition, new social movement theory, and cognitive liberation.

On the other hand, the existing literature is faulted for equating the framing concept with "any and all cultural dimensions of social movements" (McAdam, McCarthy, and Zald 1996b: 6). The solution to this problem is to "define framing rather narrowly as referring to the conscious *strategic efforts by groups of people to fashion shared understandings of the world and of themselves that legitimate and motivate collective action*" (McAdam, McCarthy, and Zald 1996b: 6; italics in original). It is hard not to read this as a "bait and switch" that claims more for the synthesis than it actually delivers.

The proposal thus anoints a hierarchy rather than producing a genuine synthesis. Resource mobilization and political process theory provide the core ideas. Framing is included as a junior partner. New social movement theory and cultural questions in general are marginalized despite nods in their direction. Put succinctly, "in spite of this effort at synthesis, political opportunities are clearly privileged, and the cultural dimension is limited to its strategic aspects. Hence, structure has the edge over culture in this book" (Giugni 1998: 373).

This view was elaborated when Jeff Goodwin and James Jasper set out to write a review of McAdam, McCarthy, and Zald's (1996a) volume. Their work mushroomed into a paper, a special issue of *Sociological Forum* (1999), and finally an edited volume with expanded content including rebuttals. It illustrates how the synthesis did not resolve differences as much as provoke ongoing debates.

These critics fault the structural bias of political process theory for leading to claims that are "tautological, trivial, inadequate, or just plain wrong" (Goodwin and Jasper 2004: 4). It is not just that structural factors are emphasized; it is also that when other factors are considered, they "are often analyzed as though they were structural factors" (Goodwin and Jasper 2004: 4).

Consider opportunity. It is typically seen in structural or political terms. It therefore directs attention to political, state-oriented movements rather than cultural or expressive movements. Finally, its widespread adoption means that it is in danger of becoming a tautological, catch-all answer for central questions about movements.

The same issues plague the synthesis itself, which they regard as an updated version of McAdam's political process model. Even while acknowledging other factors, "structural biases have led 'mobilizing structures' to be specified so *broadly* that the political process model becomes trivial, if not (once again) tautological, while 'cultural framing' has been specified so *narrowly* that it fails to capture some of the most important ways that culture matters for movements" (Goodwin and Jasper 2004: 19; italics in original).

Concerning mobilizing structures, the critics claim they are often not "pre-existing" or "indigenous," but rather result from movement strategies to create networks through the "independent importance of cultural persuasion" (Goodwin and Jasper 2004: 21). Concerning framing, there is a dual problem. The synthesis only recognizes strategic framing, reducing it to yet another "resource." Even on its own terms, however, the framing approach suffers from an ideational, cognitive bias that ignores affectual, emotional processes in collective action.

In the end, Goodwin and Jasper are wary of all invariant models, dominant paradigms, and alleged syntheses. Each relies too much on "conceptual stretching" that dilutes the clear and specific meanings of terms for the sake of incorporating other elements. Most crucially, such unitary approaches tend to obscure the ways in which "cultural and strategic processes define and create the factors usually presented as 'structural'" (Goodwin and Jasper 2004: 28).

To their credit, Goodwin and Jasper's (2004) volume contains rebuttals and responses from defenders of the synthesis as well as theorists with different takes on the entire debate. Suffice it to say that if one measure of a proposal is the attention it receives and the commentary it provokes, then the McAdam/McCarthy/Zald synthesis was a clear success in this regard.

CONCLUSION

Although the proposed synthesis was faulted on many grounds, any such undertaking was daunting at best. Just because theories address different levels of analysis or emphasize different variables, it does not follow that they can simply be combined into a synthesis. To do so ignores the differing domain assumptions, epistemological presuppositions, and theoretical styles that distinguish the philosophical, normative bent of new social movement theory; the processual, interactive emphasis of social constructionism; and the structural, organizational accent of resource mobilization and political process theory.

Combining these approaches amounts to a "shotgun marriage" yielding a weak synthesis at best. Some of its plausibility derives less from its logical coherence than from its resonance with intellectual, disciplinary, and national dynamics. Thus, the incorporation of framing reflects a larger accommodation with symbolic interactionism in sociological theory more generally; it provides both an agency-centered, processual counterweight to theoretical tendencies toward reification and determinism as well as a partial acknowledgement of the cultural turn in social theory.

The deflection of new social movement theory was foreordained because it is holistic, philosophical, and critical in precisely those places where American social theory has historically been elementarist, empirical, and objective. For better and worse, the synthesis reflects its American roots as a middle-range theory using comparative methods to explore the interaction of multiple variables to arrive at empirical generalizations.

The centrality of resource mobilization and political process theories in the synthesis also reflects their prominence in mainstream literature at the time. In the same year the proposed synthesis appeared (1996), an informal survey of *American Journal of Sociology* and *American Sociological Review* reveals numerous articles on social movements (compared with other topics and previous issues). Virtually every one, however, draws upon resource mobilization/political process assumptions and concepts (Buechler 2000: 52–53). Despite calls to bring culture back in, it remained very much "out" by this measure at this time.

A broader reading of the movement literature of the 1990s suggests not so much a synthesis but rather "conceptual poaching." This means "appropriating the language and issues of a different paradigm and incorporating them as a minor theme in a preexisting paradigm that undergoes no fundamental change in the process" (Buechler 2000: 53).

As we have seen, concepts such as collective identity and (cross-national) political opportunity were poached from new social movement theory for incorporation in the synthesis. The inclusion of framing—but only in its strategic aspects—is another poach, evident in the synthesis and in related arguments that framings of the public good (Williams 1995) or identity (Bernstein 1997) are best understood as tactical resources deployed according to the instrumental logic of resource mobilization. From another angle, the concepts of identity (Hunt et al. 1994) and opportunity (Gamson and Meyer 1996) have been poached from other perspectives by framing advocates who argued that both are as much a matter of intersubjective definition as objective reality.

Although a more meaningful synthesis *might* be in the offing, conceptual poaching suggests something quite different: the defense and expansion of an existing paradigm by appropriating and colonizing the key ideas of rival perspectives. Such poaching occurs in multiple forms and directions, but it does not amount to a coherent synthesis of rival perspectives.

Despite attempts at synthesis, social movement theory at the turn of the twenty-first century remained rife with controversy over differing assumptions and approaches. The fundamental rift between structure and culture became especially evident in these debates, foreshadowing the separate rather than synthesized work that was in gestation at the time.

Chapter Twelve

Contentious Dynamics and Passionate Politics

The proposed synthesis examined in the previous chapter was the culmination of three decades of productive theorizing, paradigm development, and extensive research. Although many did not find the synthesis entirely persuasive, it nonetheless represented a robust and productive period in theorizing collective action.

Of all the difficulties with the proposed synthesis, perhaps most fundamental was its inability to convincingly overcome the rift between a long-standing structural emphasis and an emerging cultural focus. The "culturalists" were the biggest critics of the synthesis, which ironically inspired even more cultural explorations rather than bringing scholars together under a single tent.

There are several ways to describe social movement work at the turn of the century. This chapter does so by following the ongoing divide between these two emphases. In both cases, there was bold new work that nonetheless perpetuated the divide between these traditions.

The structuralist approach morphed into an even broader framework for analyzing dynamics of contention, including but going beyond conventional social movements. The culturalist approach continued to paint with a broad palette, but the dominant colors now emphasized the diverse emotions that play an undeniable role in collective action if not in recent theories about such action.

Two key texts that appeared in the same year symbolize the divide. *Dynamics of Contention* (McAdam, Tarrow, and Tilly 2001) offers a bold, cohesive, relational alternative to previous theorizing, while *Passionate Politics* (Goodwin, Jasper, and Polletta 2001b) provides a sprawling, multifaceted, wide-ranging exploration of how culture in general and emotion in particular shape collective action. This contrast says much about social movement theory at the turn of the century.

THE CONTEXT

The immediate context for this theoretical work was the confluence of all the paradigms that had gained recognition by the end of the twentieth century. These included resource mobilization, political process, and framing approaches alongside new social movement theory, broader cultural emphases, and ongoing collective behavior insights. Whether seen as elements of a weak synthesis or simply as freestanding approaches, this theoretical field provided robust inspiration for new departures.

Transcending this historically specific context was a broader intellectual current behind the entire history of social theory. For several centuries, Western philosophy, science, and subsequently social science presumed Cartesian dualisms that privileged mind over body, rationality over emotion, and public over private (Calhoun 2001). The presumption that cognition and emotion were opposites and that the former was preferable to the latter infused social theory from the beginning.

Within sociology specifically, Weber's types of social action distinguished and elevated rational over affectual action. Durkheim's analysis of ritual and collective effervescence accentuated the difference between, if not always the superiority of, rationality over emotion. European crowd theorists and American collective behavior analysts explicitly or implicitly reproduced the bias against emotions and their presumed irrationality.

One of the biggest sea changes in social movement theory unwittingly reinforced this dualistic bias. It occurred when resource mobilization theorists transcended the "hearts and minds" approach with the rational actor model. "Emotions were banished from the study of social movements, to a very large extent, in reaction against a tradition of collective behavior analysis that ran from Le Bon through Turner and Killian and Neil Smelser" (Calhoun 2001: 48). While rescuing movements from connotations of deviance and irrationality, "[w]ith the bathwater of some very serious biases, the baby of emotions was commonly thrown out" (Calhoun 2001: 48).

This longstanding bias in social movement theory was eventually undermined in several ways. Most broadly, the cultural turn in social theory fostered suspicion toward (instrumental) rationality and greater receptivity to myth, narrative, intuition, and emotion. Within sociology, new subfields emphasizing emotions and embodiment appeared as well.

The sociological analysis of emotions introduced concepts such as emotional labor and feeling norms to understand the social construction of emotions in diverse contexts (Hochschild 1983). This approach side-stepped old debates and dualistic assumptions while legitimating sociological interpretations of emotions. Once this door was opened, it was perhaps inevitable that (some) social movement theorists would walk through it.

Not all such theorists did so, however. Advocates of the contentious dynamics paradigm acknowledge that emotions accompany such activities but have been reluctant to accord them analytical or explanatory significance. They still emphasize politicized conflicts while examining them across a broader range of geographical locations, political contexts, and collective actors. Those favoring the impact of culture in general and emotions in particular have conducted their own case studies. Both perspectives combine important conceptual arguments with rich empirical illustrations.

DYNAMICS OF CONTENTION

The proposed synthesis discussed earlier tilted toward the political process model. Hence, it was striking that only five years later, McAdam, Tarrow, and Tilly (2001) announced a qualitative departure from their own model to the dynamics of contention. The new approach incorporated criticisms of the original model and the synthesis, even if it did not always move in directions that the critics might have hoped.

The new focus is on episodes of transgressive political contention rather than life-histories of social movements. In one sense, the frame is smaller because episodes come and go while movements can persist over decades. In another sense, the frame is dramatically enlarged to include "social movements, revolutions, strike waves, nationalism, democratization, and more" (McAdam, Tarrow, and Tilly 2001: 4). What links these different phenomena is not just that they are contentious episodes but also that they can be explained through a similar set of mechanisms and processes.

This approach promises to improve upon the "classic social movement agenda" as typified by the political process model and the 1996 synthesis. The classic agenda presumed single movement actors in democratic societies and sought to explain movement emergence, mobilization, framing, and the like. It offered static images of movement variables linked by "causal arrows" while the actual causal mechanisms remained unspecified.

In seeking to move beyond the limits of this model, the authors discuss structural and rationalist analyses as well as phenomenological and cultural approaches. They acknowledge their roots in the structuralist paradigm, but recognize the "necessity of taking strategic interaction, consciousness, and historically accumulated culture into account" (McAdam, Tarrow, and Tilly 2001: 22). The result moves away from "similar large structures and sequences" to "recurrent causal mechanisms concatenating into causal processes" (McAdam, Tarrow, and Tilly 2001: 24).

The focus shifts to "smaller-scale causal mechanisms that recur in different combinations with different aggregate consequences in varying historical settings" (McAdam, Tarrow, and Tilly 2001: 24). Mechanisms may be environmental, cognitive, or relational, but in each case they alter relations among elements in similar ways across a variety of situations.

Processes are "recurring causal chains, sequences, and combinations of mechanisms" (McAdam, Tarrow, and Tilly 2001: 27); they also operate in similar ways in diverse situations. Mechanisms and processes reside on a continuum from relatively simple and narrow to more complex and intertwined causes.

Episodes of contention (rather than "movements") are the unit of analysis in which to observe mechanisms and processes. Episodes descriptively identify what is to be explained; mechanisms and processes, combined in various ways, provide the explanation. Prior static, descriptive variables of movements are now replaced by dynamic, explanatory mechanisms and processes of contentious episodes.

With this conceptual edifice in place, the book examines familiar issues of mobilization, identities, and trajectories from this more dynamic perspective. The authors revisit their signature works regarding mobilization in McAdam's (1982) analysis of the civil rights movement, identity in Tilly's (1964) study of the French Revolution, and trajectories in Tarrow's (1989) account of the Italian student movement.

The method they adopt to improve upon these accounts involves paired comparisons that reveal how "similar causal mechanisms and processes appear in quite dissimilar varieties of contentious politics . . . and appear in episodes producing massively different general outcomes" (McAdam, Tarrow, and Tilly 2001: 87).

Reviewing mobilization in the civil rights movement, they offer a more dynamic mobilization model by recasting opportunities and threats not as objective structures but as dependent upon framing and attribution as an activating mechanism. Social appropriation is another mechanism whereby groups coopt existing organizations as vehicles for politicized mobilization. Finally, framing is redefined from a strategic task of movements to an interactive contest among multiple parties in a contentious episode.

This more dynamic mobilization model is expanded by a paired comparison of the Kenyan Mau Mau revolt of the 1950s and the Philippines' Yellow Revolution of the 1980s. Despite vastly different circumstances, the authors detect similar mechanisms shaping mobilization and demobilization in both contexts.

Attributions of threat and opportunity were crucial in both situations as shared definitions of the situation were constructed and diffused to relevant populations. Social appropriation of existing spaces and collective identities was a second common mechanism in these otherwise disparate settings. And finally, brokerage was crucial in linking together previously unconnected social sites or groups that propelled the conflict. These mechanisms operated in both cases despite differing contexts and outcomes.

Reviewing collective identity in the French Revolution reveals that collective actors are not "neatly bounded, self-propelling entities with fixed attributes" but rather subject to incessant "modifications of their boundaries and attributes as they interact" with others in contentious episodes (McAdam, Tarrow, and Tilly 2001: 56). Indeed, each of the mechanisms that contributed to mobilization in the prior cases also contributed to the "contingent, collective, constructed character of actors, actions, and identities in contentious politics" (McAdam, Tarrow, and Tilly 2001: 61).

The construction of identity is elaborated by moving from revolutionary France to the paired comparison of religious identities in India and political ones in South Africa. Brokerage appears again because linking previously unconnected sites and groups creates new collective actors. Category formation also creates boundaries and hence new identities through invention, borrowing, and encounters; it is especially apparent in ethnic, religious, and national identity formation. Object shift is yet another mechanism that can alter and redraw previously established identities, whereas certification (and decertification) is a final mechanism conferring (or withholding) validation by authorities.

Reviewing movement trajectories in the Italian student movement suggests the limits of "movement career" and "protest cycles" models and the need for a more dynamic analysis of mechanisms. Competition for power is an obvious mechanism once contentious episodes are underway. Their subsequent trajectories are shaped by additional mechanisms of diffusion, repression, and radicalization. As always, the same mechanisms can lead to vastly different outcomes depending on their combination.

This becomes evident in a paired comparison of the runup to the American Civil War and the Spanish transition to democracy in the 1970s. Brokerage mechanisms shaped alliances and coalitions on both sides of both conflicts. Identity shift was also important by altering definitions of boundaries and relations between political actors. Radicalization was an additional mechanism that interacted with convergence as more moderate actors coalesced in response to the radicalization of other groups.

As the cases accumulate, it becomes evident that similar mechanisms operated in many episodes, eroding the provisional distinction between mobilization, identity, and trajectories. The authors claim several benefits of their approach over previous ones. It is dynamic rather than static; it captures the interplay among actors; it acknowledges complexities beyond strategic framing; and perhaps most important, it identifies the actual causal mechanisms left unspecified by the political process model. Finally, this approach helps transcend the compartmentalization of different types of contentious episodes by finding similar mechanisms in each.

The analysis then turns to even broader examinations of contentious episodes often treated separately: revolution, nationalism, and democratization. Although the earlier paired comparisons show that similar mechanisms operate in dissimilar settings and can lead to very different outcomes, the new strategy is to demonstrate that "small, well-chosen sets of causal mechanisms and processes explain problematic features of dissimilar episodes" (McAdam, Tarrow, and Tilly 2001: 87).

Tilly's (1978) earlier call for an integrated approach to social movements and revolutions largely fell upon deaf ears among social movement scholars. Goldstone later reiterated that "revolutions are not a genre apart, but share characteristics with social movements, rebellions, failed revolutions, and cycles of protest" (quoted in (McAdam, Tarrow, and Tilly 2001: 194). The authors build on this assumption.

Prior theories of revolution (natural histories, structural strain, structural origins, and cultural agency) are not very convincing in explaining why most revolutions fail whereas a few succeed. The reason is that each proposes a linear narrative but none deal "with the crucial interactions within contentious politics that result in new alignments, new identities, and the collapse of oppressive regimes" (McAdam, Tarrow, and Tilly 2001: 196). The dynamics of contention approach examines precisely these interactions in the form of mechanisms and processes.

The relative success of the Sandinista revolution in Nicaragua thus can be explained through a convergence of mechanisms. The Somoza regime's infringement on elite interests prompted many of them to withdraw support. There followed several "suddenly imposed grievances" through regime blunders. This prompted decertification by other governments. The concatenation of mechanisms converted a revolutionary situation into a revolutionary outcome with the rise of the Sandinistas to power.

The utter failure of the Chinese student rebellion of 1989 may be explained by a different combination of mechanisms. Despite mixed messages about democratization prior to the Beijing spring, there was no comparable elite defection from the regime. When the regime eventually repressed the movement, it prompted its growth and radicalization. Without some faction of elite support for the emboldened movement, however, radicalization "helped turn a revolutionary situation into a revolutionary failure" (McAdam, Tarrow, and Tilly 2001: 224). In this account, prior theories are not so much invalidated as incorporated: "structure, culture, and strategic calculation are not outside the mechanisms of contention but the raw material for their action and interaction" (McAdam, Tarrow, and Tilly 2001: 226).

Like revolution, nationalism is best understood not as an isolated domain for specialists but as another form of contentious politics. This is evident in a paired comparison of Italian unification in the 1860s and the disintegration of the Soviet Union in the 1980s. Similar mechanisms operated to produce radically different outcomes.

In the Italian case, opportunity spirals and identity shifts created a sense of nationalism across disparate regions and cultures. Competition and brokerage then helped produce a relatively weak but durable and integrated nation-state. In the strong state case of the Soviet Union, top-down liberalization sparked democratic movements and nationalist aspirations in a different type of opportunity spiral. This prompted new nationalistic identity shifts that fed into competition and brokerage that further weakened centralized authority and ultimately produced state disintegration.

Rather than reducing these events to grand models of state formation or imperial decline, each is better understood "by examining them closely for political mechanisms that operate in a wide range of contention" (McAdam, Tarrow, and Tilly 2001: 263). The same holds for the final case of contentious democratization.

Switzerland democratized in the mid-nineteenth century, whereas Mexico did so in the later twentieth century; they offer contrasting "weak state" and "strong state" paths to democracy. Despite historical, geographical, and cultural differences, four similar mechanisms operated to foster democratization through two distinct pathways.

Cross-class coalitions helped insulate categorical inequality from public politics. The central cooptation of intermediaries, formerly autonomous brokers, and subgroup leaders fostered the integration of trust networks into public politics. The dissolution of patron-client networks reinforced this integration, whereas brokerage reinforced all the previous processes (McAdam, Tarrow, and Tilly 2001: 276).

In this comparison, two different states followed different pathways that were nonetheless mediated by the same mechanisms to produce roughly similar outcomes. More broadly, the lessons are twofold. First, "democratic polities form through contentious politics and reshape contentious politics as they form" (McAdam, Tarrow, and Tilly 2001: 304). Second, the same mechanisms that explain other forms of contentious politics also explain democratization; contentious politics is thus a big tent encompassing democratization, nationalism, revolution, social movements, and related collective struggles under the same explanatory logic.

The authors conclude by discussing three additional mechanisms that "recur over a surprising number and broad range of episodes" (McAdam, Tarrow, and Tilly 2001: 314). Actor constitution, exemplified by the civil rights movement and Chinese Cultural Revolution, occurs when social appropriation and innovative action spark category formation and certification. Polarization, illustrated by the French Revolution and the Maluku War of Indonesia, results from the interaction of competition, opportunity/threat spirals, category formation, and brokerage. Finally, scale shift in the Italian student movement and Rwandan genocide occurred either through brokerage or diffusion that produced attributions of similarity leading to emulation and coordinated action.

The authors conclude by underscoring how their approach moves away from a single-actor, social movement focus in the democratized West to a "more dynamic and relational account of contentious politics within and across world regions" (McAdam, Tarrow, and Tilly 2001: 305). The seemingly narrower focus on contentious episodes encompasses many different collective struggles and a mind-boggling variety of cases. The approach potentially links specialists in movements, revolutions, strikes, and democratization by identifying similar dynamics across those realms. Finally, whereas the authors identify recurring mechanisms and processes, the goal is not a generalizable theory as much as a toolkit that can explain particular episodes through varying combinations of well-understood mechanisms and historically contingent factors.

CRITIQUES AND PERMUTATIONS

The contentious politics agenda represents a potential paradigm shift in social movement theory. Unlike many paradigm shifts, it came not from outsiders with fresh eyes but rather from three of the most prominent social movement theorists of the twentieth century. As prior advocates of the reigning political process theory, their effort to transcend their own hegemonic theory was quite unusual.

The significance of the new paradigm should not be underestimated. It implies the erasure of the social movement as an independent analytical category after only a twenty-five-year life span. Recall that until the mid-1970s, movements were bundled with other forms of collective behavior amenable to similar explanatory logics. It required the resource mobilization/political process paradigm shift to extricate movements from these entanglements as a phenomenon worthy of analysis and explanation in their own right.

The new proposal would once again submerge movements into a broader category alongside other types; this time the category is contentious politics rather than collective behavior. Thus, even as Tilly (2004) was polishing his historical lens for studying social movements from 1768 to 2004, he was also endorsing a conceptual shift away from movements in themselves to the contentious politics paradigm.

As might be expected, the new paradigm attracted much attention and prompted respectful discussion. Even critics applauded the move away from structural determinism toward a more interactive approach and a broader scope of analysis beyond contemporary movements in Western democracies. Although these goals found wide acceptance, the overall program met with considerable skepticism and critique.

As often happens with new proposals, McAdam, Tarrow, and Tilly were accused of constructing a straw man out of the classical agenda they sought to transcend. Critics noted that the earlier political process model and later synthesis were not as static as the authors claimed, and that they already incorporated a more interactive and dynamic emphasis (Rucht 2003).

That literature also discussed "mechanisms," but there is little acknowledgement of earlier efforts in the new approach (Koopmans 2003). Indeed, the authors seem to deliberately ignore points of continuity with previous work and to exaggerate the novelty of their approach. Finally, the classic agenda did not necessarily seek the broad explanations and generalizations that the authors found inappropriate, whereas the new approach flirted with such ambitions despite protestations to the contrary (Diani 2003).

Critics also called for greater conceptual clarification of key elements of the new approach. Contentious action was asserted more than demonstrated to be a coherent category of analysis that could replace that of social movements. In fact, the mechanisms and processes found in contentious action occur more broadly in other social settings, suggesting blurry boundaries at best around this central idea (Diani 2003; Rucht 2003). Critics thus expressed doubts that the new concepts are demonstrable improvements over the old ones (Diani 2003).

Perhaps the most significant criticism centered around the role of mechanisms. It is not clear whether they arise through some type of induction from case studies or some derivation from an established body of literature (Rucht 2003). This ambiguity makes them seem rather arbitrary; one can easily imagine an academic parlor game of inventing ad hoc mechanisms *ad infinitum*.

Whatever their origins, the mechanisms themselves were roundly criticized. Real mechanisms should have predictable effects across different situations, but that is not the case here (Koopmans 2003). Oliver (2003) claimed that the theory really proposes just processes and not mechanisms; the latter should specify how these devices really operate and the theory largely fails to do so. Put somewhat differently, the purported mechanisms cry out for explanation themselves; too little attention is paid to how and why they arise in some contexts and not others. Rather than genuine mechanisms, they function more as narrative aids (Koopmans 2003).

These difficulties pose serious problems for the explanations offered by the contentious politics paradigm. Because mechanisms are ill-defined and arbitrarily invoked, there is a danger of tautology. The accumulation of case studies does little to resolve such problems because rather than specifying conditions and effects of previous mechanisms, new ones are constantly being introduced.

Indeed, the authors posit more mechanisms than cases to be explained, abandoning any pretense of parsimonious explanation. Most generally, the resulting explanations seem arbitrary and ad hoc in their emphasis on some mechanisms rather than others (Diani 2003; Rucht 2003). Paralleling these explanatory difficulties is a plethora of competing if not conflicting statements of the actual research program of the approach (Oliver 2003).

A final set of criticisms concerned the phenomenon to be explained. Although the authors portray their approach as broadening the range from social movements to contentious politics, it remains narrow in its focus on state-centered, political activism. It simply ignores challenges to nonstate authority systems or hegemonic beliefs (Taylor 2003; Snow 2004; Van Dyke, Soule, and Taylor 2004). In this, as Taylor (2003) noted, the more things change (to contentious politics), the more they stay the same (as in political process theory). This persistent privileging of political contention is especially regrettable as new evidence of how *cultural* contention matters becomes more available (Taylor et al. 2009).

McAdam (2003) defended the approach's applicability to diverse challenges while conceding that the book focused on political ones for "pragmatic" reasons. He addressed problems with mechanisms by claiming that the proposal was never intended as a "fully ripened explanatory perspective" but rather a "highly provisional pragmatic call" for more dynamic accounts of collective action (McAdam 2003: 128). Finally, he characterized the contentious political paradigm as a logical extension of the classical social movement agenda rather than a rival paradigm.

Tarrow (2003) defended the approach by reiterating the structuralist bias of previous theory, underscoring the incorporation of framing and agency elements in the new version, and characterizing it not as an "alternative" paradigm but simply a way to "find new and more dynamic pathways from structure to action" (Tarrow 2003: 135). He suggested its relevance to nonstate conflict with brief vignettes from religious conflict, organizational contention, and transnational social movements.

A more systematic response appeared with *Contentious Politics* (Tilly and Tarrow 2007). It acknowledged "three justified complaints" about the paradigm's initial formulation: too many mechanisms and processes, lack of clarity about methods, and a confusing number of empirical illustrations. The newer volume sought to remedy these problems while remaining faithful to the logic of the overall approach.

The book reintroduces basic claims and concepts with appendices and glossaries. It continues with paired comparisons examining fewer mechanisms across many contentious interactions. In the judgment of one reviewer, "the book does not really add to the DOC project in theoretical or methodological terms" but is "quite successful" in presenting more accessible explanations of contentious interactions through combinations of mechanisms and processes (Diani 2007: 575).

The reception of this new approach among social movement scholars has been uneven at best. On one hand, there has been much sympathy with the call for more dynamic and interactive accounts over static structural explanations, and the phrase "dynamics of contention" has become widespread in social movement scholarship.

On the other hand, many who have appropriated this language have not embraced the conceptual implications of that language. Thus, many studies make reference to "contentious dynamics" while analyzing familiar variables from previous paradigms rather than identifying mechanisms and processes. Even when mechanisms and processes receive lip service, the method of paired comparisons has not been widely adopted; we rather find talk of mechanisms and processes in otherwise conventional studies of standard variables in the trajectories of single movements.

Moreover, movement scholars still focus largely on movements rather than broadening their range to other forms of contentious politics; the "social movement" lives on as an analytical category. Finally, significant clusters of scholars have rejected what they see as the hegemonic ambitions of the contentious politics paradigm. They continue to study a wider range of social movements with a cultural or constructivist emphasis and little interest in establishing or following a new theoretical orthodoxy.

BRINGING CULTURE BACK IN

Several years before McAdam, Tarrow, and Tilly put mechanisms center stage, Jasper called for increasing our explanatory reach by concentrating "*on mechanisms, not grand theories*" (1997: 378; italics in original). He also called for a more interactive, dynamic approach to deconstruct static variables of environment or opportunity into relations between strategic actors responding to each other's moves. Thus, two distinctive elements of the contentious dynamics paradigm had already been articulated by a theorist who nonetheless took them in a decidedly more cultural direction.

Cultural theorists of protest have long been in the position of counterpunchers. Since the demise of the collective behavior tradition, structure and politics have been ascendant, whereas culture and meanings have been subordinate. Thus, cultural analysts typically offered their insights as filling gaps in the dominant perspectives. This was how framing was introduced in the 1980s and accepted into the later "synthesis." New social movement theory arguably made more basic claims for cultural elements, but it was also assimilated in a piecemeal fashion into a predominantly structural analysis.

By the end of the twentieth century, however, it was argued that "recent treatments of the cultural dimensions of protest have begun to reconceptualize the very terms of movement theorizing" (Polletta 1997: 431). At the same time, even these reconceptualizations too often "remain limited ... by their retention of dichotomous conceptions of culture and structure" (Polletta 1997: 431).

This dualistic tendency is evident across many different dimensions of protest activity. Concerning protest origins, this false dichotomy obscures the inevitably cultural dimensions of supposedly structural opportunities as well as the ways in which cultural challenges are structured by, and often reproduce, power asymmetries.

Another expression of this false dichotomy juxtaposes culture to instrumental action. This obscures how supposedly instrumental decision making is infused with cultural processes. As neoinstitutionalists have revealed, organizations often make decisions less in terms of efficiency than to mimic practices of similar organizations. By the same token, practices often seen as "cultural" (e.g., participatory democracy) have been undertaken as instrumental strategies to cultivate a broader cadre of leadership.

The false dichotomy also implies that politics and culture are distinct terrains of protest. Thus, new social movements are often cited as fighting "cultural" as opposed to political battles. "In fact, many so-called new social movements continue to target the state" (Polletta 1997: 443) and the cultivation of collective identity (supposedly a "cultural" phenomenon) is often both a strategic goal and a measure of movement success. In sum, even culturalist challenges to structural or political accounts often falter by reproducing the same misleading dichotomies (see also Polletta 2004).

At the very least, these observations underscore that all movements have both political and cultural elements. Even the most "cultural" movements challenge some type of hegemonic (if not always state-based) power, whereas even the most "political" movements rest on a cultural substratum of meanings and signification. Focusing on one or the other dimension may be a valid analytical strategy but should not be reified into an ontological assertion about movements themselves (Buechler 2000).

This logic argues against a "cultural paradigm" of movements that would merely reproduce dichotomous thinking. This may be why a single unitary cultural approach to movements has never congealed. Perhaps the closest thing is Jasper's (1997) work on moral protest. As noted previously, he calls for a genuinely interactive approach, while speaking with a distinctly cultural accent that underscores the relevance of cultural elements to every aspect of collective action.

Echoing the previous discussion, Jasper's starting premise is that "[c]ulture ... should not be contrasted with structural factors because it is fused with them" (1997: xi). Three components of culture are especially relevant: "cognitive beliefs, emotional responses, and moral evaluations ... are inseparable, and together these motivate, rationalize and channel political action" (Jasper 1997: 12). These elements are intrinsic to all movements, but are especially evident in what Jasper calls postindustrial or postcitizenship movements such as antinuclear, animal rights, and environmental activism.

Jasper's distinctive claim is that protest rests on four irreducible dimensions of resources, strategies, culture, and biography. When these "autonomous" dimensions are combined in various ways, "derivative" dimensions of political structure, social networks, or formal organizations emerge. Jasper thus claims to be identifying the more foundational substratum underlying familiar theories.

Resources and strategies have been widely studied but also conflated and over-extended into tautological formulations. Jasper advocates more limited definitions and careful distinctions between them that will allow us to study their interaction both with each other and with culture and biography.

Culture itself varies along at least two major dimensions: from implicit to explicit and from interior/individual to shared/public. Both Giddens and Bourdieu are enlisted to grasp the duality of culture. Following Giddens, culture is "'both medium and outcome' of social practices, both structured and structuring" (Giddens, quoted in Jasper 1997: 50). Following Bourdieu, culture is like a structured game with rules that allow for individual discretion and creativity. This culturally constructionist approach implies that resources and strategies are "not just interpreted through a cultural lens, but are constituted and defined from the start by cultural contexts" (Jasper 1997: 53).

Biography accounts for individualized meanings as well as the diverse motives that propel people into collective action. Conscious and purposive selves fuse self-identity with moral significance and emotional valences. Claiming a fundamental status for biography brings individuals back into the study of collective action after their virtual banishment by structural models of protest.

These four factors can be studied in static ways, but must ultimately be seen as dynamic processes. This leads Jasper to emphasize the artfulness of protest. "One way to think about how all these dimensions change is through the idea of artfulness: people are aware of what they are doing, they make plans and develop projects, and they innovate in trying to achieve their goals. In their characteristic jargon, sociologists often refer to artfulness as 'agency'" (Jasper 1997: 65).

Summarizing his treatment of the four factors, Jasper succinctly notes that "nothing comes first" (1997: 67) and all these factors interact. At the same time, he seems to privilege culture as not just an independent dimension but also as constitutive of the other dimensions (e.g., what counts as a movement resource is culturally defined). Thus, "[s]ometimes culture is a simple causal factor; ... at other times (or in other ways) it helps define these other factors too" (Jasper 1997: 41).

Jasper further distinguishes his culturally accented approach from other cultural theories. He suggests that framing and identity approaches have overextended these concepts by asking them to do too much; the result is vacuous or tautological formulations in which all ideas become frames, or all cultural elements are reduced to identity. He also claims that "[f]ar more attention has been given to cognition than to morals or especially emotions" (Jasper 1997: 70). His alternative is consistently committed to recognizing thinking, feeling, and judging as coequal cultural capacities.

This theoretical edifice is then applied to various dimensions of "postcitizenship" movements, incorporating rich empirical evidence from antinuclear, animal rights, and environmental movements. The role of emotions is nicely illustrated by evidence from movements responding to suddenly imposed grievances or moral shocks. The contribution of moral judgment is exemplified by whistleblowers whose commitment to principles overrides other motives and generates protest. The importance of cognitive appeals is effectively explored in the animal rights movement, in which protesters have strategically opted for logical, rational arguments specifically to deflect criticisms of sentimentality and playing to emotions.

If culture looms large in mobilization and recruitment, it may loom even larger in sustaining movements. Antinuclear activism at Diablo Canyon in the 1980s provides vivid examples of how rituals and emotions sustained activist identities even as that particular battle was being lost. A biographical lens helps focus on the satisfactions of protest and underscores how "[v]irtually all the pleasures that humans derive from social life are found in protest movements" (Jasper 1997: 220).

In exploring tactics, it becomes evident that activist subcultures and generations often have different "tastes" in tactics, which *represent important routines, emotionally and morally salient in these people's lives*" (Jasper 1997: 237; italics in original). Consumer boycotts provide a final example of how moral outrage generates and sustains protest, albeit with differing dynamics for local boycotts using direct action as opposed to national ones relying on indirect action.

The role of rhetoric and the arts of persuasion are additional cultural factors that help account for the differential success of otherwise similar movements. Thus, environmental movements can often use a globalizing rhetoric to advance their goals, whereas movements with more localized grievances are less able to do so. Finally, an examination of successful strategies suggests that they are not just logical solutions to game theory dilemmas but rather are infused with cultural elements; it is culture that "sets limits to strategic repertoires through know-how, tactical tastes and identities, virtuosity, and learning processes" (Jasper 1997: 301).

Jasper's work (1997) is thus among the most far-reaching of many attempts to restore a cultural dimension to the study of collective action and to explore the implications for prevailing paradigms and familiar concepts. Even where culture had previously been recognized, however, it was typically done with a cognitive bias receptive to logic but blind to emotion. Thus, the call to bring not only culture but emotions back into the study of social movements merits a separate discussion.

PASSIONATE POLITICS

There are intimate connections between emotions and culture. "Emotions are but the entering wedge for many aspects of politics and protest that have been neglected by the structural paradigm of the last thirty years, a whole world of psychological and cultural processes that have been considered too 'soft' or too messy for empirical investigation" (Goodwin, Jasper, and Polletta 2001a: 24).

For many decades, emotions were part of the study of collective behavior but they attracted "the wrong kind of attention" (Goodwin, Jasper, and Polletta 2000). In theories of crowd behavior and their derivatives from the 1890s into the 1960s, emotions were equated with irrationality and other pejorative judgments about participants in protest. While this work pathologized emotions and protest, at least emotions were part of the analysis.

With the paradigm shifts of the 1970s came the "great silence" (Goodwin, Jasper, and Polletta 2000: 70). Maintaining a view of emotions as irrational but substituting the contention that movements are rational banished any consideration of emotions in the study of movements. The conceptual bias against emotion was matched by methodological strategies that marginalized subjective states.

The great silence was followed in the 1980s by a focus on "cognition without emotions" (Goodwin, Jasper, and Polletta 2000: 72). Some cultural elements were addressed through concepts of framing and identity, but even these important factors were addressed as if movement actors were "Spock-like beings, devoid of passion and other human emotions" (Benford, quoted in Goodwin, Jasper, and Polletta 2000: 73).

Thus, it was not until the 1990s that emotions regained legitimacy in the analysis of collective action. As noted earlier, this was facilitated by the cultural turn in social theory and the emergence of a sociological approach to emotions in general. Additional factors included an influx of women into the discipline, the rise of feminist scholarship, and renewed interest in a self comprised of emotions as well as cognitions (Goodwin, Jasper, and Polletta 2000). Under these influences, students of movements began to seriously investigate the role of emotions.

The sociology of emotions views them as culturally constructed. "In the constructionist view ... emotions are constituted more by shared social meanings than automatic physiological states" (Jasper 1998: 400). Partly because of their common roots in shared meanings, emotions are intertwined with both cognitive beliefs and moral rules. The sociology of emotions has identified various dimensions of emotions, while also distinguishing long-term affective states from short-term reactive emotions.

Protest activities provide a rich laboratory for investigating emotion in social life. Affective emotions like hostility, solidarity, or trust; reactive emotions such as anger, outrage, or shame; and intermediate moods including envy, compassion, or pride can recruit members and sustain protest or dampen support and hasten protest decline.

Acknowledging a role for emotions quickly reveals how many conventional concepts in movement studies rest on an emotional substratum. Thus, many "suddenly imposed grievances" in fact involve moral shocks with strong emotional valences. While networks may aid in recruiting friends, emotionally laden moral shocks may be equally important in recruiting strangers to movements (Jasper and Poulsen 1995).

Many aspects of framing are also profoundly rooted in emotional states. Diagnostic framing attributes blame for a problem that is as much an emotional as a cognitive process. Motivational framing is clearly rooted in emotional states even though conventional treatments have emphasized beliefs and values over emotions and affect. Injustice frames, as Gamson et al. (1982) recognized early on, rest on "hot cognitions," which is an indirect acknowledgment of how emotions shape beliefs.

Much the same may be said for McAdam's notion of "cognitive liberation," given that "'liberation' implies heady emotions that 'cognitive' then denies" (Goodwin, Jasper, and Polletta 2001a: 7).

Collective identity is yet another popular concept often conceptualized in cognitive terms despite the seemingly obvious role of affective bonds in such identities. Indeed, collective identities often combine reciprocal emotions that protesters feel toward each other with commonly shared emotions toward external objects. The combination can create a powerful "we-feeling" and a "libidinal economy" (Goodwin 1997) within movements that helps account for the often tenacious grip of such identities even in the face of insurmountable odds and opponents.

Beyond its relevance for collective identity, emotional energy may be seen as the social glue that binds many forms of collective action. Following Durkheim, Collins argues that "at the center of every highly mobilized social movement is … 'collective effervescence'" (2001: 28). Such "high ritual density" occurs when people are physically assembled together with a mutual shared focus of attention. Such gatherings result in group solidarity, emotional energy, symbolic rituals, and moral sensibilities. They can both amplify and transform emotional states; social movements are especially in the business of transforming such states into action toward movement goals.

As noted earlier, the edited volume *Passionate Politics* (Goodwin, Jasper, and Polletta 2001b) underscored emotions in social movements (at the very same time that the dynamics of contention paradigm appeared). Two striking examples include the pull of nationalist identities in fascist Italy (Berezin 2001) and the role of shame in animating the Christian right's culture war (Stein 2001). The linking of emotions to "bad" or "irrational" movements is an ironic if unintended consequence of this effort to revive a presumably non-judgmental approach to emotions in social movements.

Several other themes in this volume demonstrate how attending to emotions can complement, refine, improve, or overturn conventional explanations of movement dynamics. One example bridges the divide between rationality and emotion by illustrating how the emotional benefits of solidarity can provide a powerful selective incentive for participation that overcomes the free-rider problem. This seems especially evident in cases of high-risk activism in El Salvadoran insurgency (Wood 2001) and the U.S. and East German civil rights movements (Goodwin and Pfaff 2001).

Another theme illustrates the strategic implications of emotional states and the volatile swings that occur when movement participants possess ambivalent emotions. This is evident in "how emotions and their expression—notably shame, fear, pride, grief, indignation, and anger—shaped lesbian and gay responses to the AIDS epidemic, sometimes encouraging lesbian and gay quiescence or community self-help, at other times animating militant political activism" (Gould 2001: 136; see also Gould 2004).

A third theme challenges standard accounts of political opportunity as the gateway to emerging collective action. In both Gould's (2001) study of militant AIDS activism and Wood's (2001) analysis of Salvadoran insurgency, mobilization increased in the face of demonstrably *narrowing* rather then widening political opportunities. In both cases, the emotional response to less favorable external conditions fostered more rather than less activism.

A final theme again suggests the proximity rather than opposition of rationality and emotion and how both may be mediated by considerations of movement strategy. In both the animal rights movement (Groves 2001) and the campaign against child abuse (Whittier 2001), activists made deliberate, strategic choices to frame their appeals in calm, logical, rational terms so as not to be dismissed as overly emotional. This surface rationality attests less to a "rational actor" model than to a complex strategic response to the interplay of logic and emotion in these movements.

Such work demonstrates that culture and emotion can no longer be taken for granted or relegated to the background in studies of collective action. Movements have always been hotbeds of cultural processes and emotional dynamics. The study of movements has finally begun to reflect that reality.

CONCLUSION

Social movements remain a robust research topic. In much of this research, attention to cultural elements or the terminology of contentious politics has become more common. Even so, the lion's share of recent work still relies on the triumvirate of political opportunity, mobilizing structures, and framing processes.

In theoretical terms, the most striking story is the persistence of a major fault line between a structural/relational focus and a cultural/emotional emphasis. The split is ironic given some surface agreements. Both sides advocate a search for mechanisms, and both have endorsed a more dynamic, interactive understanding of the often volatile flow of events that comprise a social movement or a contentious episode.

These commonalities mask underlying differences. The mechanisms detailed by the contentious politics paradigm remain primarily structural or relational, occasionally acknowledging framing and attribution while ignoring emotions. The unit of analysis is also distinctive; social movements have moved from center stage to merely one type of contentious episode. The scope broadens beyond movements, but remains narrowly interested in challenges to state-based authority. While raising new questions, this seems a premature closure on traditional movement studies.

Cultural approaches also stress the interaction of different factors, but their "starting line-up" is quite different. Recall Jasper's cultural approach based on resources, strategy, culture, and biography. The latter two are largely absent in structural approaches, and even strategy has often been downplayed in favor of more macro-level factors. On the other hand, Jasper regards the familiar factors of opportunity, mobilization, and framing as secondary derivations from the starting lineup.

A second thrust of the cultural approach has been to insist that all the more familiar variables have irreducible cultural dimensions. In this sense, culture is not just another factor but is fundamentally constitutive of *all* other factors such as re-sources, opportunities, strategy, identity, and the like. For all these reasons, the gulf between structural and cultural approaches remains a fundamental one.

It might nonetheless be bridged by more studies of the relative contribution of both sets of factors. Examples already exist wherein "cultural" work explicitly positions itself as a supplement or corrective to political process explanations, while other studies directly challenge key tenets of the reigning orthodoxy (Polletta and Amenta 2001). This theoretical strategy is perhaps inevitable when a challenging paradigm confronts a dominant one, but it has led to some very provocative studies (as noted previously).

Two additional bridges across the gulf might also be built. First, if proponents of the political process/contentious dynamics approach would take cultural factors as seriously as cultural proponents have taken structural factors, it would provide a richer test of the viability of both and perhaps some accommodation between them.

Finally, if advocates of a cultural emphasis would do more to investigate the conditions under which cultural and emotional processes affect the course of a conflict, it would strengthen their position. Such a strategy would take us beyond a weak acknowledgment that culture and emotions are "always there" to a specifi-cation of how and when they acquire a predominant causal role that overrides the influence of more familiar structural, relational, and political factors (Polletta and Amenta 2001).

Chapter Thirteen

New Directions

Social movement theory has a history of classical thinkers and major paradigms reaching back well more than a century. Although there have been pendulum swings between contrasting approaches, and although certain ideas have gone in and out of (and sometimes back in) fashion, the cumulative result is a rich set of concepts about collective action.

This toolkit continues to expand, as does the variety of movements that comprise our subject matter. This expansion is currently less about entirely new paradigms than about permutations on existing models, efforts to complement paradigms with insights from rival camps, and suggestions for synthesizing elements of different paradigms. At the same time, new types of collective action require a rethinking of familiar frameworks.

This chapter reviews some of the more promising branches of current theorizing, as well as some new movement arenas that have helped stimulate these developments.

THE CONTEXT

Across the social sciences, social theory has entered a postpositivist era in which a widening array of theoretical foundations and conceptual models are available to practitioners of specific disciplines. Although obvious in anthropology, sociology, and psychology, it is even becoming evident in the "harder" sciences of political science and economics.

Consider the rise of behavioral economics. Confronted with the limits of neoclassical models of rational choice, behavioral economists have reintroduced psychological dynamics into explanations of decision making, particularly in situations of risk and uncertainty. This shift parallels sociology's own rethinking of the rational actor model as a basis for explaining participation in collective action.

As social science disciplines become more theoretically diverse and reflexive about their premises, it increases the likelihood of two developments. First, other disciplines may develop their own understandings of collective action. Second, interdisciplinary explanations of social movements may become more common. This would help realize one goal of the "dynamics of contention" program: to break down barriers between specialized subfields across disciplines and thereby foster richer understandings of their often strikingly similar subject matter.

Within sociology, similar trends involving diverse concepts and permeable boundaries between subfields promise more robust approaches to analyzing collective action as well. Three examples must suffice here.

Cultural sociology continues to pose fresh questions about movement processes. The framing approach has been a fruitful source of hypotheses since the 1980s. The cognitive bias of the framing approach was subsequently criticized and emotions were added to the cultural palette. More recently, culturalist approaches have evolved to focus on discourses, narratives, stories, speech acts, strategies, and more.

Political sociology brings another promising dimension to the analysis of collective action. The oft-neglected issue of movement success or outcomes dovetails with questions about determinants of public policy. As more movement scholars examine movement impacts and more policy analysts include collective action among their "variables," fresh insights on movement dynamics are beginning to emerge.

Organizational sociology is a third subfield that informs questions about collective action. Practitioners of "new" and "neo" institutionalist paradigms have catalogued diverse movement organizational forms and their variable consequences. More broadly, they have identified dynamics that can account for both institutional patterns and movement trajectories more convincingly than abstract models of rational actors.

Social movement theory thus continues to be conceptually "pushed" by innovations in other subfields and disciplines. It is also empirically "pulled" by new movements and movement forms. These include the rise of computer-mediated communications and the virtualization of human experience. Studies of "cyberactivism" and "cyberprotest" have begun to explore the consequences of such new technologies for movement origins, trajectories, and impacts.

Another example concerns globalization. Like all social change, this one creates "winners" and "losers," thereby fostering new grievances and corresponding targets.

Globalization can facilitate the mobilization of many movements, but it most obviously expands the transnational movement sector in ways that both support and challenge standard accounts of collective action.

These conceptual and empirical developments promise to reshape the study of collective action in significant ways. Hence, they form a fitting conclusion to this history of social movement theories.

STRUCTURAL PERMUTATIONS

Some of the more promising recent developments are permutations on the structural/relational approaches of resource mobilization, political process, and contentious dynamics. Four clusters of such work may be briefly mentioned here: the political mediation approach, organizational analyses, new emphases on leadership and strategy, and world-system perspectives on collective action.

The political mediation model enlists political sociology to understand the role of collective action in shaping public policy. A precursor is Edwin Amenta's (1998) analysis of the New Deal that generated an "institutional politics" theory explaining how varying combinations of political structures, domestic bureaucrats, and electoral regimes shape the likelihood that any contender will achieve their policy objectives.

Amenta (2006) subsequently focused on the prospects for social movement success in particular, leading to a political mediation model of collective action. To say that collective action is politically mediated means that it "must influence the calculations and actions of institutional political actors" (Amenta et al. 1999: 1) to be successful. It follows that political circumstances influence the effectiveness of movement strategies; their "productivity" depends on the specific contexts in which they are deployed.

Some contextual conditions greatly reduce the chances for any significant movement impact. These include strong restrictions on democratic practices and the prevalence of patronage-oriented political parties; this combination largely insulates the political system from the influence of most outsider challengers and strategies.

Even when a polity is more open, the regime's orientation to the challenger's constituency and state bureaucrats' stance toward the challenger's interests are crucial. In the most promising case, in which elected officials and state bureaucrats are supportive of movement goals, sheer mobilization and limited protest may be sufficient to win movement objectives. In the least favorable scenario, in which both are opposed, much more assertive movement strategies will be required to have even a chance of success.

In the mixed cases of favorable elected officials with an intransigent bureaucracy or sympathetic bureaucrats with antagonistic elected officials, movements must deploy negative sanctions and calculated strategies to create new state bureaus or displace elected officials in order to achieve much success. Empirical evidence from the Townsend movement illustrates the contingent interactions between movement strategy and political structure; we must attend to their reciprocal influence if we are to better understand *When Movements Matter* (Amenta 2006; see also Soule 2004).

Although this work bridges political sociology and social movements, other efforts have linked organizational sociology with collective action. For a long time, the "core images and boundaries" of these areas were quite different. "In the collective behavior version, social movements were seen as a kind of spontaneous combustion," whereas "[f]ormal organizations, by way of contrast, were seen as cool, rational, and planned arrangements" (Zald 2008: 569). As the organizational aspects of movements and the informal dimensions of organizations gradually came to the forefront of scholarly attention, these bifurcated images began to break down.

An important predecessor of these trends in the movements literature was Elisabeth Clemens's (1996, 1997) study of the rise of "the people's lobby" at the beginning of the twentieth century. She traces how labor, agrarian, and women's groups adopted and politicized distinct organizational forms and then creatively deployed them to foster mobilization and bolster collective identity among their respective constituencies.

More systematic attention has since been drawn to parallels in recent work on organizations and movements. Both trace the trajectories or path-dependent evolution of their subject matter. Both address framing and diffusion processes. Both analyze when and how states repress or facilitate organizational development or movement mobilization. Because they focus on similar causal mechanisms, both subfields have much to contribute to the other (Campbell 2005).

This convergence is also occurring on an empirical level where "processes of economic globalization, changing forms of production, the spread of information and communication technologies, and changing poles of power from states to corporations generate pressures for convergence in the processes of movements and organizations" (Davis and Zald 2005: 337). Given this, it is not surprising to find similar causal mechanisms in play, further promoting cross-fertilization between these subfields.

One of the most systematic treatments of these questions reveals independently developed but parallel conceptual tools that emerged in both fields. For example, the organizational language of institutional actors, institutional logics, and governance structures mirrors the movement vernacular of mobilizing structures, framing processes, and political opportunities, respectively (McAdam and Scott 2005).

Despite these similarities, organizational studies have traditionally stressed structure, established organizations, institutional authority, and localized regimes; movement scholars have emphasized process, emergent organizations, transgressive contention, and societal regimes (McAdam and Scott 2005). The fact that similar conceptual tools emerged from differing empirical arenas suggests the value of a common framework whereby each subfield could complement the other.

One such proposal identifies the organizational field as a unit of analysis containing dominants, challengers, and governance units embedded in a broader environment of external actors and larger governance units. In this field, social actors following institutional logics periodically set off destabilizing processes that in turn spark reactive mobilization. Key mechanisms are attributions of threat or opportunity, social appropriation, and the impact of new actors and innovative action. The outcome is a shift in strategic alignments, reconstituting the organizational field for the next round of contention. (McAdam and Scott 2005).

Although this proposal resonates with the contentious dynamics paradigm, other scholars have also been rethinking the role of organization in social movement theory and research. For example, Elisabeth Clemens and Debra Minkoff note that for too long, researchers faced an unfortunate "choice between the thin and homogenized sense of organization within resource mobilization research and the distrust of organization that stemmed from an emphasis on disruption and spontaneity" (2004: 155).

With a renewed appreciation of symbolic interactionist insights, however, "organizations take center stage as arenas of interaction. Rather than being homogenized as a 'resource,' particular organizations sustain distinctive cultures of interaction and shape trajectories of mobilization" (Clemens and Minkoff 2004: 157). Clemens's (1997) study of the people's lobby is one oft-cited example of how a richer notion of organizational repertoires can inform movement analysis. Another example is Elizabeth Armstrong's (2002, 2005) study of gay mobilization, in which prior homophile interest group organization was displaced by new organizational forms fostered by the New Left that facilitated a fundamentally new gay identity and liberation movement.

A final example of convergence among various subfields examines the "contentiousness of markets." Economic sociologists have long recognized that markets are politically mediated in a variety of ways; this insight has now been extended to the diverse ways in which movements as political actors not only challenge corporations but also create new pathways to market change and new market categories for entrepreneurial innovation (King and Pearce 2010).

All these developments have made it possible to see movements and organizations as "ships riding the same waves" or "twins separated at birth" (Davis et al. 2008: 389–390); this interface certainly promises to be one of the most productive avenues for new work on movements in the foreseeable future.

Alongside this emphasis on political and organizational factors is renewed attention to leadership and strategy. Ironically enough, it was not the structuralists but rather James Jasper's (1997) cultural approach that began deconstructing resources and organizations to reveal how skillful leaders artfully deploying novel strategies can succeed against strong opponents.

This story of David defeating Goliath is explicitly told in an analysis of how the resource-poor United Farm Workers led a successful union-organizing campaign in the 1960s and 1970s (Ganz 2000, 2009). In this case, the (high) quality of resourcefulness compensated for the (low) quantity of resources, producing victory against all odds and in contrast to the failures of similarly situated campaigns.

Resourcefulness is a matter of access to, and heuristic use of, salient information coupled with strategic capacity. The latter is enhanced to the extent that a "leadership team includes insiders and outsiders, strong and weak network ties, and access to diverse yet salient, repertoires of collective action and also if an organization conducts regular, open, authoritative deliberation, draws resources from multiple constituencies, and roots accountability in those constituencies" (Ganz 2000: 1005).

By emphasizing strategic capacity, this argument does not endorse a particular strategy but rather underscores the process of discovering effective strategies for a given set of challenges. Marshall Ganz sees this as an interactive learning process whereby experienced and resourceful leaders derive cumulative lessons from prior campaigns and that researchers can discover only by studying organizations over time.

A final permutation on structural approaches to collective action examines antisystemic movements in the world-capitalist system. The French Revolution unleashed such movements that ultimately led to social democratic politics in core countries, communist parties in the semiperiphery, and nationalist regimes in the periphery. In a second historical wave, these world-system zones were subsequently challenged by new social movements, antibureaucratic challenges, and renewed resistance to Westernization, respectively (Wallerstein 1990).

Global structures are relevant to understanding movements with more limited goals as well. Thus, core countries often provide resources and opportunities rarely seen elsewhere, fostering a permanent movement sector with diverse goals, frames, and strategies (McCarthy and Zald 1977). In other zones of the world system, restricted resources and opportunities contribute to the more episodic if occasionally explosive character of collective action.

World-system dynamics also shape movement activity. For example, the hegemonic maturity of the United States in the 1950s blunted working-class challenges, whereas the U.S. effort to maintain that hegemony a decade later in Southeast Asia sparked antiwar challenges that contributed to the 1960s protest cycle in many core countries. Thus, even domestic movement dynamics can be better understood by locating activism in the global structure and dynamics of the world-capitalist system (Buechler 2000).

Subsequent research has revealed waves of worldwide social movements since 1750 whose causes, dynamics, and potentials can be understood from a world-system perspective (Martin 2008a, 2008b). Such work is noted here as an ambitious example of macrostructural theorizing about movements; we will return to these arguments in the discussion of transnational movements and activism.

CULTURAL EMBELLISHMENTS

Cultural approaches have also explored new pathways in social movement analysis. From the mid-1980s to the mid-1990s, culture was essentially equated with the framing approach. Jasper (1997) then broadened the range of cultural questions to include biography, emotions, artfulness, and morality to counter the cognitive bias of framing approaches. Some recent cultural work shares framing theory's concern with symbolic representations, but seeks to transcend familiar framing topics and questions.

One problem with the framing paradigm has been a tendency to treat frames as overly static and ignore ongoing processes of framing, reframing, and counterframing (Benford 1997). Ingrid Miethe (2009) has suggested that by returning to Goffman's original notion of keying as an individual activity linked to biographical dispositions, framing can again be seen as a dynamic process that can explain otherwise unexpected alternations in movement trajectories and individual participation.

Framing theory has also been faulted for emphasizing cognition over discourse, leading to an "overly instrumentalist and individualistic theoretical outlook" that obscures the "collective, i. e. cultural nature of interpretation" (Ignatow 2009: 158). A corrective may be found in cognitive linguistics, which reveals that a primary function of language is to provide figurative signs, metaphors, and tropes. Such devices are collective, taken-for-granted elements of idioculture; focusing on them helps move beyond the individual cognitions typically addressed by conventional framing theory.

Yet another departure from framing uses speech act theory to explore the normative dimensions underlying protest. In the conventional view, protest is a strategic, instrumental conflict in which resources—including frames—are deployed by competing parties. Communication is simply part of the instrumental struggle to persuade audiences to support a particular side.

Speech act theory (as developed by John Austin [1962] and elaborated by Jürgen Habermas [1984/1987]) proposes a more basic role for communicative action in which "validity claims are raised, criticized, and rejected or accepted by participants" (Klimova 2009: 108). Communicative action highlights norms that are presumably shared by protesters and authorities alike. In this view, the struggle is less about garnering support and more about using discourse to invoke shared normative frameworks and "calling out" power holders who fail to abide by them.

Cultural emphases have also revealed additional dimensions of movement form and strategy. Concerning the former, the annual World Social Forum held to protest World Economic Forums has created a template "of an open and inclusive public space ... [in which] (p)articipation is open to all civil society groups" (Della Porta 2009: 183). This space is intentionally designed to foster deliberative democracy built upon discursive preference transformation rather than mere vote aggregation; it does so through rational argument oriented to the public good and striving for a consensus based on equality, inclusiveness, and transparency. Like the prefigurative politics of an earlier generation, such forms privilege symbolic meanings over instrumental efficiency.

Other work suggests that this may be a false dichotomy. Citing cultural-historical activity theory, John Krinsky and Colin Barker (2009) argue that when movements cultivate ongoing internal dialogues, it encourages developmental learning so that strategy becomes a collective, relational accomplishment rather than an individual leader's responsibility. By this logic, deliberative democracy may actually promote more effective strategizing.

Yet another thread in recent cultural work examines storytelling and narratives as "discursive processes that precede the formation of movement organizations or that take place outside their auspices" (Polletta 1998: 138). In her study of the Southern sit-in movement, Francesca Polletta (2006) repeatedly heard stories of how the tactic spread "like a fever." Such accounts acknowledged the spontaneity of the tactic, but interpreted it as an expression of local initiative, independence from adult leadership, and moral imperatives rather than simply an unplanned or accidental development

These narratives fostered a powerful collective identity that propelled increasing numbers of students into high-risk activism. Such narratives are often more "action-compelling" than conventional frames "by virtue of narrative's combination of familiarity and undecidability, convention and novelty, and truth (representing reality) and fiction (constituting reality)" (Polletta 1998: 152). It was the combination of "ambiguity, risk and mystery within a familiar discursive form" (Polletta 1998: 152) that motivated participants more effectively than conventional motivational framing.

Subsequent research on other movements confirms that the power of narratives in movements derives not "from the clarity of their moral message but from their allusiveness, indeed, their ambiguity" (Polletta 2009: 33). At the same time, cultural norms operate as significant constraints on how such stories must be told if they are to be effective in galvanizing supporters and neutralizing opposition.

Thus, one disadvantage movement storytellers face is the cultural hegemony of mainstream stories reinforced in many variations so as to entrench a "common sense" worldview that is difficult to dislodge with counternarratives. This is why ambiguity and ambivalence in movement narratives may be effective where didactic polemics are not.

A second obstacle concerns cultural norms about how stories are told, heard, evaluated, or believed. Such norms vary by issue, historical period, and setting, so that stories about "victims" that are persuasive in one setting or in a mass media context may be less so at other times or in a court of law. One strategic lesson is that personal narratives are highly effective when there is widespread skepticism about expert knowledge and opinion. Where personal stories can be dismissed as "merely" anecdotal, however, activists may be better advised to compose statistical "stories" that resonate with scientific norms of evidence and credibility (Polletta 2009).

Others have examined how movement storytelling claims credit for movement successes and the conditions under which such stories become credible and widespread (Meyer 2009). Still others have tackled the different issue of how movements besmirched by disreputable followers must develop narratives that accomplish boundary maintenance and reputational defense (Fine 2009). The breadth of these examinations of narrative suggests that it will be a major emphasis of ongoing cultural work on social movements.

SYNTHESIS 2.0?

The foregoing suggests that even the most recent developments in social movement theory still cluster around structural and cultural poles. The fault line examined in the previous chapter between contentious dynamics (and structural approaches in general) and passionate politics (and cultural analyses more broadly) has thus persisted through the first decade of the twenty-first century.

Advocates of the contentious dynamics approach have pursued their agenda in a number of books and anthologies. Although they have acknowledged cultural factors by recognizing framing and attributional processes, they have not fundamentally wavered from their original conception of their subject matter.

This conception maintains that social movements (in the earlier political process approach) or contentious dynamics (in the newer paradigm) involve public, episodic, and conflictual claims-making in which at least one of the parties is a government. Put more succinctly, these structural approaches have been resolutely state-centered; conflicts not involving states are dismissed by definition from their conceptualization of their subject matter.

As noted previously, this unwavering focus has been widely criticized. Here we examine one line of criticism in more detail because it has opened the door to a new proposal for another synthesis that might bridge the gap between structural and cultural approaches. Unlike the synthesis of 1996, this one comes from the "culturalist" side of the divide in social movement theory.

Thus, a major proponent of framing theory has criticized contentious politics as "an emerging conceptual hegemony" (Snow 2004) that marginalizes all non–state-centered forms of collective action. This conceptual hegemony leads to a categorical straitjacket by virtually excluding religious, expressive, communal, or identity-based social movements from consideration. Such hegemony can also be challenged on empirical grounds. A recent analysis of protest events (including civil rights, gay and lesbian, and women's movements) reveals that they frequently target public opinion or other nonstate institutions (Van Dyke, Soule, and Taylor 2004). These, too, are excluded in the contentious dynamics paradigm.

This paradigm also has conceptual limitations. It endorses only one focal organizing concept (contentious dynamics) in a field that has historically embraced several, such as social movement organizations, networks of interaction, or ideologically structured action. It privileges institutional and political contention even as its proponents acknowledge the ubiquity of contention in various settings (Snow 2004: 9). Finally, it constricts our notion of social change to political and institutional realms at the expense of cultural, personal, or symbolic transformation.

These criticisms support calls for a more "inclusive and elastic conceptualization" (Snow 2004: 10) that encompasses nonstate, collective challenges; recognizes multiple levels of social life; and acknowledges diverse organizational forms. David Snow (2004) proposes the concept of structures or systems of authority that can be the target of collective challenges across a range of institutional settings.

These ideas were subsequently elaborated in the development of a "multi-institutional politics approach to social movements" (Armstrong and Bernstein 2008). This model is explicitly contrasted with the political process/contentious politics approach, which has a number of "awkward moments" or blind spots.

As noted, movements that target cultural hegemony, civil society, or corporations do not easily fit the contentious politics model. The latter's materialist conception of politics marginalizes identity politics, symbolic challenges, and movement participation by white middle-class people who have no obvious structural grievances. Not only does the contentious politics paradigm fail to recognize constituencies pursuing cultural goals or prefigurative strategies, it also has difficulty recognizing how cultural challenges can be consequential for political change (Taylor et al. 2009).

Invoking an old dichotomy in movement theory, Elizabeth Armstrong and Mary Bernstein see the contentious dynamics approach as focusing on the *how* of collective action while ignoring or assuming the *why* of such action. To restore an appreciation of the latter, the authors borrow an insight from new social movement theory "that study of the relationship between forms of domination and forms of challenge should be central to the study of movements" (Armstrong and Bernstein 2008: 81).

If social forms and movement challenges are linked as new social movement theorists have traditionally claimed, then "the investigation of the goals and strategies of movements are opportunities for insight into the nature of domination in contemporary societies" (Armstrong and Bernstein 2008: 82).

This suggests a conception of society as a multi-institutional field in which different institutions operate with distinct logics or organizing principles. The state is one, but it is by no means the only or necessarily the most important such institution. All such institutions exercise both material and symbolic power, so that meaning is constitutive of structure every bit as much as structures shape meanings. All such institutions may provoke collective challenges to their authority, and each challenge is a legitimate topic of study.

Although Armstrong and Bernstein are careful not to overstate their case, their argument suggests a second-generation synthesis in social movement theory. Whereas the earlier synthesis of 1996 sought to fuse two structural approaches (resource mobilization and political process) with one cultural approach (framing) and privileged the former, this synthesis strikes a somewhat different balance.

In this newer version, there is more genuine appreciation of the truly interactive and mutually constitutive roles of the material and the symbolic or the political and cultural realms. Informed by the theoretical work of Anthony Giddens, Pierre Bourdieu, and Michel Foucault, as well as organizational theories and neoinstitutional approaches, this newer synthesis has the potential to transcend older, theoretically debilitating dualisms and dichotomies. It denies nothing in the structural paradigm other than its claim to privileged status; it rather broadens conceptions of movement actors, targets, goals, and strategies in provocative ways. The fact that this paper won the 2009 "Outstanding Article Award" from the Collective Behavior and Social Movements section of the ASA suggests its potential impact on the field.

MOVEMENTS IN CYBERSPACE

Alongside these theoretical permutations, embellishments, and syntheses, two new "spaces" for collective action are receiving systematic attention: "cyberactivism" on the Internet and transnational activism around the globe. Movement developments in these spaces are closely related as well.

Although the Internet may be new, it is hardly the first technological innovation to impact collective action. It fits a trend whereby technological developments decrease intrinsic costs of mobilization and organization but increase extrinsic costs of repression (Tilly 1978). In the case of the Internet, more profoundly qualitative changes in the very texture of activism and the repertoire of contention may also be emerging.

Computer-mediated communications lower costs of recruitment, organization, and mobilization in numerous ways. They provide virtually free publicity about organizations, events, meetings, and protests. They facilitate coordinated activity that could be difficult or costly by other means. They can minimize intrinsic challenges of organizational maintenance over time. Finally, they can develop or extend collective identities beyond face-to-face networks. The Internet has thus become a potentially major resource, opportunity, or organizational substitute facilitating collective action.

Such potentials are captured in the very title of *Click on Democracy: The Internet's Power to Turn Political Apathy into Action* (Davis, Elin, and Reeher 2002), which documents Internet-inspired activism during the 2000 election. These accounts illustrate the Web's potential for providing social capital and nourishing civic engagement. Although mindless web surfing can sedate users, these accounts suggest the Internet's capacity to propel people into political activism (Elin 2003).

The Internet's potential for altering the texture of social relations is suggested in claims that it can promote communal, gemeinschaft-like relations (Elin 2003: 109) and that it may approximate Habermas's notion of the public sphere. Although falling short of the ideal speech situation, computer-mediated communications can foster nonhierarchical, self-reflexive discourse that is difficult to achieve in conventional settings and that many regard as central to progressive activism (Salter 2003).

For every claim about how cyberspace facilitates collective action, there are counterclaims or reservations about its impact as well. One of the earliest cautions acknowledged that email networks have an "obvious capacity to reduce transaction costs and transmit information quickly across national lines, but they do not promise the same degree of crystallization, of mutual trust and collective identity, as do the interpersonal ties in social networks" (Tarrow 1998: 241). The extent to which e-ties can substitute for interpersonal ones remains to be clarified (Calhoun 1998; Galusky 2003; Lebert 2003).

Glowing accounts of the Internet's potential also need to be tempered with reminders that it remains a form of instrumental rationality with its own logic. It is a space subject to commodification and corporatization that in turn has inspired activism to preserve net neutrality and democratic access. Although it can promote collective identities, they are frequently categorical rather than interpersonal (Calhoun 1998), and they can be readily deployed to target advertising and channel consumption rather than promote collective action (McLaine 2003; J. Gamson 2003).

Computer-mediated communications are also an "equal opportunity" technology available to reactionary or terrorist movements as well as social control agents.

They facilitate new tactics such as "hacktivism," but they also expose movements to new forms of surveillance, sabotage, and e-repression. More generally, it appears that for every account of how the Internet may complement traditional activism (Kidd 2003), there are others in which it redirects movement energy into more trivial pursuits (Ayers 2003).

Empirical work at three distinct levels of analysis illustrates the Internet's potentials and pitfalls. Its greatest impact on collective action may be at the global level. Thus, the Hemispheric Social Alliance "has employed Internet technologies to communicate, strategize, educate and pressure state authorities in an effort to promote an alternative social-developmental vision" (Ayres 2005: 35). In this case, Internet activism has complemented conventional collective action, enriching the repertoire of contention and expanding collective protest beyond nation-state boundaries.

This raises the question of whether "the Internet can be used *for* protest, or does it simply *support* RL [real life] protests?" (McCaughey and Ayers 2003: 5; italics in original). One answer emerges from a national-level analysis of the movement for strategic voting in the 2000 presidential election whereby voters "traded" Gore votes in close states for Nader votes in safely Democratic ones.

This "strategic voting movement was dominated by on-line activity and organizing" (Earl and Schussman 2003: 159) to the virtual exclusion of conventional activism. As an exclusively e-movement, it dispensed with the costs of sustaining a traditional social movement organization; indeed, webmasters actually declined financial contributions, noting that "web sites are cheap" (quoted in Earl and Schussman 2003: 178). In lieu of organization, movement entrepreneurs assumed a central role as they orchestrated the campaign and shifted the locus of movement decision making.

A local animal rights movement provides a third distinct story. In this case, conventional movement organizations experienced significant factionalism and their members suffered from high levels of burnout. In response, movement leaders turned to the Internet to create a virtual abeyance structure that not only maintained movement continuity but provided new strategies and tactics of collective action (Sin 2009).

Unlike conventional abeyance structures, this virtual one reduced internal costs, dampened schisms, fostered decentralization, and actually promoted more action-oriented tactics during a period of seeming abeyance and latency than during the height of organizational dominance. This trajectory suggests how Internet-based activism may require rethinking of conventional movement concepts and propositions (Sin 2009).

These cases suggest that cyberactivism can complement, substitute for, or evolve out of more conventional collective action. Missing from this *tableau* are movements that originate in cyberspace and then evolve into real-space activism; this may be the acid test of the Internet's importance for collective action. In any event, this work illustrates both the potentials and pitfalls of cyberactivism for social movements.

TRANSNATIONAL ACTIVISM

Sometimes intertwined with cyberactivism, new forms of transnational activism are also attracting increasing attention. As many have noted, the modern social movement arose as an autonomous, modular, and cosmopolitan form of action alongside the nation-state; the latter often provoked grievances and provided a target (Tilly 2004). For the political process and contentious dynamics paradigms, movements are essentially defined as political challenges to national governments.

By a similar logic, the emergence of transnational movements is intertwined with the rise of multinational organizations and multilateral institutions in economic and political realms. Their appearance continues the scale shift from local particular collective actions (e.g., bread riots) to autonomous national social movements, to transnational challenges confronting global institutions and processes.

For well over a decade, scholars have been mapping the transnational social movement sector, revealing movement clusters advocating human rights, women's rights, environmental preservation, peace, and development causes. This sector also displays increasing linkages and geographical dispersion among transnational social movements, intergovernmental, and non-governmental organizations (Smith 1997).

In response to the globalization of movements, scholars undertook the globalization of social movement theory (McCarthy 1997). Early efforts sought to demonstrate that familiar social movement concepts and processes such as movement sectors, mobilizing structures, framing strategies, resource mobilization, political opportunities, and contentious repertoires could be extended from national to transnational movements (Smith, Pagnucco, and Chatfield 1997; McCarthy 1997).

Subsequent work addressed how transnational activism might challenge the premises of mainstream movement theory. For example, the "strong" transnational movement thesis asserts that national political opportunity structures are giving way to transnational ones, that states are losing their capacity to constrain movements, that electronic communication has fundamentally altered movement processes, and that a new transnational civil society is developing (Tarrow 1998).

Such assertions should be treated with caution. On the one hand, claims about the novelty of transnational activism are dubious given the long history of abolitionist, women's rights, humanitarian, and pacifist movements. On the other hand, it is also doubtful whether the interpersonal networks that have proven so vital to national activism can be constructed for transnational activism; "even with … structural preconditions, the transaction costs of linking the indigenous groups of a variety of countries into integrated transnational networks would be difficult for any social movement to overcome" (Tarrow 1998: 235).

Such complexities suggest a typology of transnational collective action that distinguishes genuine movements from other forms. Many so-called transnational movements involve either temporary campaigns or nonintegrated domestic social networks, exemplified by cross-border diffusion, transnational issue networks, and political exchange. If genuine transnational movements require both integrated domestic networks and sustained campaigns, they are rarer than casual use of the term implies (Tarrow 1998; see also Della Porta and Kriesi 1999, and Tarrow 2002).

This conceptual clarification eventually led to a working definition of transnational collective action as *"coordinated international campaigns on the part of networks of activists against international actors, other states, or international institutions"* (Della Porta and Tarrow: 2005a: 2–3; italics in original). This definition clarifies that some forms of transnational action involve familiar processes addressed by prior movement theory.

This applies, for instance, to diffusion whereby activists in one locale adopt issues, forms, or frames from other settings. It also applies to internalization or domestication, where conflicts originating externally are played out in a domestic setting. It finally applies to externalization, in which movements appeal to international bodies to intervene in or resolve national conflicts (Della Porta and Tarrow 2005a).

Three types of changes have promoted new features of transnational collective action. These include environmental changes such as the collapse of the Soviet bloc, increases in electronic communication and international travel, and the "growing power of transnational corporations and international institutions" (Della Porta and Tarrow 2005a: 8). Second, cognitive changes have allowed protesters to learn and mimic successful frames and tactics from protesters in distant locales. Finally, relational changes have promoted more horizontal, transnational coalitions, leading to "a movement of movements" (Della Porta and Tarrow 2005a).

Although these changes have not produced a truly global civil society, they have led to a "complex internationalism" consisting of a "triangular set of relationships among states, international institutions, and nonstate actors" (Della Porta and Tarrow 2005b: 231). This system creates new multilevel political opportunities and constraints for transnational activism. It also creates a new activist stratum of "rooted cosmopolitans" with multiple belongings and flexible identities that provide a heterogeneous social base of people who "combine the resources and opportunities of their own societies with ... 'activism beyond borders'" (Della Porta and Tarrow 2005b: 238).

This applies to the empirical case of the global justice movement, which qualifies as a transnational movement on several grounds (Della Porta 2007). It employs frames that reflect global identities, issues, and concerns opposing neoliberal globalization. It consists of organizational networks that operate in multiple countries, rely upon a horizontal, network structure, and embrace internal movement democracy. Finally, the movement pursues multiple coequal issues through the confrontational tactics of nonviolent direct action and civil disobedience.

The underlying reasons for this globalization of protest flow from changes in the global political economy. Just as new social movement theory argued that new social structures call forth new types of movements, the globalization of economic profit making and political policy formulation has provoked correspondingly transnational movement challenges. Given the manner in which globalization has reduced state capacity and undermined democratic decision making, the globalization of resistance is a perfectly logical response to shifts in the global political economy (Smith 2005).

This conflict involves contested versions of globalization. On one side is a neoliberal vision of a globalized world organized around market principles. Its proponents include (some) national governmental bodies, transnational corporations, global financial institutions, currency speculators, and commercial media outlets. On the other side is a vision of democratic globalism built on participation from below. Its proponents include civil society groups; local, national, and transnational movement organizations; elements of progressive political parties; and independent media organizations (Smith 2008: 6ff).

Situating the movement for global justice (Della Porta 2007) or global democracy (Smith 2008) in the context of this conflict with neoliberal globalizers reveals how both sides are engaged in building organizations, mobilizing resources, and developing frames that advance their respective visions. This oppositional dance is nicely illustrated in the episodic gatherings of the neoliberal World Economic Forum on one side and the democratic World Social Forum on the other (Smith et al. 2008).

Transnational movements have been addressed in rather different terms by world-system theorists (Wallerstein 1990). These scholars operate with a global unit of analysis—the world-capitalist system—that provides an overarching context for several centuries of global collective action. Although this approach is less focused on the minutiae of recruitment, frames, organization, or resources, it offers some provocative insights into global activism.

World-system theorists are in perhaps the best situation to remind us that transnational movements are not historically new. They are particularly interested in antisystemic movements, and the hypothesis that "for at least several hundred years there have been successive waves of movements that have attacked and destabilized the capitalist world-economy, its hegemonic powers, and dominant geocultures, and yet, at the same time, have come to provide legitimacy and the foundation for a new ordering of accumulation and political rule on a world scale" (Martin 2008a: 1).

In this view, recent transnational activism may signify the crest of a new wave of antisystemic movements. Whereas conventional movement theory emphasized the rationalization, normalization, and institutionalization of movements in the 1980s and 1990s, recent transnational movements have exhibited highly confrontational tactics and decidedly anticapitalist and antistate stances. As a result, "fewer and fewer movements can be neatly encapsulated in the models that came to focus upon national, normative, and institutionalized movement activity and organizations" whereas "[a]ttempts to inflate dominant nation-state models to cover disruptive, noninstitutionalized, and transnational movements have flourished, but with mixed success at best" (Martin 2008a: 3–4).

Antisystemic movement waves can be dated from at least the "long eighteenth century" (1750–1850) when a remarkable range of transformative movements sought to "defend the possibility of social life outside the clutches of capitalism" (Agartan et al. 2008: 47). Historical accounts of this period reveal a "startling transnational and transoceanic connection among local movements, something that is often held to be possible only in today's age of globalization" (Agartan et al. 2008: 47).

Such activity became full-fledged antisystemic movements between 1848 and 1917. As labor, anarchist, antislavery, and anticolonial movements challenged the imperatives of the world-capitalist system, they paradoxically strengthened state structures by "pulling antisystemic resistance within safer bounds for the ongoing operations of historical capitalism" (Bush 2008: 51). At the same time, such challenges prompted transformations in regimes of accumulation, as when effective national labor movements inadvertently pushed domestic capital to seek cheaper labor abroad.

In the next broad period, from 1917 to 1968, formerly antisystemic challengers assumed or at least shared state power and thereby lost their antisystemic character. As labor and social democratic forces entered the system they formerly challenged, "antisystemic struggle was taken up by radical nationalists in the colonial world" (Bush and Morris 2008: 84). By the end of this period, formerly antisystemic forces were wielding state power to wage wars against national liberation movements, stoking not only anticolonial movements but also a new wave of antisystemic resistance in the form of student, antiwar, and New Left movements in the core and subsequent popular uprisings in the Soviet bloc and the "Third World."

In the most recent historical period, from 1968 to the present, the expansion and penetration of the capitalist mode of production has proceeded along vectors of culture, consumption, subjectivity, and identity. "These developments have in turn reawakened identities and localized groups based on common interest, religion, ethnicity, or 'tribe' ... while the ideological forces inherent in socialism, nationalism, and communism have weakened" (Kalouche and Mielants 2008: 164).

Given the relative decline of national states and the diffusion of capitalist control strategies, it is not surprising that contemporary global activism is more likely to target international bodies and organizations (the UN, WTO, IMF, World Bank, and so on) than individual states and corporations. Such activities pose an antisystemic challenge to capitalist world-system equilibrium, but they "do not yet ... constitute an 'antisystemic movement' with an organizational infrastructure that sustains the effective power of consistent, recurring, and threatening actions" (Kalouche and Mielants 2008: 165).

A world-system perspective thereby reveals clusters of worldwide, antisystemic activity that have been occurring for more than two centuries. Moreover, "transcontinental linkages are evident in all our epochs, even centuries before the recent focus on globalization and antiglobalization movements" (Martin 2008b: 169). Finally, these waves of activism have periodically been able to change "the contours and processes that form the world-economy" and alter "the conditions within which future movements form, and the forces against which they protest" (Martin 2008b: 170).

CONCLUSION

Over the last three decades, social movement theory has seen the sequential appearance of several robust paradigms for analyzing collective action. Beginning in the late 1970s, the resource mobilization, political process, and framing approaches arose. They were soon joined by new social movement theories, diverse cultural insights, and the contentious dynamics paradigm. Although various attempts at synthesis across these perspectives have not been completely convincing, there has been notable cross-fertilization and enrichment across paradigms that are particularly striking when set against the theoretical lethargy found in some other sociological subfields.

This diversity of movement paradigms resonates with the broader, postpositivist era of competing epistemological frameworks across the social sciences. It means that social movement scholars not only have a rich toolkit but also that this diversity of approaches and the novel combinations of concepts it encourages enjoys scholarly legitimacy and continues to foster rigorous criticism and productive debates.

If there was a danger that movement theory would settle into overly familiar, institutionalized patterns (like many movements themselves), it has been at least partially offset by new types of activism on the Internet and around the globe. These movements provide natural empirical laboratories for testing whether and how concepts, propositions, and hypotheses that were developed for one era and type of activism require modification, specification, or replacement to adequately capture these new forms. This combination of conceptual "pushes" and empirical "pulls" should continue enriching social movement theory into the foreseeable future.

Epilogue

Social movements first arose amid broad social changes that ushered in the modern age. These social changes included the expansion of markets, the building of states, the industrialization of production, the proletarianization of labor, and the growth of cities. Such changes provoked grievances and provided targets for social movements, which emerged as challengers developed new repertoires of contention that allowed them to intervene repeatedly in national affairs to make claims through large-scale coordinated action (Tilly 2004). For more than two centuries, social movements have evolved alongside the other defining elements of modernity itself.

The same changes that sparked the social movement as a form of collective action also contributed to the rise of sociology as an academic discipline. Both social movements and sociology share a basic premise that the world is a social construction. For social movements, it is a construction that stands in need of transformation; for sociology, it is a construction that stands in need of explanation. Although they responded differently to this shared social constructionist premise, it has nonetheless linked social activism and the study of that activism from the beginning (Buechler 2000).

This volume has presented a sociological history of social movement theory. Such theory has obviously changed dramatically over the many decades that sociologists have studied social movements. The philosophy of science offers various explanations of theoretical evolution in scientific endeavors, though they only roughly fit the story we have told.

For instance, Karl Popper (1965) proposed that science advances not by establishing "truths" but rather by proposing conjectures that are tested and inevitably refuted. By this refutationalist logic, the rejection of inferior explanations gradually allows a science to develop better explanations even though all remain vulnerable to future refutations.

Although instructive in the natural sciences and occasionally applicable to the social sciences, this story rarely fits the sociological study of social movements. One exception might be the prediction emerging out of mass society theory that socially isolated individuals are most prone to become involved in collective behavior.

Subsequent research on social networks, preexisting organizations, and bloc recruitment convincingly rejected this logic.

More generally, however, sociological theory is not as linear, deductive, rigorous, or deterministic as Popper's vision implies, and it can rarely conduct the definitive experiment or generate the conclusive data that warrants the complete refutation of a given hypothesis. Finally, sociological theory (and, less obviously, natural science theory) is subject to extra-scientific, social influences that Popper's model ignores.

Another vision of scientific progress is Thomas Kuhn's (1962) study of paradigm shifts and scientific revolutions. In this view, "normal science" proceeds within the premises of a given paradigm until unavoidable anomalies emerge that cannot be explained within that paradigm. This circumstance may then trigger a paradigm shift to a qualitatively different set of premises that resolves the anomaly and allows scientific theory and research to pursue fundamentally different questions.

This vision also has limited applicability to the study of social movements. Sociology has rarely had a single dominant paradigm, much less a set of anomalies so basic as to precipitate a fundamental shift from one paradigm to another across the entire discipline. Having said that, the idea of a "paradigm shift" has been popularized in a more casual sense to refer to shifting perspectives within a field or subfield.

In this more casual usage, perhaps the biggest paradigm shift in the study of social movements occurred with the decline of the collective behavior approach and the rise of the resource mobilization alternative in the late 1970s, The longer history of social movement theory, however, suggests that this was a relative rather than an absolute shift, and that both before and after the shift the work being done was less "normal science" within a single paradigm than a congeries of different approaches or perspectives that have always commingled within the field of social movements.

Despite these examples, the evolution of social movement theory has departed from both Popper's model of conjectures and refutations and Kuhn's vision of normal science and paradigm shifts. Rather than following either of these grand theories of scientific development, "the study of social movements is one whose history is less a story of the cumulation of knowledge moving toward a goal than a collection of separate issues and problems with diverse orientations and perspectives" (Gusfield 1978: 122). Hence, the more modest approach taken in this volume has been to identify the multiple influences at work in different sociohistorical periods that have shaped the concepts, questions, answers, and very subject matter of collective action.

This account is thus much closer to Mayer Zald's (1995) argument that progress and cumulation in the human sciences occurs within epistemic communities that develop their own cultures, organize around specific topics, preserve certain consensually defined findings, and dispense their own organizational rewards and punishments. Because sociology is a fragmented field, questions of progress and cumulation are best posed at the level of subfields rather than the discipline as a whole.

Consistent with this vision, this study has emphasized three sets of contextual issues that bear on the study of social movements. The first involves the matrix of social science disciplines and the division of labor between disciplines and within subfields, and how they have changed over time. This has allowed us to trace a story that began before social science disciplinary boundaries and identities were even firmly drawn, through their establishment and entrenchment, to the corresponding constrictions and opportunities this created. Although things rarely come full circle, it is striking that in recent work there have been both calls for and evidence of more interdisciplinary efforts that synthesize work previously segregated into distinct disciplines and subfields.

A second contextual factor has been the prevailing intellectual climate, currents and trends, and how changes in them have affected the study of movements. This revealed another dimension of the story. Social movements were once subsumed under a generic category of collective behavior with connotations of spontaneous, episodic, emotional, or irrational activity. The rational actor model (originating in economics and subsequently diffusing across the social sciences) then provided a conceptual crowbar that pried social movements loose from the confines of the collective behavior tradition. Shortly thereafter, the cultural turn in social theory challenged this rational actor model, and sought to restore emotions as well as other cultural dynamics that had been relegated to the sidelines. More recently, the quest for a more dynamic or relational approach to contentious processes has threatened to subsume social movements under a broader category once again.

The third contextual factor has obviously involved the kinds of movements that operate in a given historical period and how they shape prevailing conceptions of what movements are and which questions are posed about them. Here, our story began with revolutionary challenges to capitalist industrialization, proceeded to the linkages between movements, parties, and their institutionalization or oligarchization, and moved on to the role of crowds and crowd behavior. The latter eventually received more refined and analytically careful attention in the collective behavior tradition. As extremist movements supporting authoritarian, totalitarian, communist, or fascist regimes moved center stage, both collective behavior and political sociology analyzed these groups. The 1960s protest cycle then sparked one of the most innovative periods in social movement theorizing as resource mobilization and political process theory arose to analyze movements that did not easily fit within earlier paradigms. Although the cycle abated, it created a climate that nurtured symbolic, or identity-based, movements that in turn provoked new paradigms emphasizing cultural dynamics and underscoring what was "new" about these movements and the structures they challenged. As of this writing, still other new forms of activism (including cyberprotest and transnational activism) are stimulating fresh conceptual developments and innovative empirical investigations.

The theoretical developments of the last three decades in particular have made the field of social movements one of the most vibrant areas within sociology. In part, this is due to the constantly evolving, often dramatic, and sometimes unanticipated forms that collective action takes. It is also due to the dialogues that proponents of different approaches have cultivated and sustained. When compared with many

References

Abbott, Andrew. 1999. *Department and Discipline.* Chicago: University of Chicago Press.

Adorno, Theodor, Else Frenkel-Brunscik, Daniel J. Levinson, and R. Nevitt Sanford. 1950/1982. *The Authoritarian Personality,* abridged edition. New York: Norton.

Agartan, Tuba, Woo-Young Choi, and Tu Hunyh. 2008. "The Transformation of the Capitalist World, 1750–1850." In William G. Martin, ed., *Making Waves: Worldwide Social Movements, 1750–2005,* pp. 10–49. Boulder, CO: Paradigm.

Aguirre, Benigno E. 1994. "Collective Behavior and Social Movement Theory." In Russell R. Dynes and Kathleen J. Tierney, eds., *Disasters, Collective Behavior and Social Organization,* pp. 257–272. Newark, DE: University of Delaware Press.

Aguirre, Benigno E. and E. L. Quarantelli. 1983. "Methodological, Ideological, and Conceptual-Theoretical Criticisms of the Field of Collective Behavior: A Critical Evaluation and Implications for Future Study. *Sociological Focus* 16: 195–216.

Amenta, Edwin. 1998. *Bold Relief.* Princeton, NJ: Princeton University Press.

———. 2006. *When Movements Matter: The Townsend Plan and the Rise of Social Security.* Princeton, NJ: Princeton University Press.

Amenta, Edwin, Drew Halfmann, and Michael P. Young. 1999. "The Strategies and Contexts of Social Protest: Political Mediation and the Impact of the Townsend Movement in California." *Mobilization* 4: 1–23.

Anderson, Charles. 1974. *The Political Economy of Social Class.* Englewood Cliffs, NJ: Prentice-Hall.

Andreas, Joel. 2007. "The Structure of Charismatic Mobilization: A Case Study of Rebellion During the Chinese Cultural Revolution." *American Sociological Review* 72: 434–458.

Armstrong, Elizabeth. 2002. *Forging Gay Identities: Organizing Sexuality in San Francisco, 1950–1994.* Chicago: University of Chicago Press.

———. 2005. "From Struggle to Settlement: The Crystallization of a Field of Lesbian/Gay Organizations in San Francisco, 1969–1973." In Gerald Davis, Doug McAdam, W. Richard Scott, and Mayer N. Zald, eds., *Social Movements and Organization Theory,* pp. 161–187. Cambridge: Cambridge University Press.

Armstrong, Elizabeth and Mary Bernstein. 2008. "Culture, Power, and Institutions: A Multi-Institutional Politics Approach to Social Movements." *Sociological Theory* 26: 74–99.

Asch, Solomon. 1952. *Social Psychology.* New York: Prentice-Hall.

Austin, John L. 1962. *How to Do Things with Words.* Cambridge, MA: Harvard University Press.

Ayers, Michael D. 2003. "Comparing Collective Identity in Online and Offline Feminist Activists." In Martha McCaughey and Michael Ayers, eds., *Cyberactivism: Online Activism in Theory and Practice,* pp. 145–164. New York: Routledge.

Ayres, Jeffrey M. 2005. "Transnational Activism in the Americas: The Internet and Innovations in the Repertoire of Contention." In Patrick Coy, ed., *Research in Social Movements, Conflicts and Change* 26: 35–61. Oxford, England: Elsevier.

Bell, Daniel. 1960. *The End of Ideology.* Glencoe, IL: Free Press.

———(ed). 1955. *The New American Right.* New York: Criterion.

———(ed). 1964. *The Radical Right.* New York: Anchor.

Bellah, Robert. 2005. "Durkheim and Ritual." In Jeffrey Alexander and Philip Smith, eds., *The Cambridge Companion to Durkheim,* pp. 183–210. Cambridge: Cambridge University Press.

Benford, Robert. 1997. "An Insider's Critique of the Social Movement Framing Perspective." *Sociological Inquiry* 67 (4): 409–430.

Berezin, Mabel. 2001. "Emotions and Political Identity: Mobilizing Affection for the Polity." In Jeff Goodwin, James Jasper, and Francesca Polletta, eds., *Passionate Politics,* pp. 83–98. Chicago: University of Chicago Press.

Berger, Peter and Thomas Luckmann. 1966. *The Social Construction of Reality.* Garden City, NY: Anchor.

Bernstein, Mary. 1997. "Celebration and Suppression: The Strategic Uses of Identity by the Lesbian and Gay Movement." *American Journal of Sociology* 103: 531–565.

Blau, Peter. 1964. *Exchange and Power in Social Life.* New York: Wiley.

Blumer, Herbert. 1951. "The Field of Collective Behavior." In A. M. Lee, ed., *Principles of Sociology,* pp. 167–222. New York: Barnes & Noble.

———. 1969. *Symbolic Interactionism: Perspective and Method.* Englewood Cliffs, NJ: Prentice-Hall.

Boggs, Carl. 1986. *Social Movements and Political Power.* Philadelphia: Temple University Press.

Bourdieu, Pierre. 1977. *Outline of a Theory of Practice.* New York: Cambridge University Press.

Brand, Karl-Werner. 1990. "Cyclical Aspects of New Social Movements: Waves of Cultural Criticism and Mobilization Cycles of New Middle-Class Radicalism." In Russell J. Dalton and Manfred Kuechler, eds., *Challenging the Political Order,* pp. 24–42. New York: Oxford University Press.

Buechler, Steven M. 1993. "Beyond Resource Mobilization Theory?" *The Sociological Quarterly* 34: 217–235.

———. 1995. "New Social Movement Theories." *The Sociological Quarterly* 36: 441–464.

———. 2000. *Social Movements in Advanced Capitalism: The Political Economy and Cultural Construction of Social Activism.* New York: Oxford University Press.

———. 2004. "The Strange Career of Strain and Breakdown Theories of Collective Action." In David A. Snow, Sarah Soule, and Hanspeter Kriesi, eds., *The Blackwell Companion to Social Movements,* pp. 47–66. Malden, MA: Blackwell.

———. Forthcoming. "Mass Society Theory." In David A. Snow, Donatella Della Porta, Bert Klandermans, and Doug McAdam, eds., *The Blackwell Encyclopedia of Social and Political Movements.* Oxford: Blackwell.

Bush, Caleb. 2008. "Reformers and Revolutionaries: The Rise of Antisystemic Movements and the Paradox of Power, 1848–1917." In William G. Martin, ed. *Making Waves: Worldwide Social Movements, 1750–2005,* pp. 50–81. Boulder, CO: Paradigm.

Bush, Caleb and Rochelle Morris. 2008. "Empires Crumble, Movements Fall: Antisystemic Struggle, 1917–1968." In William G. Martin, ed. *Making Waves: Worldwide Social Movements, 1750–2005*, pp. 82–127. Boulder, CO: Paradigm.

Calhoun, Craig. 1993. "'New Social Movements of the Nineteenth Century." *Social Science History* 17: 385–427.

———. 1998. "Community without Propinquity Revisited: Communications Technology and the Transformation of the Urban Public Sphere." *Sociological Inquiry* 68: 373–397.

———. 2001. "Putting Emotions in their Place." In Jeff Goodwin, James Jasper, and Francesca Polletta, eds., *Passionate Politics*, pp. 45–57. Chicago: University of Chicago Press.

Campbell, John L. 2005. "Where Do We Stand? Common Mechanisms in Organizations and Social Movement Research." In Gerald Davis, Doug McAdam, W. Richard Scott, and Mayer N. Zald, eds., *Social Movements and Organization Theory*, pp. 41–68. Cambridge: Cambridge University Press.

Castells, Manuel. 1978. *City, Class and Power*. New York: St. Martin's.

———. 1983. *The City and the Grassroots: A Cross-Cultural Theory of Urban Social Movements*. Berkeley: University of California Press.

Clemens, Elisabeth. 1996. "Organizational Form as Frame: Collective Identity and Political Strategy in the American Labor Movement, 1880–1920." In Doug McAdam, John D. McCarthy, and Mayer N. Zald, eds., *Comparative Perspectives on Social Movements: Political Opportunities, Mobilizing Structures, and Cultural Framings*, pp. 205–226. Cambridge: Cambridge University Press.

———. 1997. *The People's Lobby: Organizational Innovation and the Rise of Interest Group Politics in the United States, 1890–1925*. Chicago: University of Chicago Press.

Clemens, Elisabeth and Debra C. Minkoff. 2004. "Beyond the Iron Law: Rethinking the Place of Organizations in Social Movement Research." In David A. Snow, Sarah Soule, and Hanspeter Kreisi, eds., *The Blackwell Companion to Social Movements*, pp. 155–170. Malden, MA: Blackwell.

Cohen, Jean. 1982. "Between Crisis Management and Social Movements: The Place of Institutional Reform." *Telos* 52: 21–40.

———. 1983. "Rethinking Social Movements." *Berkeley Journal of Sociology*: 28: 97–113.

———. 1985. "Strategy or Identity: New Theoretical Paradigms and Contemporary Social Movements." *Social Research* 52: 663–716.

Collins, Randall. 1994. *Four Sociological Traditions*. New York: Oxford University Press.

———. 2001. "Social Movements and the Focus of Emotional Attention." In Jeff Goodwin, James Jasper, and Francesca Polletta, eds., *Passionate Politics*, pp. 27–44. Chicago: University of Chicago Press.

Coser, Lewis. 1956. *The Functions of Social Conflict*. New York: Free Press.

———. 1977. *Masters of Sociological Thought*, 2nd edition. New York: Harcourt, Brace, Jovanovich.

Crossley, Nick. 2002. *Making Sense of Social Movements*. Buckingham, England: Open University Press.

Currie, Elliott and Jerome Skolnick. 1970. "A Critical Note on Conceptions of Collective Behavior." *Annals of the American Academy of Political and Social Science* 391: 34–45.

Dahrendorf, Ralf. 1959. *Class and Class Conflict in Industrial Society*. Stanford, CA: Stanford University Press.

Dalton, Russell J. and Manfred Kuechler. 1990. *Challenging the Political Order: New Social and Political Movements in Western Democracies*. New York: Oxford University Press.

Dalton, Russell J., Manfred Kuechler, and Wilhelm Burklin. 1990. "The Challenge of the New Movements." In Russell J. Dalton and Manfred Kuechler, eds., *Challenging the Political Order*, pp. 3–20. New York: Oxford University Press.

Darnovsky, Marcy, Barbara Epstein, and Richard Flacks. 1995. "Introduction." In Marcy Darnovsky, Barbara Epstein, and Richard Flacks, eds., *Cultural Politics and Social Movements*, pp. vi–xxiii. Philadelphia: Temple University Press.

Davies, James. 1962. "Toward a Theory of Revolution." *American Sociological Review* 27 (1): 5–19.

Davis, Gerald and Mayer N. Zald. 2005. "Social Change, Social Theory, and the Convergence of Movements and Organizations." In Gerald Davis, Doug McAdam, W. Richard Scott, and Mayer N. Zald, eds., *Social Movements and Organization Theory*, pp. 335–350. Cambridge: Cambridge University Press.

Davis, Gerald, Calvin Morrill, Hayagreeva Rao, and Sarah A. Soule. 2008. "Introduction: Social Movements in Organizations and Markets." *Administrative Science Quarterly* 53: 389–394.

Davis, Steve, Larry Elin, and Grant Reeher. 2002. *Click on Democracy: The Internet's Power to Turn Political Apathy into Action*. Boulder, CO: Westview Press.

Della Porta, Donatella. 2007. *The Global Justice Movement: Cross-National and Transnational Perspectives*. Boulder, CO: Paradigm.

———. 2009. "Making the New Polis: The Practice of Deliberative Democracy in Social Forums." In Hank Johnston, ed., *Culture, Social Movements, and Protest*, pp. 181–208. Surrey, England: Ashgate.

Della Porta, Donatella and Hanspeter Kriesi. 1999. "Social Movements in a Globalizing World: An Introduction." In Donatella Della Porta, Hanspeter Kriesi, and Dieter Rucht, eds., *Social Movements in a Globalizing World*, pp. 3–22. New York: St. Martin's Press.

Della Porta, Donatella and Sidney Tarrow. 2005a. "Transnational Processes and Social Activism: An Introduction." In Donatella Della Porta and Sidney Tarrow, eds., *Transnational Protest and Global Activism*, pp. 1–17. Lanham, MD: Rowman & Littlefield.

———. 2005b. "Conclusion: 'Globalization,' Complex Internationalism, and Transnational Contention." In Donatella Della Porta and Sidney Tarrow, eds., *Transnational Protest and Global Activism*, pp. 227–246. Lanham, MD: Rowman & Littlefield.

Diani, Mario. 2003. "The Terrestrial Emporium of Contentious Knowledge." *Mobilization* 8: 109–112.

———. 2007. "Contentious Politics." *Contemporary Sociology* 36: 574–575.

Durkheim, Émile. 1893/1964. *The Division of Labor in Society*. New York: Free Press.

———. 1895/1950. *The Rules of the Sociological Method*. Glencoe, IL: Free Press.

———. 1897/1951. *Suicide*. New York: Free Press.

———. 1915/1965. *The Elementary Forms of the Religious Life*. New York: Free Press.

Earl, Jennifer and Alan Schussman. 2003. "The New Site of Activism: On-Line Organizations, Movement Entrepreneurs, and the Changing Location of Social Movement Decision Making." In Patrick Coy, ed., *Research in Social Movements, Conflicts and Change* 24: 155–187. Oxford, England: Elsevier.

Eder, Klaus. 1993. *The New Politics of Class*. Newbury Park, CA: Sage.

Elin, Larry. 2003. "The Radicalization of Zeke Spier." In Martha McCaughey and Michael Ayers, eds., *Cyberactivism: Online Activism in Theory and Practice*, pp. 97–114. New York: Routledge.

Epstein, Barbara. 1991. *Political Protest and Cultural Revolution: Nonviolent Direct Action in the 1970s and 1980s*. Berkeley: University of California Press.

Evans, Sara and Harry Boyte. 1986. *Free Spaces.* Chicago: University of Chicago Press.

Eyerman, Ron and Andrew Jamison. 1991. *Social Movements: A Cognitive Approach.* University Park, PA: Pennsylvania State University Press.

Ferree, Myra. 1992. "The Political Context of Rationality." In Aldon Morris and Carol McClurg Mueller, eds., *Frontiers in Social Movement Theory,* pp. 29–52. New Haven, CT: Yale University Press.

Festinger, Leon. 1957. *A Theory of Cognitive Dissonance.* Evanston, IL: Row, Peterson.

Fine, Gary A. 1995. *A Second Chicago School? The Development of a Postwar American Sociology.* Chicago: University of Chicago Press.

———. 2009. "Notorious Support: The America First Committee and the Personalization of Policy." In Hank Johnston, ed., *Culture, Social Movements, and Protest,* pp. 77–102. Surrey, England: Ashgate.

Fireman, Bruce and William Gamson. 1979. "Utilitarian Logic in the Resource Mobilization Perspective." In Mayer N. Zald and John McCarthy, eds., *The Dynamics of Social Movements,* pp. 8–44. Cambridge, MA: Winthrop.

Flacks, Richard. 1988. *Making History: The American Left and the American Mind.* New York: Columbia University Press.

Friedrichs, Robert. 1970. *A Sociology of Sociology.* New York: Free Press.

Fromm, Erich. 1941. *Escape from Freedom.* New York: Rinehart.

Galbraith, John Kenneth. 1958. *The Affluent Society.* Boston: Houghton Mifflin.

Galusky, Wyatt. 2003. "Identifying with Information: Citizen Empowerment, the Internet, and the Environmental Toxins Movement." In Martha McCaughey and Michael Ayers, eds., *Cyberactivism: Online Activism in Theory and Practice,* pp. 185–205. New York: Routledge.

Gamson, Joshua. 2003. "Gay Media, Inc.: Media Structures, the New Gay Conglomerates, and Collective Sexual Identities." In Martha McCaughey and Michael Ayers, eds., *Cyberactivism: Online Activism in Theory and Practice,* pp. 255–278. New York: Routledge.

Gamson, William. 1975. *The Strategy of Social Protest.* Belmont, CA: Wadsworth.

———. 1988. "Political Discourse and Collective Action." *International Social Movement Research* 1: 219–244.

———.1990. *The Strategy of Social Protest,* 2nd edition. Belmont, CA: Wadsworth.

———. 1992. *Talking Politics.* Cambridge: Cambridge University Press.

Gamson, William, Bruce Fireman, and Steven Rytina. 1982. *Encounters with Unjust Authority.* Homewood, IL: Dorsey Press.

Gamson, William and David S. Meyer. 1996. "Framing Political Opportunity." In Doug McAdam, John D. McCarthy, and Mayer N. Zald, eds., *Comparative Perspectives on Social Movements: Political Opportunities, Mobilizing Structures, and Cultural Framings,* pp. 275–290. Cambridge: Cambridge University Press.

Gamson, William and Gadi Wolfsfeld. 1993. "Movements and Media as Interacting Systems." *Annals of the American Academy of Political and Social Science* 528: 114–125.

Ganz, Marshall. 2000. "Resources and Resourcefulness: Strategic Capacity in the Unionization of California Agriculture." *American Journal of Sociology* 105: 1003–1062.

———. 2009. *Why David Sometimes Wins: Leadership, Organization, and Strategy in the California Farm Workers Movement.* Oxford: Oxford University Press.

Garfinkel, Harold. 1967. *Studies in Ethnomethodology.* Englewood Cliffs, NJ: Prentice-Hall.

Garner, Roberta Ash and Mayer N. Zald. 1987. "The Political Economy of Social Movements Sectors." In Mayer N. Zald and John D. McCarthy, eds., *Social Movements in an Organizational Society: Collected Essays,* pp. 293–317. New Brunswick, NJ: Transaction.

Geschwender, James. 1968/1997. "Explorations in the Theory of Social Movements and Revolutions." In Steven M. Buechler and F. Kurt Cylke, eds., *Social Movements: Perspectives and Issues,* pp. 97–107. Mountain View, CA: Mayfield.

Giddens, Anthony. 1986. *The Constitution of Society.* Berkeley: University of California Press.

Giugni, Marco. 1998. "Structure and Culture in Social Movement Theory." *Sociological Forum* 13 (2): 365–375.

Goffman, Erving. 1959. *The Presentation of Self in Everyday Life.* Garden City, NY: Anchor.

———. 1961. *Encounters.* Indianapolis, IN: Bobbs-Merrill.

———. 1974. *Frame Analysis.* Boston: Northeastern University Press.

Goldstone, Jack. 1991a. "An Analytical Framework." In Jack Goldstone, Ted Robert Gurr, and Farrokh Moshiri, eds., *Revolutions of the Late Twentieth Century,* pp. 37–51. Boulder, CO: Westview Press.

———. 1991b. *Revolution and Rebellion in the Early Modern World.* Berkeley: University of California Press.

———. 2002. "Theory Development in the Study of Revolutions." In Joseph Berger and Morris Zelditch, Jr., eds., *New Directions in Contemporary Sociological Theory,* pp. 194–226. Lanham, MD: Rowman & Littlefield.

Goodwin, Jeff. 1997. "The Libidinal Constitution of a High-Risk Social Movement: Affectual Ties and Solidarity in the Huk Rebellion 1946–1954." *American Sociological Review* 62: 53–69.

Goodwin, Jeff and James M. Jasper. 2004. "Caught in a Winding, Snarling Vine: The Structural Bias of Political Process Theory." In Jeff Goodwin and James M. Jasper, eds., *Rethinking Social Movements: Structure, Meaning and Emotion,* pp. 3–30. Lanham, MD: Rowman and Littlefield.

Goodwin, Jeff, James Jasper, and Francesca Polletta. 2000. "The Return of the Repressed." *Mobilization* 5: 65–84.

———. 2001a. "Introduction: Why Emotions Matter." In Jeff Goodwin, James Jasper, and Francesca Polletta, eds., *Passionate Politics,* pp. 1–24. Chicago: University of Chicago Press.

——— eds. 2001b. *Passionate Politics: Emotions and Social Movements.* Chicago: University of Chicago Press.

Goodwin, Jeff and Steven Pfaff. 2001. "Emotion Work in High-Risk Social Movements: Managing Fear in the U. S. and East German Civil Rights Movement." In Jeff Goodwin, James Jasper, and Francesca Polletta, eds., *Passionate Politics,* pp. 282–302. Chicago: University of Chicago Press.

Gould, Deborah. 2001. "Rock the Boat, Don't Rock the Boat Baby: Ambivalence and the Emergence of Militant AIDS Activism." In Jeff Goodwin, James Jasper, and Francesca Polletta, eds., *Passionate Politics,* pp. 135–157. Chicago: University of Chicago Press.

———. 2004. "Passionate Political Processes: Bringing Emotions Back into the Study of Social Movements." In Jeff Goodwin and James M. Jasper, eds., *Rethinking Social Movements: Structure, Meaning and Emotion,* pp. 155–175. Lanham, MD: Rowman and Littlefield.

Gouldner, Alvin. 1970. *The Coming Crisis of Western Sociology.* New York: Basic.

Gramsci, Antonio. 1971. *Selections from the Prison Notebooks.* New York: International Publishers.

Groves, Julian M. 2001. "Animal Rights and the Politics of Emotion: Folk Constructions of Emotion in the Animal Rights Movement." In Jeff Goodwin, James Jasper, and

Francesca Polletta, eds., *Passionate Politics*, pp. 212–229. Chicago: University of Chicago Press.

Gurr, Ted. 1970. *Why Men Rebel.* Princeton: Princeton University Press.

Gusfield, Joseph. 1963/1986. *Symbolic Crusade: Status Politics and the American Temperance Movement.* Urbana: University of Illinois Press.

———. 1978. "Historical Problematics and Sociological Fields: American Liberalism and the Study of Social Movements." *Research in Sociology of Knowledge, Sciences and Art* 1: 121–149.

———. 1994. Gusfield, Joseph R. "The Reflexivity of Social Movements: Collective Behavior and Mass Society Theory Revisited." In Enrique Larana, Hank Johnston, and Joseph R. Gusfield, eds., *New Social Movements: From Ideology to Identity*, pp. 58–78. Philadelphia: Temple University Press.

Habermas, Jürgen. 1975. *Legitimation Crisis.* Boston: Beacon.

———. 1981. "New Social Movements." *Telos* 49: 33–37.

———. 1984. *The Theory of Communicative Action: Reason and the Rationalization of Society* (Volume 1). Translated by Thomas McCarthy. Boston: Beacon Press.

———. 1987. *The Theory of Communicative Action: Lifeworld and System* (Volume 2). Translated by Thomas McCarthy. Boston: Beacon Press.

Halmos, Paul, ed. 1970. *The Sociology of Sociology.* Keele: University of Keele.

Heberle, Rudolf. 1951. *Social Movements: An Introduction to Political Sociology.* New York: Appleton-Century-Crofts.

Hochschild, Arlie. 1983. *The Managed Heart: Commercialization of Human Feeling.* Berkeley: University of California Press.

Hoffer, Eric. 1951. *The True Believer.* New York: Harper & Row.

Homans, George. 1974. *Social Behavior: Its Elementary Forms.* New York: Harcourt, Brace, Jovanovich.

Hunt, Scott A., Robert D. Benford, and David A. Snow. 1994. "Identity Fields: Framing Processes and the Social Construction of Movement Identities." In Enrique Larana, Hank Johnston, and Joseph R. Gusfield, eds., *New Social Movements: From Ideology to Identity*, pp. 185–208. Philadelphia: Temple University Press.

Ignatow, Gabriel. 2009. "Figurative Speech and Cognition: Metaphoric Analysis of a Shipyard Union Dispute." In Hank Johnston, ed., *Culture, Social Movements, and Protest*, pp. 157–178. Surrey, England: Ashgate.

Inglehart, Ronald. 1990. "Values, Ideology, and Cognitive Mobilization in New Social Movements." In Russell J. Dalton and Manfred Kuechler, eds., *Challenging the Political Order*, pp. 43–66. New York: Oxford University Press.

Jasper, James. 1997. *The Art of Moral Protest: Culture, Biography and Creativity in Social Movements.* Chicago: University of Chicago Press.

———. 1998. "The Emotions of Protest: Affective and Reactive Emotions in and Around Social Movements." *Sociological Forum* 13: 397–424.

Jasper, James and Jane Poulsen. 1995. "Recruiting Strangers and Friends: Moral Shocks and Social Networks in Animal Rights and Anti-Nuclear Protests." *Social Problems* 42: 493–512.

Jenkins, J. Craig. 1983. "Resource Mobilization Theory and the Study of Social Movements." *Annual Review of Sociology* 9: 527–553.

Johnston, Hank and Bert Klandermans. 1995. "The Cultural Analysis of Social Movements." In Hank Johnston and Bert Klandermans, eds., *Social Movements and Culture*, pp. 3–24. Minneapolis: University of Minnesota Press.

Johnston, Hank, Enrique Larana, and Joseph R. Gusfield. 1994. "Identities, Grievances and New Social Movements." In Enrique Larana, Hank Johnston, and Joseph R. Gusfield, eds., *New Social Movements: From Ideology to Identity,* pp. 3–35. Philadelphia: Temple University Press.

Kalouche, Fouad and Eric Mielants. 2008. "Transformations of the World-System and Antisystemic Movements: 1968–2005." In William G. Martin, ed. *Making Waves: Worldwide Social Movements, 1750–2005,* pp. 128–167. Boulder, CO: Paradigm.

Kauffman, L. A. 1990. "The Anti-Politics of Identity." *Socialist Review* 20: 67–80.

Kidd, Dorothy. 2003. "Indymedia.org: A New Communications Commons. In Martha McCaughey and Michael Ayers, eds., *Cyberactivism: Online Activism in Theory and Practice,* pp. 47–69. New York: Routledge.

King, Brayden and Nicholas A. Pearce. 2010. "The Contentiousness of Markets: Politics, Social Movements, and Institutional Change in Markets." *Annual Review of Sociology* 36: 249–267.

Klandermans, Bert. 1984. "Mobilization and Participation: Social-psychological Expansions of Resource Mobilization Theory." *American Sociological Review* 49: 583–600.

———. 1994. "Transient Identities? Membership Patterns in the Dutch Peace Movement." In Enrique Larana, Hank Johnston, and Joseph R. Gusfield, eds., *New Social Movements: From Ideology to Identity,* pp. 168–184. Philadelphia: Temple University Press.

Klandermans, Bert and Dirk Oegema. 1987. "Potentials, Networks, Motivations, and Barriers: Steps Toward Participation in Social Movements." *American Sociological Review* 52: 519–531.

Klandermans, Bert and Sidney Tarrow. 1988. "Mobilization into Social Movements: Synthesizing European and American Approaches." In Bert Klandermans, Hanspeter Kriesi, and Sidney Tarrow, eds., *International Social Movement Research, Vol.1: From Structure to Action,* pp. 1–38. New York: JAI Press.

Klimova, Sveta. 2009. "Speech Act Theory and Protest Discourse: Normative Claims in the Communicative Repertoire of Three Russian Movements." In Hank Johnston, ed., *Culture, Social Movements, and Protest,* pp. 105–133. Surrey, England: Ashgate.

Koopmans, Ruud. 2003. "A Failed Revolution—But a Worthy Cause." *Mobilization* 8: 116–119.

Kornhauser, William. 1959/2008. *The Politics of Mass Society.* New York: Free Press.

Kriesi, Hanspeter. 1989. "New Social Movements and the New Class in the Netherlands." *American Journal of Sociology* 94: 1078–1116.

Kriesi, Hanspeter, Ruud Koopmans, Jan Willem Duyvendak, and Marco G. Guigni. 1995. *New Social Movements in Western Europe: A Comparative Analysis.* Minneapolis: University of Minnesota Press.

Krinsky, John and Colin Barker. 2009. "Movement Strategizing as Developmental Learning: Perspectives from Cultural-Historical Activity Theory." In Hank Johnston, ed., *Culture, Social Movements, and Protest,* pp. 209–225. Surrey, England: Ashgate.

Kuhn, Thomas. 1962. *The Structure of Scientific Revolutions.* Chicago: University of Chicago Press.

Laclau, Ernesto and Chantal Mouffe. 1985. *Hegemony and Socialist Strategy: Toward a Radical Democratic Politics.* London: Verso.

Larana, Enrique, Hank Johnston, and Joseph R. Gusfield, eds. 1994. *New Social Movements: From Ideology to Identity.* Philadelphia: Temple University Press.

Lebert, Joanne. 2003. "Wiring Human Rights Activism: Amnesty International and the Challenges of Information and Communication Technologies." In Martha McCaughey and Michael Ayers, eds., *Cyberactivism: Online Activism in Theory and Practice*, pp. 209–231. New York: Routledge.

Le Bon, Gustave. 1896/1960. *The Crowd.* New York: Viking Press.

Lemert, Charles. 2008. *Social Things,* 4th edition. Lanham, MD: Rowman and Littlefield.

Lenin, Vladimir. 1917/1937. *Imperialism: The Highest Stage of Capitalism.* New York: International Publishers.

———. 1902/1988. *What Is to Be Done?* Harmondsworth, England: Penguin (1902).

Lipset, Seymour Martin. 1950/1967. *Agrarian Socialism.* Berkeley: University of California Press.

Lipset, Seymour Martin and Earl Raab. 1970. *The Politics of Unreason.* Chicago: University of Chicago Press.

———. 1977. *The Politics of Unreason,* 2nd edition. Chicago: University of Chicago Press.

Lipset, Seymour Martin and Stein Rokkan (eds.). 1967. *Party Systems and Voter Alignments: Cross-National Perspectives.* New York: Free Press.

Lipset, Seymour, Martin A. Trow, and James S. Coleman. 1956. *Union Democracy.* New York: Free Press.

Mannheim, Karl. 1936/1952. *Ideology and Utopia.* New York: Harcourt, Brace, Jovanovich.

Martin, William G. 2008a. "Introduction: The Search for Antisystemic Movements." In William G. Martin, ed. *Making Waves: Worldwide Social Movements, 1750–2005*, pp. 1–9. Boulder, CO: Paradigm.

———. 2008b. "Conclusion: World Movement Waves and World Transformations." In William G. Martin, ed. *Making Waves: Worldwide Social Movements, 1750–2005*, pp. 168–180. Boulder, CO: Paradigm.

Marx, Gary. 1972. "Issueless Riots." In James F. Short and Martin Wolfgang, eds., *Collective Violence*, pp. 47–59. New York: Aldine Atherton.

Marx, Gary and James L. Wood. 1975. "Strands of Theory and Research in Collective Behavior." *Annual Review of Sociology* 1: 363–428.

Marx, Karl. 1867/1967. *Capital.* New York: International Publishers.

———. 1964. *Economic and Philosophic Manuscripts of 1844.* New York: International Publishers.

Marx, Karl and Friedrich Engels. 1848/1964. *The Communist Manifesto.* New York: Washington Square Press.

McAdam, Doug. 1982. *Political Process and the Development of Black Insurgency.* Chicago: University of Chicago Press.

———. 1994. "Culture and Social Movements." In Enrique Larana, Hank Johnston, and Joseph R. Gusfield, eds., *New Social Movements: From Ideology to Identity*, pp. 36–57. Philadelphia: Temple University Press.

———. 2003. "'Eehh, What's Up (with) DOC?' Clarifying the Program." *Mobilization* 2003: 126–134.

———. 2007. "From Relevance to Irrelevance: The Curious Impact of the Sixties on Public Sociology." In Craig Calhoun, ed., *Sociology in America: A History*, pp. 411–426. Chicago: University of Chicago Press.

McAdam, Doug, John D. McCarthy, and Mayer N. Zald (eds.). 1996a. *Comparative Perspectives on Social Movements: Political Opportunities, Mobilizing Structures, and Cultural Framings.* Cambridge: Cambridge University Press.

McAdam, Doug, John D. McCarthy, and Mayer N. Zald (eds.). 1996b. "Introduction: Opportunities, Mobilizing Structures, and Framing Processes—Toward a Synthetic,

Comparative Perspective on Social Movements." In Doug McAdam, John D. McCarthy, and Mayer N. Zald, eds., *Comparative Perspectives on Social Movements: Political Opportunities, Mobilizing Structures, and Cultural Framings*, pp. 1–20. Cambridge: Cambridge University Press.

McAdam, Doug and W. Richard Scott. 2005. "Organizations and Movements." In Gerald Davis, Doug McAdam, W. Richard Scott, and Mayer N. Zald, eds., *Social Movements and Organization Theory*, pp. 4–40. Cambridge: Cambridge University Press.

McAdam, Doug, Sidney Tarrow, and Charles Tilly. 2001. *Dynamics of Contention.* Cambridge: Cambridge University Press.

McCarthy, John D. 1997. "The Globalization of Social Movement Theory." In Jackie Smith, Charles Chatfield, and Ron Pagnucco, eds., *Transnational Social Movements and Global Politics*, pp. 243–259. Syracuse, NY: Syracuse University Press.

McCarthy, John D. and Mayer N. Zald. 1973/1987. *The Trend of Social Movements in America: Professionalization and Resource Mobilization.* Morristown, NJ: General Learning Press.

———. 1977. "Resource Mobilization and Social Movements: A Partial Theory." *American Journal of Sociology* 82:1212–1241.

———. 2002. "The Enduring Vitality of the Resource Mobilization Theory of Social Movements." In Jonathan Turner, ed., *Handbook of Sociological Theory*, pp. 533–565. New York: Kluwer/Plenum.

McCaughey, Martha and Michael D. Ayers. 2003. "Introduction." In Martha McCaughey and Michael Ayers, eds., *Cyberactivism: Online Activism in Theory and Practice*, pp. 1–21. New York: Routledge.

McLaine, Steven. 2003. "Ethnic Online Communities: Between Profit and Purpose." In Martha McCaughey and Michael Ayers, eds., *Cyberactivism: Online Activism in Theory and Practice*, pp. 233–254. New York: Routledge.

Melucci, Alberto. 1980. "The New Social Movements: A Theoretical Approach." *Social Science Information* 19: 199–226.

———. 1981. "Ten Hypotheses for the Analysis of New Movements." In Diana Pinto, *Contemporary Italian Sociology*, pp. 173–194. Cambridge: Cambridge University Press.

———. 1988. "Getting Involved: Identity and Mobilization in Social Movements." In Bert Klandermans, Hanspeter Kriesi, and Sidney Tarrow, eds., *International Social Movement Research, Vol.1: From Structure to Action*, pp. 329–348. New York: JAI Press.

———. 1989. *Nomads of the Present: Social Movements and Individual Needs in Contemporary Society.* Philadelphia: Temple University Press.

———. 1996. *Challenging Codes.* Cambridge: Cambridge University Press.

Merton, Robert. 1957. *Social Theory and Social Structure.* Glencoe, IL: Free Press.

Meyer, David. 2009. "Claiming Credit: Stories of Movement Influence as Outcomes." In Hank Johnston, ed., *Culture, Social Movements, and Protest*, pp. 55–76. Surrey, England: Ashgate.

Michels, Robert. 1915/1958. *Political Parties.* Glencoe, IL: Free Press.

Miethe, Ingrid. 2009. "Frames, Framing and Keying: Biographical Perspectives on Social Movement Participation." In Hank Johnston, ed., *Culture, Social Movements, and Protest*, pp. 135–156. Surrey, England: Ashgate.

Mills, C. Wright. 1959. *The Sociological Imagination.* New York: Free Press.

Moore Jr., Barrington. 1966. *The Social Origins of Dictatorship and Democracy.* Boston: Beacon Press.

Mueller, Carol. 1994. "Conflict Networks and the Origins of Women's Liberation." In Enrique Larana, Hank Johnston, and Joseph R. Gusfield, eds., *New Social Movements: From Ideology to Identity*, pp. 234–263. Philadelphia: Temple University Press.

Neidhardt, Friedhelm and Dieter Rucht. 1991. "The Analysis of Social Movements: The State of the Art and Some Perspectives for Further Research." In Dieter Rucht, ed., *Research on Social Movements: The State of the Art in Western Europe and the USA*, pp. 422–464. Boulder, CO: Westview Press.

Neumann, Sigmund. 1942. *Permanent Revolution.* New York: Harper and Brothers.

Oberschall, Anthony. 1973. *Social Conflict and Social Movements.* Englewood Cliffs, NJ: Prentice-Hall.

Offe, Claus. 1985. "New Social Movements: Challenging the Boundaries of Institutional Politics." *Social Research* 52: 817–868.

———. 1990. "Reflections on the Institutional Self-transformation of Movement Politics: A Tentative Stage Model." In Russell J. Dalton and Manfred Kuechler, eds., *Challenging the Political Order*, pp. 232–250. New York: Oxford University Press.

Oliver, Pam. 2003. "Mechanisms of Contention." *Mobilization* 8: 119–122.

Olson, Mancur. 1965. *The Logic of Collective Action.* Cambridge, MA: Harvard University Press.

Park, Robert. 1972. *The Crowd and the Public and Other Essays.* Chicago: University of Chicago Press.

Park, Robert and Ernest Burgess. 1921. *Introduction to the Science of Sociology.* Chicago: University of Chicago Press.

Parsons, Talcott. 1951. *The Social System.* Glencoe, IL: Free Press.

Perrow, Charles. 1979. "The Sixties Observed." In Mayer N. Zald and John D. McCarthy, eds., *The Dynamics of Social Movements*, pp.192–211. Cambridge, MA: Winthrop.

Piven, Frances F. and Richard Cloward. 1979. *Poor People's Movements.* New York: Vintage.

———. 1992. "Normalizing Collective Protest." In Aldon Morris and Carol Mueller, eds., *Frontiers in Social Movement Theory*, pp. 301–325. New Haven, CT: Yale University Press.

Polletta, Francesca. 1997. "Culture and Its Discontents." *Sociological Inquiry* 67: 431–450.

———. 1998. "'It Was Like a Fever … ' Narrative and Identity in Social Protest." *Social Problems* 45: 137–159.

———. 2004. "Culture is Not Just in Your Head." In Jeff Goodwin and James M. Jasper, eds., *Rethinking Social Movements: Structure, Meaning and Emotion*, pp. 97–110. Lanham, MD: Rowman & Littlefield.

———. 2006. *It Was Like a Fever: Storytelling in Protest and Politics.* Chicago: University of Chicago Press.

———. 2009. "Storytelling in Social Movements." In Hank Johnston, ed., *Culture, Social Movements, and Protest*, pp. 33–54. Surrey, England: Ashgate.

Polletta, Francesca and Edwin Amenta. 2001. "Conclusion: Second that Emotion? Lessons from Once-Novel Concepts in Social Movement Research." In Jeff Goodwin, James Jasper, and Francesca Polletta, eds., *Passionate Politics*, pp. 303–316. Chicago: University of Chicago Press.

Popper, Karl. 1965. *Conjecture and Refutations: The Growth of Scientific Knowledge.* London: Routledge and Kegan Paul.

Riesman, David. 1950. *The Lonely Crowd.* New Haven, CT: Yale University Press.

Ritzer, George. 1991. *Metatheorizing in Sociology.* Lexington, MA: Lexington Books.

Rucht, Dieter. 1988. "Themes, Logics and Arenas of Social Movements: A Structural Approach." In Bert Klandermans, Hanspeter Kriesi, and Sidney Tarrow, eds., *International Social Movement Research, Vol.1: From Structure to Action,* pp. 305–328. New York: JAI Press.

———. 2003. "Overcoming the 'Classical Model'?" *Mobilization* 8: 112–116.

Rule, James. 1988. *Theories of Civil Violence.* Berkeley: University of California Press.

Salter, Lee. 2003. "Democracy, New Social Movements, and the Internet: A Habermasian Analysis." In Martha McCaughey and Michael Ayers, eds., *Cyberactivism: Online Activism in Theory and Practice,* pp. 117–144. New York: Routledge.

Schilling, Chris. 2005. "Embodiment, Emotions, and the Foundations of Social Order: Durkheim's Enduring Contribution." In Jeffrey Alexander and Philip Smith, eds., *The Cambridge Companion to Durkheim,* pp. 211–238. Cambridge: Cambridge University Press.

Schwartz, Michael. 1976. *Radical Protest and Social Structure.* New York: Academic Press.

Sewell, William. 2005. *Logics of History: Social Theory and Social Transformation.* Chicago: University of Chicago Press.

Shils, Edward. 1980. "Tradition, Ecology, and Institution in the History of Sociology." In Edward Shils, *The Calling of Sociology and Other Essays on the Pursuit of Learning,* pp. 165–256. Chicago: University of Chicago Press.

Sin, Ray. 2009. "Sustaining Continuity During the Doldrums—Constructing a Virtual Abeyance Structure." Unpublished paper.

Skocpol, Theda. 1979. *States and Social Revolutions.* Cambridge: Cambridge University Press.

Skolnick, Jerome. 1969. *The Politics of Protest.* New York: Ballantine.

Smelser, Neil. 1962. *Theory of Collective Behavior.* New York: Free Press.

Smith, Jackie. 1997. "Characteristics of the Modern Transnational Movement Sector." In Jackie Smith, Charles Chatfield, and Ron Pagnucco, eds., *Transnational Social Movements and Global Politics,* pp. 42–58. Syracuse, NY: Syracuse University Press.

———. 2005. "Globalization and Transnational Social Movement Organizations." In Gerald Davis, Doug McAdam, W. Richard Scott, and Mayer N. Zald, eds., *Social Movements and Organization Theory,* pp. 226–248. Cambridge: Cambridge University Press.

———. 2008. *Social Movements for Global Democracy.* Baltimore: Johns Hopkins University Press.

Smith, Jackie, Marina Karides, Marc Becker, Dorval Brunelle, Christopher Chase-Dunn, Donatella Della Porta, Rosable I. Garza, Jeffrey S. Juris, Lorenzo Mosca, Ellen Reese, Peter (Jay) Smith, and Rolando Vazquez. 2008. *Global Democracy and the World Social Forums.* Boulder, CO: Paradigm.

Smith, Jackie, Ron Pagnucco, and Charles Chatfield. 1997. "Social Movements and World Politics: A Theoretical Framework." In Jackie Smith, Charles Chatfield, and Ron Pagnucco, eds., *Transnational Social Movements and Global Politics,* pp. 59–77. Syracuse, NY: Syracuse University Press.

Snow, David A. 2004. "Social Movements as Challenges to Authority: Resistance to an Emerging Conceptual Hegemony." *Research in Social Movements, Conflicts, and Change* 25: 3–25.

Snow, David A. and Robert Benford. 1988. "Ideology, Frame Resonance, and Participant Mobilization." *International Social Movement Research* 1: 197–217.

———. 1992. "Master Frames and Cycles of Protest." In Aldon Morris and Carol Mueller, eds., *Frontiers in Social Movement Theory,* pp. 133–155. New Haven, CT: Yale University Press.

Snow, David A., Daniel M. Cress, Liam Downey, and Andrew W. Jones. 1998. "'Disrupting the Quotidian:' Reconceptualizing the Relationship between Breakdown and the Emergence of Collective Action." *Mobilization* 3: 1–22.

Snow, David A. and Phillip W. Davis. 1994. "Turner's Contributions to the Study of Collective Behavior: An Elaboration and Critical Assessment." In Gerald Platt and Chad Gordon, eds., *Self, Collective Action, and Society: Essays Honoring the Contriutions of Ralph H. Turner,* pp. 97–115. Chicago: University of Chicago Press.

———. 1995. "The Chicago Approach to Collective Behavior." In Gary A. Fine, ed., *A Second Chicago School?,* pp. 188–220. Chicago: University of Chicago Press.

Snow, David A., E. Burke Rochford, Jr., Steven K. Worden, and Robert D. Benford. 1986. "Frame Alignment Processes, Micromobilization, and Movement Participation." *American Sociological Review* 51: 464–481.

Soule, Sarah. 2004. "When Do Movements Matter? The Politics of Contingency and the Equal Rights Amendment." *American Sociological Review* 69: 473–497.

Stein, Arlene. 2001. "Revenge of the Shamed: The Christian Right's Emotional Culture War." In Jeff Goodwin, James Jasper, and Francesca Polletta, eds., *Passionate Politics,* pp. 115–131. Chicago: University of Chicago Press.

Stoecker, Randy. 1995. "Community, Movement, Organization: The Problem of Identity Convergence in Collective Action." *The Sociological Quarterly* 36: 111–130.

Tarrow, Sidney. 1989. *Democracy and Disorder: Protest and Politics in Italy 1965–1974.* Oxford: Oxford University Press.

———. 1991. "Struggle, Politics and Reform: Collective Action, Social Movements, and Cycles of Protest." Western Societies Program, Occasional Paper No. 21, Center for International Studies. Ithaca, NY: Cornell University Press.

———. 1994. *Power in Movement.* Cambridge: Cambridge University Press.

———. 1998. "Fishnets, Internets, and Catnets: Globalization and Transnational Collective Action." In Michael Hanagen, Leslie Page Moch, and Wayne te Brake, eds., *Challenging Authority: The Historical Study of Contentious Politics,* pp. 228–244. Minneapolis: University of Minnesota Press.

———. 2002. "From Lumping to Splitting: Specifying Globalizaiton and Resistance." In Jackie Smith and Hank Johnston, eds. *Globalization and Resistance,* pp. 229–249. Lanham, MD: Rowman & Littlefield.

———. 2003. "Confessions of a Recovering Structuralist." *Mobilization* 8: 134–141.

Taylor, Verta. 2003. *"Plus ca change, plus c'est le meme chose."* *Mobilization* 8:122–126.

Taylor, Verta, Katrina Kimport, Nella Van Dyke, and Ellen Ann Andersen. 2009. "Culture and Mobilization: Tactical Repertoires, Same-Sex Weddings, and the Impact on Gay Activism." *American Sociological Review* 74: 865-890.

Taylor, Verta and Nancy E. Whittier. 1992. "Collective Identity in Social Movement Communities: Lesbian Feminist Communities." In Aldon Morris and Carol Mueller, eds., *Frontiers in Social Movement Theory,* pp. 104–129. New Haven, CT: Yale University Press.

Thompson, E. P. 1963. *The Making of the English Working Class.* New York, Vintage.

Tilly, Charles. 1964. *The Vendee.* Cambridge, MA: Harvard University Press.

———. 1978. *From Mobilization to Revolution.* Reading, MA: Addison-Wesley.

———. 1995. *Popular Contention in Great Britain, 1758–1834.* Cambridge, MA: Harvard University Press.

———. 2004. *Social Movements: 1768–2004.* Boulder, CO: Paradigm.

Tilly, Charles and Sidney Tarrow. 2007. *Contentious Politics.* Boulder, CO: Paradigm.

Tilly, Charles, Louise Tilly, and Richard Tilly. 1975. *The Rebellious Century, 1830–1930.* Cambridge, MA: Harvard University Press.

Tolbert, Pamela S. and Shon R. Hiatt. 2009. "On Organizations and Oligarchies: Michels in the Twenty-First Century." In Paul Adler, ed., *Sociological Classics and Organizational Research,* pp. 174–199. London: Oxford University Press.

Touraine, Alain. 1977. *The Self-Production of Society.* Chicago: University of Chicago Press.

———. 1981. *The Voice and the Eye: An Analysis of Social Movements.* New York: Cambridge University Press.

———. 1985. "An Introduction to the Study of Social Movements." *Social Research* 52: 749–787.

———. 1988. *Return of the Actor: Social Theory in Post-Industrial Society.* Minneapolis: University of Minnesota Press.

———. 1992. "Beyond Social Movements." *Theory, Culture and Society* 9: 125–145.

Touraine, Alain, Michel Wieviorka, and Francois Dubet. 1987. *The Worker's Movement.* Cambridge: Cambridge University Press.

Trotsky, Leon. 1930/1965. *History of the Russian Revolution.* London: Gollancz.

Tucker, Kenneth H. 1991. "How New Are the New Social Movements?" *Theory, Culture and Society* 8 (2):75–98.

Turner, Ralph and Lewis Killian. 1957. *Collective Behavior.* Englewood Cliffs, NJ: Prentice-Hall.

———. 1972. *Collective Behavior,* 2nd edition. Englewood Cliffs, NJ: Prentice-Hall.

———. 1987. *Collective Behavior,* 3rd edition. Englewood Cliffs, NJ: Prentice-Hall.

Turner, Stephen Park and Jonathan H. Turner. 1990. *The Impossible Science.* Newbury Park, CA: Sage.

Useem, Bert. 1998. "Breakdown Theories of Collective Action." *Annual Review of Sociology* 24: 215–238.

Van Dyke, Nella, Sarah A. Soule, and Verta A. Taylor. 2004. "The Targets of Social Movements: Beyond a Focus on the State." *Research in Social Movements, Conflicts, and Change* 25: 27–51.

Wallerstein, Immanuel. 1974. *The Modern World-System: Capitalist Agriculture and the Origins of the European World-Economy in the 16th Century.* New York: Academic Press.

———. 1980. *The Modern World-System II: Mercantilism and the Consolidation of the European World-Economy, 1600–1750.* New York: Academic Press.

———. 1989. *The Modern World-System III: The Second Era of Great Expansion of the Capitalist World-Economy, 1730–1840.* New York: Academic Press.

———. 1990. "Antisystemic Movements: History and Dilemmas." In Samir Amin, Giovanni Arrighi, Andre G. Frank, and Immanuel Wallerstein, eds., *Transforming the Revolution,* pp. 13–53. New York: Monthly Review Press.

Walsh, Edward. 1981. "Resource Mobilization and Citizen Protest in Communities Around Three Mile Island." *Social Problems* 29: 1–21.

Weber, Max. 1904/1958. *The Protestant Ethic and the Spirit of Capitalism.* New York: Scribners.

———. 1978. *Economy and Society.* Berkeley: University of California Press.

Whittier, Nancy. 1995. *Feminist Generations: The Persistence of the Radical Women's Movement.* Philadelphia: Temple University Press.

———. 2001. "Emotional Strategies: The Collective Reconstruction and Display of Oppositional Emotions in the Movement against Child Sexual Abuse." In Jeff Goodwin, James Jasper, and Francesca Polletta, eds., *Passionate Politics,* pp. 233–250. Chicago: University of Chicago Press.

Williams, Rhys H. 1995. "Constructing the Public Good: Social Movements and Cultural Resources." *Social Problems* 42: 124–144.

Wood, Elisabeth J. 2001. "The Emotional Benefits of Insurgency in El Salvador." In Jeff Goodwin, James Jasper, and Francesca Polletta, eds., *Passionate Politics,* pp. 267–281. Chicago: University of Chicago Press.

Wright, Erik O. 1989. *The Debate on Classes.* London: Verso.

Zald, Mayer N. 1995. "Progress and Cumulation in the Human Sciences after the Fall." *Sociological Forum* 10: 455–479.

———. 2007. "Changing Movements, Changing Methods, and Changing Theories: A Sociological Approach to the History of the Study of Social Movements." Unpublished lecture.

———. 2008. "Epilogue: Social Movements and Political Sociology in the Analysis of Organizations and Markets." *Administrative Science Quarterly* 53: 568–574.

Zald, Mayer N. and Roberta Ash. 1966. "Social Movement Organizations: Growth, Decay and Change." *Social Forces* 44: 327–340.

Zald, Mayer N. and John D. McCarthy (eds.). 1979. *The Dynamics of Social Movements.* Cambridge, MA: Winthrop.

———. 1987a. *Social Movements in an Organizational Society: Collected Essays.* New Brunswick, NJ: Transaction.

———. 1987b. "Social Movement Industries: Competition and Conflict Among SMOs." In Mayer N. Zald and John D. McCarthy, eds., *Social Movements in an Organizational Society: Collected Essays,* pp. 161–179. New Brunswick, NJ: Transaction.

Zald, Mayer N. and Bert Useem. 1987. "Movement and Countermovement Interaction: Mobilization, Tactics, and State Involvement." In Mayer N. Zald and John D. McCarthy, eds., *Social Movements in an Organizational Society: Collected Essays,* pp. 247–272. New Brunswick, NJ: Transaction.

Index

Action, 153; mass, 39; mobilization, 148; political, 160; public, 170; social movement, 121, 155; value-rational, 30, 33. *See also* Collective action; Social action

Activism, 5, 34, 178, 182, 203, 208, 222, 229, 231; antinuclear, 151, 205; class-based, 160; decrease in, 113; global, 225; high-risk, 207, 218; Internet, 221, 222, 227; movement, 110, 160, 161; political, 10, 126, 207; progressive, 221; social, 21, 37, 161, 162, 183, 229; social landscape and, 139; transnational, 216, 220, 223–227, 231; union, 123, 137. *See also* Cyberactivism

Adorno, Theodore, 84, 85, 86

Affirmative action, 151, 152

Amenta, Edwin, 213

American Jewish Committee, 84, 85

American Sociological Association (ASA), 142, 178, 220

Anarchism, 10, 226

Andreas, Joel, 40

Animal rights movement, 20, 178, 203, 204, 205, 222

Anomie, 46, 47, 53, 54, 71, 127

Anti-Semitism, 84, 85

Anticolonialism, 93, 109, 226

Antinuclear movement, 15, 120, 178, 203, 204, 205

Antisystemic movements, 159, 216, 226

Aristotle, democracy and, 82

Armstrong, Elizabeth, 220

Asch, Solomon, 92

Ash, Roberta, 38, 39

Austin, John, 217

Authoritarianism, 84, 85, 86, 88, 100

Authority, 30–33, 37; charismatic, 32, 33, 34–35, 38, 40; legitimation and, 31, 32; rational, 32, 33; traditional, 32, 35

Barker, Colin, 217

Behavior, 60, 99, 143, 182; conventional, 100; institutional, 61, 74; mass, 71; noninstitutional, 111; organized, 69, 74; self-destructive, 46; social, 63, 67. *See also* Collective behavior

Bell, Daniel, 86, 87, 92

Benford, Robert, 146, 148, 149, 156, 187

Bernstein, Mary, 220

Blumer, Herbert, 55, 67, 69, 70, 73, 142, 156; Chicago School and, 94; collective behavior and, 63–66; reform movement and, 72; social movements and, 65, 66

Bourdieu, Pierre, 142, 204, 220

Breakdown theory, 101–102, 103, 105, 129, 143; solidarity and, 104, 115

Bureau of Applied Social Research, 76

Bureaucracy, 25, 27, 34, 37, 38, 71, 81, 85, 135, 163

Burgess, Ernest, 62, 63, 64, 66, 67, 69, 70, 73, 156; Chicago School and, 59, 93, 94

Calvin, John, 27

Calvinism, 27, 28

Capitalism, 1, 10, 16, 17, 18–19, 22, 25, 30, 42, 87, 124, 158, 166, 226;

249

About the Author

Steven M. Buechler is Professor of Sociology at Minnesota State University. His previous books include *Critical Sociology* (Paradigm, 2008) and *Social Movements in Advanced Capitalism: The Political Economy and Cultural Construction of Social Activism* (Oxford, 2000).